THE
·Basic·Basics·

BAKING

MARGUERITE PATTEN

GRUB STREET · LONDON

Published in 2018 by
Grub Street
4 Rainham Close
London
SW11 6SS

Email: food@grubstreet.co.uk
Web: www.grubstreet.co.uk
Twitter: @grub_street
Facebook: Grub Street Publishing

The moral right of the author has been asserted

A CIP catalogue record for this book is available from the British Library

ISBN 978-1-911621-13-3

Printed and bound in India

CONTENTS

INTRODUCTION

This book is to enable everyone to enjoy the art and pleasure of home-baking. Even if you are new to cooking, with this guide you can achieve excellent results.

As you will see the title of this book is *The Basic Basics Baking Handbook* – that is because every step is explained clearly, so there can be no uncertainty about the method of producing all kinds of cakes and biscuits or cookies plus a few special easy-to-make and popular breads and practical meat patties and pies.

Although this is a basic book it does not mean a limited selection of dishes.

You will find a wide range of cakes; from those for special occasions, such as a refreshing moist Lemon Cake, a rich Coffee and Walnut Cake, with a mouth-watering filling, and a simple, but delicious, Chocolate Cake and many others.

We have a wealth of traditional recipes in Britain – both savoury and sweet – and some of the most interesting are included. A home-made Cornish Pasty or a Steak Pie and ever popular Sausage Rolls bear no resemblance to those made commercially. You will produce melt-in-the-mouth pastry with a succulent meat filling. Several counties in England compete for the best Apple Cake; I think you will agree that the cake baked from the recipe on page 76 is a winner.

Ireland is represented by light soda and tea breads, made without yeast, and from Scotland there is a selection of crisp shortbreads and Baps (light rolls) that give a good introduction to modern easy-to-use yeast. If you have never tasted home-made Welsh Cakes you have missed a treat. These and Scotch Pancakes are made without using the oven, and are included in the book, along with other British regional recipes.

During the past few years we have started to enjoy a number of baked goods from other countries, such as American Muffins – ideal to serve on many occasions, including a leisurely week-end breakfast time. We have also become used to buying American Cookies and Cornbread. Two simple and delicious versions are on pages 151 and 152.

Nutritionists advise us to include more unsaturated fats in our diet, particularly olive oil, so I have included a number of recipes based on oils, which give excellent results.

If you are someone who is intolerant to wheat you will be pleased to find a few mentions that use alternative ingredients, such as gluten-free and rice flours.

Today most households have a freezer, so you will find information with each recipe as to whether the dish freezes well or should not be frozen.

This means you can plan your baking when you have a suitable time. So when you are busy you will be able to take muffins, scones, bread and cakes from your freezer. Home-made biscuits will keep well in an airtight container.

Microwave ovens save a considerable amount of cooking time, so I have included a few microwaveable recipes together with hints where a specific recipe could be cooked in the microwave with satisfactory results.

Before you first embark on baking please do read the important points beginning on page 6, these stress the essentials to achieve perfect results.

This section gives advice on the correct use of kitchen equipment, including an electric mixer and food processor and some special terms used when you prepare foods for baking, are explained. There is also advice on the wise choice of ingredients.

I am confident you will enjoy baking as much as I do and it is certain your family and friends will greet your successful efforts with great enthusiasm.

Marguerite Patten

FACTS TO ENSURE SUCCESS

To achieve 100% success it is important to appreciate the following points.

CHOOSE THE RIGHT INGREDIENTS

Each recipe gives the preferred kind of fat, sugar and flour but in many cases alternatives are given so you need not rush out shopping if you don't have the first choice. Alternative names of ingredients are shown for American readers of this book.

WEIGH OR MEASURE CAREFULLY

Baked dishes are based on the correct proportions of the various ingredients so follow the recipes carefully when making a baked dish. A carefully tested recipe will be based on a well-balanced choice of ingredients. After making the recipe with success you can adapt the flavouring given by spices, herbs or extracts for that will not spoil the balance of fat, flour, etc.

MIXING THE INGREDIENTS

Use the recommended method of mixing the ingredients. The way in which the ingredients are incorporated makes a great deal of difference to the result. There are four basic techniques of mixing, these are:

Rubbing-in
In this method the fat is incorporated into the flour with your fingers, although a food processor or electric mixer can be used, see page 109.

Creaming
In this method the fat and sugar, or sugar and other ingredients, are beaten together until soft and light. There is a variation on this method known as 'one-stage mixing', which can be achieved thanks to the soft fats now on the market. The technique of successful creaming by hand or electric appliances is explained on pages 70 to 72.

Melting
In this method some of the ingredients are heated in a saucepan or a suitable container in the microwave. Details are on page 48.

Whisking
A technique used when making very light cakes or whisking egg whites. See page 53.

Each recipe in the book clearly shows the appropriate mixing technique in the method.

Other words are used in recipes, such as 'folding'. This is described on pages 72 and 100. The terms **'mixing'** or **'blending'** simply mean combining the ingredients with a fairly brisk movement.

COOKING THE FOOD

The temperature at which baked food is cooked is of the utmost importance. Unless stated to the contrary it is always advisable to preheat the oven before adding the prepared dish. In the case of an electric oven this is clearly indicated by the oven thermostat. Allow 15 minutes to preheat a gas oven to the recommended setting.

Try to use the same sized cake tin (pan) or dish recommended in the recipe. If you use a slightly wider cake tin than stated in the recipe the mixture will be spread over a larger area, but it will be more shallow, so the cake will take a slightly shorter cooking time. If smaller in diameter you will have a greater depth of mixture so the cooking time will be slightly longer. The way to adjust cooking times is given on page 182 under Questions and Answers.

If you have an electric fan oven (convection oven) you will need to adjust the basic cooking temperatures. In some cases this means lowering it by 10°C, in others by 20°C. Although advice is clearly shown in each recipe consult your manufacturer's book too.

One of the best investments to make for good baking is an oven thermometer. This will enable you to check the temperature of your oven at all times. Oven thermometers can be purchased quite cheaply. Lakeland Limited is a good source as well as for all kitchen equipment. www.lakelandlimited.co.uk or 015394 88100.

POSITIONS IN THE OVEN

Fan ovens: all parts should provide the same heat so you can put the food where convenient. This oven is known as a convection type in America.

Ordinary electric and gas ovens: towards the top for muffins, scones, small cakes and buns. Sandwich sponges go just above the centre.

Large cakes, loaves of bread, substantial pastry tarts, pies and pasties together with biscuits, should be placed in the centre of the oven.

TESTING

Test baked foods carefully. Individual ovens vary slightly, so although the baking time in each recipe is based on careful testing you may find the cake, or bread takes a few minutes longer or shorter cooking time in **your** oven. The method of testing each kind of baked dish is given in the introduction to the various sections, see pages 28, 33, 184.

STORING

Never store cakes and biscuits (cookies) in the same tin and keep any biscuit containing oatmeal, such as Flapjacks (page 49) apart from other biscuits as oatmeal absorbs moisture from cakes and other biscuits and oatmeal cookies or biscuits become over-soft in storage. If the recipes states the cake or biscuits keep well, put them into an *airtight* tin when they are cold. If in doubt about the keeping time then freeze the cake or bread or other food. Each recipe states whether the dish will freeze.

FREEZING

Most cakes, bread, muffins and meat patties or pies freeze well.

It is a good idea to cut a large cake or loaf of bread into slices before freezing. You can put a piece of baking parchment or greaseproof paper (wax paper) between each slice before freezing. This will enable you to take out the number of slices required without defrosting the whole cake or loaf.

If you want to defrost any frozen baked dishes
   a)   allow them to defrost slowly in the refrigerator or
   b)   heat slowly in the oven set to a low temperature or
   c)   thaw out in the microwave on the defrost setting or even a lower setting in the case of pastry.

BASIC INGREDIENTS USED IN BAKING

The following are the most essential ingredients in baking.

FLOUR

The flour used in the majority of recipes is made from wheat. For the majority of basic dishes the flours below are those you will need.

As there is considerable interest in organic foods today you may well find you need to choose between organic and non-organic brands of flour. Whichever you buy it will not affect the quantity of flour used in the recipes and it will not make a great deal of difference to the results.

If flour is sifted before use it makes it lighter in texture and there is no possibility of it forming small lumps, see page 18.

WHITE FLOURS
These are produced by extracting the bran and the wheat germ in milling. It leaves between 72 to 74% of the whole wheat grain.

The three types of white flour on sale are:

Plain (all-purpose) flour. This is the flour to use in pastry, some biscuits (cookies) and certain tea breads. Plain flour can be used in other recipes with the addition of baking powder or other raising agents, such as yeast.

Self-raising flour. In this flour the millers have incorporated baking powder. The proportion used is suitable for a wide range of cakes and other recipes. There is a special form of self-raising flour known as **Supreme Sponge** self-raising flour. It is ideal for very light sponges as on page 101.

Strong flour. The wheat used has a higher gluten content than the weaker plain flour. Strong flour is particularly suitable for preparing a yeast dough used in bread making. A mixture made from this flour expands well, has a good texture and shape. It produces good puff, rough puff and flaky pastry.

BROWN FLOURS

Brown flour is produced from a mixture of half white and half wheatmeal flour. From a nutritional point of view we are urged to eat wheatmeal or wholemeal bread and to use these flours in cooking. Both these flours are available as plain flour, self-raising flour and strong flour.

Wheatmeal flour contains most of the bran and wheat germ and between 80 and 90% of the whole wheat germ.
Wholemeal flour contains all the bran and wheat germ, so you have 100% of the wheat grain.

SPECIALIST FLOURS

Occasionally you may find flours on sale that are described as 'stone ground'. Modern flours are milled using metal rollers but some are ground between stones, as in the past. Stone ground flour can be used in the recipes.

A few specialist flours are used in this book. One of the most popular is from **maize** (easily available as **polenta**). This is used to make the Cornbreads (see page 151 and 152). **Cornflour (cornstarch)** and **rice flour** are both good ingredients particularly in some biscuits.

Some people are allergic or intolerant to wheat and other grains containing gluten, so I have given a few simple adaptations on some recipes. These are based on **gluten-free flour**, either by itself or combined with suitable ingredients.

FATS (SHORTENING)

In practically all the recipes in this book some kind of fat is required. This gives a pleasant moistness to the cake, pastry or other dishes.
What kind of fats can you use?

Butter. This can be obtained as salted and unsalted. In most cases either can be used. Butter is a hard fat so it is not easy to cream if taken straight from the refrigerator. It should be kept at room temperature for a time.

However there is now a large range of 'spreadable' butters available. As the name suggests these are sufficiently soft to cream or spread even when brought straight from the refrigerator. Spreadable butters can be used in any recipe instead of ordinary butter or margarine. It is possible to buy lighter butters, in which the fat content is lower, but their use in baking is limited.

Margarines. These are produced from edible oils, mostly of vegetable origin. They vary considerably in taste, so experiment until you find the brand you prefer. Margarine comes in various basic types.

Hard margarine. Used in the same way as butter for which they are an excellent alternative. They should be removed from the refrigerator some time before use, if being used for the creaming or rubbing-in methods.
Soft margarine. Sold in tubs and are better used straight from the refrigerator; they should not be left at room temperature. Best in one-stage recipes, the first example of which is on page 72.
Poly-unsaturated margarine. Soft and a good choice for anyone following a low cholesterol diet; can be used in the same way as ordinary soft margarines.

Use margarines for biscuits (cookies), cakes and pastry. It is less good than butter for cake fillings.

In addition there is the type of spread that has been formulated to help reduce cholesterol. This can be used in cooking.

Lard (shortening). This is a hard animal fat. It is not suitable for creaming. Use in shortcrust pastry with butter or margarine and Lardy Cake on page 171.

Suet. This is obtainable in two forms, i.e. from animal sources and from vegetarian ingredients. It is not used in any recipes in this book.

OILS

During the past decade there has been a great interest in the use of oil in all forms of cooking. You can use oil very successfully in many forms of baking, in fact it is an extremely good choice for a wider range of cakes.

Olive oil is of great value nutritionally. There is no need to choose extra virgin olive oil for baking.

Sunflower oil is another very good type for baking and so is corn oil.

I find the very light type of cakes, where good creaming is important, are less good made with oil than with butter or margarine. The less delicate textured cakes are excellent made with oil instead of other fats, recipes begin on page 76.

If you want to replace butter or margarine in a recipe by using oil, substitute 115 g/4 oz (½ cup) of the fat with 120 ml/4 fl oz (½ cup) of oil. All recipes will state clearly when you can use oil as the fat. By using oil you have a very speedy method of mixing the ingredients.

SUGARS

Sugar plays an important part in baking, for it not only sweetens cakes, biscuits, scones and other baked goods, but it helps to lighten the mixture, or make it crisp. If you cut down on the sugar in a cake you lose some sweetness and lightness too. If you cut down on sugar in biscuits, some of the crispness is lost.

When buying sugar today you will find there are certain basic words used on some brands. Some sugars are grown organically and this point will be given on packets. It means no artificial fertilizers or sprays were used in the culture of the sugar.

Another term used on some sugars is 'natural'. This indicates the sugar has not been blanched or treated in any way to enhance the colour, and does give a slight change of flavour in a few cases.

These are sugars used in baking.

WHITE SUGARS

Caster sugar. The very fine white sugar. This is ideal for sponges and many light cakes, as the granules dissolve quickly and easily. It can be used for many biscuits, scones and other baked goods.

Granulated sugar. Coarser than caster sugar, it is not as good in light cakes, but excellent for many biscuits (cookies), for family-type 'rubbed-in' mixtures, for scones and bread, and some boiled icings.

Icing (confectioners) sugar. Not only the correct sugar for many icings, but it can be used as an ingredient in meringues and some biscuits. Use a hair or nylon sieve to remove lumps; if you push icing sugar through a metal sieve with a metal spoon it can become greyish in colour. There is a 'natural' golden icing sugar, produced from unrefined sugar. This does not spoil the colour of a filling or icing.

BROWN SUGARS

Some are known as unrefined (or natural) sugars and they do give an excellent flavour to many cakes, biscuits and breads. Others are called refined brown sugars and most tend to have a less definite taste than the unrefined sugars (except Demerara).

Unrefined granulated sugar. Not particularly well-known, slightly darker than ordinary granulated, a pale golden colour. Use as granulated sugar.

Demerara (raw) sugar. There are two kinds, the unrefined type, which is milder in taste than the refined (London) type Demerara. Use in cakes where you want a slightly 'nutty' taste, this sugar dissolves reasonably well, so is quite good for light cakes. The refined type has larger granules, so is better for biscuits than cakes. Other brown sugar can be substituted if necessary.

Light brown sugar. A refined moist sugar with fine granules like caster sugar, so dissolves easily in creaming. Use in semi-light cakes or where indicated in the recipe; gives a good colour to the mixture.

Dark brown sugar. A refined moist sugar with fine granules like caster sugar. Use in rich cakes; good in some biscuits.

Barbados sugar. A strongly flavoured natural sugar. Good for Christmas and similar cakes. There is a light and dark variety of Barbados sugar. It is used in the cake on page 78.

Molasses sugar. A very strong flavoured sugar, used in rich Christmas type cakes or gingerbreads only. Not used in recipes in this book.

Muscovado sugar. Use as Barbados sugar.

NOTE: If dark brown sugars harden in the pack, stand it over a pan of very hot water for a time and it will soften, or put into a food processor to break up into granules once more.

Always keep sugar in a tightly sealed container when removed from the packet.

OTHER INGREDIENTS FOR SWEETENING

Golden Syrup (Corn Syrup) and Black Treacle (Molasses). These are used in some recipes as a means of sweetening. They also create a pleasantly moist and/or sticky texture. Never exceed the recommended quantity for it can cause a cake to be heavy. Where spoon measures are given this means *level* spoons, page 79 gives hints on measuring these sweetenings.

Honey. This is another form of sweetening in certain recipes. Unless stated to the contrary use clear (thin) honey. Measure as syrup or treacle.

EGGS

Eggs help to make cakes and other baked dishes light in texture; they also add interest and richness to a mixture.

When buying eggs check the dates on egg boxes to make certain you are buying fresh eggs. Free-range eggs mean the hens have not been confined to batteries but were free to wander and feed freely.

Egg whites and yolks

In some recipes the egg whites are separated from the yolks. To do this quickly and easily first have two small bowls or containers ready.

Give the egg shell a sharp tap on the edge of one of the bowls. Carefully pull the two halves of the shell apart so allowing the egg white to drop into one bowl. To make certain you have extracted ALL the egg white tip the shell to one side then back again. Finally tip the yolk into the second bowl. When a recipe states that the eggs or egg whites should be whisked, it is better to use eggs that are 48 hours old. Absolutely new-laid eggs do not whisk well. Eggs whisk better when removed from the refrigerator for a time so they are at room temperature.

Size of eggs

Very large eggs weigh	over	70 g/2½ oz
Large eggs weigh	from	60 to 70 g/ 2 to 2½ oz
Medium eggs weigh		50 to 55 g/2 oz to a scant 2¼ oz
Small eggs weigh	under	40 to 50 g/ 1½ to 2 oz

The recommended egg sizes are given in recipes where this is very important. If no egg size is given use medium eggs.

FLAVOURINGS

These add interest to many baked dishes.

SPICES

Spices of all kinds deteriorate with long keeping so always buy small containers.

There are certain spices used in a wide range of baked recipes. You buy these as ground spices in small containers. Keep the lids tightly closed so the spices remain as fresh as possible. The most usual are:

Allspice from the tree of this name. It has a flavour rather like a mixture of cinnamon, cloves and nutmeg.

Cinnamon comes from the dried bark of a tree. It is a very common spice for baking.

Cloves are the closed buds of an evergreen tree. In an Apple Pie (page 117) the apples can be flavoured with a few whole dried cloves.
It is possible to buy ground cloves too. It is strong so use sparingly.
Oil of cloves is not used in this book.

Coriander is sold as seeds or a ground spice. It is popular in savoury dishes but less important in sweet ones.

Ginger is one of the most interesting spices. In most forms of baking it is used as ground ginger but fresh ginger from the underground stem of the plant is ideal for savoury dishes.

Ginger is also sold as a crystallized ingredient or preserved in syrup. Both of these forms of ginger can be used to enhance Gingerbreads, see pages 78 to 82.

Mixed spice as the name suggests is a mixture of most spices on this page. It is prepared by the manufacturers and different makes vary somewhat. It is not unlike allspice.

Nutmeg is another suitable spice in baking. It is sold as the large seed from the fruit of the nutmeg tree. This must be grated prior to use. Ground nutmeg is also available.

Mace is the dried outer skin of nutmeg used in a variety of cakes.

Vanilla is the pod (bean) of a climbing orchid. Today one can buy dried vanilla pods easily.

The best way to use these for baking is to put one or two vanilla pods into a jar of caster sugar or of icing (confectioners') sugar. Within a very short time the sugar becomes flavoured by the vanilla so when a recipe needs sugar and vanilla flavouring you simply weigh or measure out the required amount from the jar.

Do not forget to refill the jar with more sugar.

Vanilla-flavoured sugar can be purchased from supermarkets.

Vanilla essence and extract give a liquid form of this flavouring. The better flavour is available from the extract rather than the essence.

HERBS

In some of the savoury dishes in this book herbs are used. Each recipe gives advice on the right choice of herbs, both fresh and dried.

You will find that you need less of the dried herb for, in drying, the flavour is intensified.

ADDITIONAL INGREDIENTS IN BAKING

A variety of ingredients are added to various mixtures in this book.

DRIED FRUITS

The most used are currants, raisins and sultanas (seedless white raisins) sold in packs. Today most dried fruits are sold as 'ready-cleaned' but do inspect them well before using to make sure there are no small pieces of stalk.

If not labelled 'ready-cleaned' then the fruits should be washed in cold water, drained well and left to dry on flat dishes for 48 hours. Drying is important for damp fruit could spoil a cake by making it heavy.

In recipes sultanas or currants could be substituted for raisins although it is advisable to use the fruit recommended if possible.

Dried dates are used in a number of recipes. These give a good flavour and moist texture. For economy choose cooking dates (which are generally stoneless (pitted)).

Apricots, figs and **prunes** are excellent in some sweet and savoury baked dishes. The modern version of these fruits is called 'ready-to-eat' as they have been treated to tenderize them and to avoid the necessity of pre-soaking.

Some of these fruits are obtainable as 'organic'.

GLACÉ (CANDIED) AND CRYSTALLIZED FRUITS

Glacé cherries are frequently used in baking. The 'natural' version of these sweetened cherries are darker in colour than the usual red glacé fruit. If having to cut up glacé cherries you will find the job easier using kitchen scissors, rather than a knife.

Expensive **glacé pineapple, lemon** and **orange slices** and other fruits are sometimes used for decorating cakes.

Peel is sold as crystallized or candied peel. The modern version of the peel is ready-chopped which makes it quick and easy to use. You can however obtain large pieces of candied peel which need chopping.

Lemon, lime, and orange candied peel give a good flavour to many baked dishes.

Angelica is the crystallized stem of a plant that needs chopping.

FRESH FRUITS

Many recipes refer to the juice of oranges, lemons or limes to give flavour to the mixture. Halve and squeeze out the amount required.

In some recipes you are required to use the **fruit rind** or the **fruit zest**. The two things are not identical. The rind means you grate the orange or lemon or lime against the side of a grater. Where the recipe states 'fruit rind' it means that a *little* white pith could be included whereas 'fruit zest' means just the very tender coloured part only. The fruit rind or zest gives a strong flavour to food.

USING NUTS IN BAKING

Always make absolutely certain that no one is allergic to nuts or has an intolerance towards them.

Nuts for baking are generally sold in packets with the outer shells removed and they are already dried.

Supermarkets and Health Food Stores sell a good range.

Nuts add a pleasant taste and texture to many cakes, breads and biscuits (cookies) and are an interesting extra in some savoury dishes. They are ideal alternatives to meat for vegetarians.

Blanching nuts

This is the term used to denote removing the skin around the nuts. The most usual way to remove the skins from many nuts is to immerse them in boiling water for about one minute, remove them then strip away the skins. Dry the nuts well before adding them to the rest of ingredients.

The other way is to heat the nuts in a moderate oven for about 10 minutes then rub off the skins.

Chopping nuts

Place the nuts on a chopping board and cut to the desired size with a sharp knife. The safest way to do this is to hold the handle of the knife with your right hand and rotate this in a clockwise manner while supporting the top of the blade with your left hand. However it is better and easier to use a food processor. Either switch on and off or use the pulse action to obtain the required texture. Small amounts of nuts can be chopped in a liquidizer. Recipes will state whether the nuts should be chopped finely or coarsely.

Here are the most popular nuts to use.

ALMONDS

These are obtainable as whole nuts, with or without the skins. They are also available blanched and ready-chopped or flaked (cut into very thin slices) or slivered (cut into narrow strips lengthways).

Blanch these by the boiling water method above.

Ground almonds are used in a number of recipes and they give a pleasantly moist texture in a cake, adding crispness to biscuits (cookies) particularly Macaroons (see page 54).

BRAZILS

Used less often in baking but they do impart a very sweet taste.

Blanch these by baking in the oven, as described above.

CASHEWS

Not used often in sweet dishes but more in savoury ones.

HAZELNUTS (FILBERTS)

These are some of the most popular nuts in a variety of dishes.

Blanch by the oven method (see page 14).

PEANUTS

Although not a true nut it is used as one in many recipes. It is the ingredient to which many people, including children, are allergic.

Peanut butter is used in some recipes and it gives a very pleasant taste.

PECANS (HICKORY NUTS)

Sold as halved nuts for baking, they do not need skinning. An excellent alternative to walnuts.

PISTACHIOS

These small green nuts are used a great deal in cake decoration but they are a very good ingredient in both sweet and savoury dishes.

Blanch by the boiling water method.

WALNUTS

These are obtainable as halved walnuts and as walnut pieces, which are cheaper and quite suitable for chopping. Walnuts do not need skinning.

MEASUREMENTS IN RECIPES

The weights and measures in each recipe are clearly given so should be easy to follow.

Spoon Measures
When measuring any ingredient with a spoon make sure that it is only a level spoonful to ensure accuracy.

It is worthwhile purchasing a set or proper measuring spoons for often those in a cutlery set are not accurate.

A standard British (imperial) tablespoon is equivalent to 15 ml.

A standard British (imperial) teaspoon is equivalent to 5 ml.

An American teaspoon is the same size as a British teaspoon but an American tablespoon is smaller so always allow 1¼ American tablespoons instead of 1 British tablespoon.

HANDY MEASURES

If you have no scales available here are a few handy measures.

Soft Breadcrumbs
25 g/1 oz equals 5 imperial tablespoons or 6¼ American tablespoons.

Dried Fruit
25 g/1 oz equals 2½ imperial tablespoons or scant 3 American tablespoons.

Fats
25 g/1 oz equals 1⅔ imperial tablespoons or 2 American tablespoons.

Flour, cocoa, cornflour (corn starch)
25 g/1 oz equals 3 imperial tablespoons or 3¾ American tablespoons or ¼ cup.

Golden syrup (maple syrup), jam and honey
25 g/1 oz equals 1 imperial tablespoon or 1¼ American tablespoons.

Sugar (caster or granulated)
25g/1 oz equals 1⅔ imperial tablespoons or 2 American tablespoons.

Icing (confectioners) sugar
25g/1 oz equals 3½ imperial tablespoons or 4¼ American tablespoons.

EQUIPMENT FOR PREPARATION

The following list gives the equipment needed for preparing the majority of dishes in this book; on pages 19 to 21 you will find equipment for baking. While it is tempting to buy a great selection of cake tins (pans) there may be few occasions to use many of these.

Basins and mixing bowl
If you possess a large electric mixer, the bowl supplied can take the place of a large mixing bowl. If you do not own an electric mixer then you will need one large bowl. Small basins will be useful; heat resistant glassware are the most practical, although there are many other types from which to choose.

Boards
A flat board on which to roll out pastry or biscuit (cookie) dough unless the surface of your kitchen units is suitable.

A wooden board is easily cleaned.

It is recommended that a special board is kept for cutting up meat and poultry.

A small board for chopping purposes is also important, although this job can be done on the board used for pastry.

Always wash and dry boards well before storing.

Brush
A small pastry brush is useful for
> a) coating tins (pans) with melted fat or oil before baking, although this is less important today when many non-stick and modern baking parchment for lining tins is readily available (see under lining tins page 20).
> b) brushing beaten egg over certain dishes.

Always wash and dry the brush well.

Dredger
This is the name given to the container that holds flour. The perforated lid enables you to shake a small amount of flour over the board when rolling out pastry.

Grater
This is of general use apart from baking. Make sure you choose a grater with various sized cutting edges. You need this for grating cheese for savoury dishes, for grating lemon or orange rind, etc.

A grating attachment on an electric mixer or food processor is ideal for dealing with larger amounts but a small grater is still useful. Buy one of good quality, preferably stainless steel if possible, for this keeps its good finish.

Knives and spatulas
Good knives are invaluable for all kinds of food preparation. For baking purposes you need a sharp knife to cut or chop nuts. You also need a flat-bladed knife often called a palette knife or spatula, which is ideal for blending ingredients together.

A plastic pliable spatula is the best utensil for removing soft cake mixtures from the mixing bowl.

Measuring jug

This is important to ensure accurate measurements of liquid ingredients and the American measures.

There are various sizes of measuring jugs. When buying one select the jug that gives millilitres and fluid ounces or ¼ pint, ½ pint etc. and then you are prepared for all measures. An American cup is equivalent to 8 fl oz.

Scales

As correct preparations of ingredients are so important scales are essential when making cakes, pastry, biscuits (cookies) etc. unless you prefer to use American cup measures.

There is a very wide choice of scales available today ranging from the traditional type with a selection of weights to those that register the weight on a gauge.

Sieve

While this may not be essential, a sieve is important, for most recipes state 'sift the flour'. This ensures it is smooth, it also lightens flour by incorporating air and sieving makes certain that additional ingredients, such as baking powder, are evenly mixed with the flour. The sieve is placed over the basin or bowl so choose one that fits over the bowl or basin you will use.

A fine nylon sieve is the most useful when baking or sifting icing sugar to make sure it is free from lumps.

Spoons

The most important spoons used in baking are
   a) for measuring, i.e. a teaspoon, a tablespoon and an American tablespoon if you want to follow these measurements (see page 16).
   b) a wooden spoon for creaming fat and sugar, etc. Even if you have an electric mixer or food processor there will be times when you will find a wooden spoon useful.

Whisk

In many recipes the term 'whisk' is used. If you have an electric mixer you will use the whisking attachment on many occasions but if most of the ingredients are already being prepared in the electric mixer you will need to whisk the egg whites in a separate bowl.

A balloon or rotary type whisk is good for all purposes but a flatter type, often called a coil whisk, is even better if you intend to prepare a light sponge mixture by hand (see page 101).

The advantages of a small electric whisk are outlined on page 23.

Wire cooling tray

When most biscuits (cookies), cakes and other baked dishes are cooked you are advised to remove them from the tin (pan) on to this tray. This means the air can circulate around the food and cool it. In some cases you are advised to leave the food in or on the baking tin or tray. This is because it may break if removed too early. In most cases an early removal from the baking equipment is important to prevent unwanted condensation as the food cools.

EQUIPMENT FOR BAKING

The following gives the tins (pans) and other equipment used in recipes in this book. Shops generally sell cake tins by measurements, rather than capacity of food.

GOOD CAKE TINS

It is worthwhile buying the best quality tins you can afford for they contribute to good baking results and will last in perfect condition for many years.

Many cake tins have a 'non-stick' finish, so you may feel it is not necessary to grease and flour or line the tins. That may be true when the tins are new but it is advisable after the tins have been used several times. However when tins with any surface are new

a) follow the manufacturer's instructions about washing and preparing them before use. It is important NOT to use abrasive cleaners.

b) grease and flour them if appropriate.

c) if you are stacking the tins one on top of another it is sensible to put a sheet of kitchen paper between each tin so there is no fear of the finish being damaged.

Non-stick tins (pans) of all kinds are readily available. As the name indicates, this means that most food will not stick to the surface during the baking time and that lining or greasing the tins(s) is not essential. There are still cases when it is better to line or grease the tin, because the ingredients used may make it likely that the particular mixture could stick. This advice is clearly stated in the recipe.

Look after 'non-stick' tins with great care for their surface can be spoiled by too abrasive cleaning. Buy the best quality tins you can afford, they will keep their shape and finish always.

Special oven-proof rubber cake, muffin and patty tins (pans) are a modern development. These do not need lining or greasing and food does not stick.

Small cake trays
These are often known as patty tins and you have one tin with a number of small cavities. These are required for baking little cakes, small pastry cases or tarts and could be used to bake muffins, although true muffin tins are somewhat larger.

You can buy trays of 6, 9 or 12, the most useful being 12.

Large cakes
If buying just one cake tin I would choose a 20 cm/8 inch round one. It is useful though to have a second 18 cm/7 inch tin for smaller cakes.

If you prefer to make square, rather than round cakes, you would need an 18 cm/7 inch square tin to take the place of the 20 cm/8 inch round one. The amount of ingredients and baking time would be the same. A 15 cm/6 inch square tin is equivalent to an 18 cm/7 inch round one.

Muffin tins
We have become so fond of American-style muffins in this country that special muffin tins are readily available. They are deeper and slightly larger in diameter than the usual patty tins; generally sold in a tray of 6.

Flat baking trays or sheets
One or two of these are essential for baking biscuits (cookies), scones (biscuits) and many kinds of bread. Choose trays or sheets of good quality that will not 'buckle' and become out of shape with continual use. A baking sheet is often supplied with the cooker.

A special tray with a shallow rim around it is used especially for making a Swiss roll (Jelly roll). It can be used for other purposes too. An ideal size for this is 25 x 18 cm/10 x 7 inches.

Oblong loaf tin
If you intend making bread this is a useful tin, although instructions for loaves in this book also contain advice for forming the dough into a suitable shape to bake on a flat baking tray or sheet.

The most useful sized loaf tin would be a 450 g/1 lb size. If you become very enthusiastic about bread-making you may require more than one tin so you can make a larger batch of bread, eat some while fresh and freeze the remainder.

Sandwich tins
These are important for layer cakes. The most useful for baking the recipes in this book is two 18 cm/7 inch tins.

TO LINE TINS

Although non-stick tins (cake pans) often mean that lining them is not essential, there are recipes where the ingredients are inclined to stick, also you may not possess non-stick tins. In this case it is important to use baking parchment or greased greaseproof (wax) paper and insert this into the tin before adding the mixture. Re-usable baking silicone is available and as the name suggests this can be used over and over again. Simply wipe and dry after use. It is sensible to cut out shapes to fit the tins (pans) you use most.

Greasing
To grease the greaseproof paper use a little olive oil or melted butter or melted lard and spread this over the surface of the greaseproof paper with a pastry brush. Baking parchment rarely needs greasing. The fat could be melted in a small dish in the microwave.

It is possible to buy rounds of baking parchment of various sizes to fit the base of tins.

To line the bottom of a tin: stand the tin on greaseproof paper or baking parchment. Draw round the tin, cut out the paper shape. Put a very little grease on the inside of the tin base to hold the paper in position, put in the paper; grease, or grease and flour, the inside of the tin and paper.

To line the sides and bottom of a round tin: make a round as above. Cut a band of single or double thickness greaseproof or waxed paper or baking parchment 2.5 to 3.5 cm/1 to 1½ inches deeper than the depth of the tin and the full length of the circumference of the cake tin. Make cuts at regular intervals to a depth of about 1.5 cm/½ inch. Grease the bottom and side of the tin in one or two places to hold the bands in position.

Put in the band of paper, with the cut edges at the bottom. These will open out to make a snug fit on the tin base.

Put the round of paper for the base on top then grease, or grease and flour, the paper. If using baking parchment this greasing step is not necessary; unless stated it should be done.

To line an oblong tin: *Method 1:* cut two pieces of greaseproof paper or waxed paper or baking parchment, one to line the sides and base of the tin and the other to line the ends and base.

Method 2: cut the paper sufficiently large to completely cover the inside and sides of the tin, mitring (cutting down) the corners. Line a square tin in the same way.

Small paper cases
Some small cakes and muffins should be baked in paper cases to prevent any possibility of sticking to the tins or breaking as they come out.

These cases are sold in packs.

EQUIPMENT FOR PASTRY DISHES

The simplest and most popular form of pastry is known as shortcrust (basic pie dough).

Full directions for making this begin on page 108 followed by a selection of sweet and savoury dishes in which pastry is an important part. Dishes using light puff and filo pastry are on pages 127 to 130 and 136.

PASTRY MAKING

In order to make pastry by hand, rather than using an electric mixer or food processor, described on page 109, you need the following equipment.

Scales or a **measure** – if following American quantities – it is important to have the right proportions of fat and flour.

A large **bowl** in which to mix the ingredients together; a container of water plus a **tablespoon**, so you add the liquid gradually. When the pastry is mixed you need a **rolling-pin**, (see below) and a **flour dredger** (see page 22). The dough will be rolled out on a flat surface so you need a **board** (see page 17).

Rolling-pin

There are many attractive ceramic rolling-pins on the market, these have the disadvantage that they are breakable. The most popular type is made of wood. Before buying a rolling-pin handle it to see if it feels a comfortable length and weight. If deciding on a wooden kind check to see that the surface is absolutely smooth. Some rolling-pins have handles at either end, there is no great advantage in these, it is just a matter of personal choice.

Wash and dry rolling-pins well, particularly if they are made of wood.

Cutters

These are essential for cutting around the pastry to make rounds to fit into small tins (pans) for tartlets. They are also used when making various biscuits (cookies). Cutters are made of metal or of plastic, either are efficient. Metal gives a slightly sharper edge to the rounds but are more easily bent out of shape than plastic. They must be dried with great care after washing them.

While you can buy individual cutters they are often sold in sets, giving a choice of sizes. A size that is useful to fit most patty tins is 7.5 cm/ 3 inches.

FOR BAKING PASTRY

One of the most popular pastry dishes in Britain is a sweet or savoury pie, i.e. a dish with fruit or meat or other ingredients in a deep dish with a covering of pastry; for this you require a pie dish.

Pie dishes

These are sold by capacity, rather than by measurements and are made in heat-proof ceramic or glassware.

To make a pie that gives two average sized portions you need a dish of 600 ml/1 pint (2½ cup) capacity; for four portions a 1.2 litre/2 pint (5 cup) dish.

It is easier to remove a hot, and quite heavy, pie dish from the oven if it is placed on a baking sheet when first placed in to the oven.

Flan rings, tins (pie pans) and dishes

There are several recipes for open tarts or flans in this book. The Quiche on page 135 is one example of these. In order to bake the pastry shape you need a suitable container. This can be obtained in several ways.

1. **Flan tin (pan).** Undoubtedly pastry is better baked in metal, rather than in a dish, (see Flan dish). The cooked pastry will be more crisp. Most flan tins have a removable base which makes it easy to lift the pastry case, or filled pastry, out of the tin.

   Choose an 18 to 20 cm/7 to 8 inch tin and one of at least 2.5 cm/ 1 inch in depth. They can be obtained with plain edges or serrated ones. The latter may be slightly more difficult to line with pastry when you start cooking but it looks more attractive.

2. **Flan ring.** This is just a metal ring and in order to use this it must be placed on a metal baking sheet, to provide the base.

   The advantage of using a flan ring, rather than a flan tin, is that it is easier to *slide* the baked pastry from the metal sheet, rather than lifting it from the tin.

It is less suitable to use a flan ring if you are filling the pastry with a very liquid mixture, as in a quiche, as this gives less support.

3. **Flan dish.** These are made in heat-resistant ceramics or glassware. They look attractive and have the advantage that the cooked pastry can be served in the dish. Undoubtedly pastry is less crisp when cooked in a dish rather than a tin, but there is advice on how to get the best results on page 125. Choose a similar size as for a flan tin.

More equipment

As time goes by you may find you need some extra containers that will enable you to make different kinds of dishes. Some of these, such as a soufflé dish, are mentioned in the recipes for microwave cakes, page 107. In each case though I have suggested making the dish in an alternative basic container.

Oven gloves
These are an essential for all forms of cooking so invest in at least one pair.

They are obtainable as two separate gloves or a long strip with two pockets in which to put your hands.

When buying either type check they are really *well-padded*, so you give adequate protection to your hands when handling hot food. Thin oven gloves – like teacloths (dish towels), give inadequate protection against hot utensils.

ELECTRIC MIXERS

These are of great value for many of the stages when preparing certain biscuits (cookies), bread and cakes. They are less efficient than a food processor for preparing the 'rubbed-in' mixture for shortcrust pastry (basic pie dough), scones (biscuits) and some biscuits (cookies).

Small hand-held electric mixers are reasonably economical to buy and can deal with small quantities of ingredients very efficiently. They are ideal for whisking eggs, egg whites and cream and for creaming small amounts of fat and sugar. You can use them with any of the basins you possess although some models are sold with a stand and their own mixing bowl.

The comments about the correct speed (see page 24) apply with a small electric mixer just as they do with the larger models.

Large electric mixers save much time and energy as they will cream or whisk the various ingredients while you continue with other jobs.

It is essential to appreciate the fact that the action of any mixer is very energetic and the large mixers have a considerable amount of power. You must therefore adjust the *speed* of mixing and watch the *timing* so that food is not over-mixed.

Speed: adjust the speed on the electric mixer to approximate that of hand mixing. When creaming fat and sugar by hand one uses a steady, relatively slow action, copy this by setting the mixer to the lowest speed. As the fat and sugar soften you can raise the speed slightly.

Too rapid an action throws the ingredients to the side of the bowl.

When whisking ingredients by hand we use a brisk movement, this can be copied with the mixer by using a higher speed.

Kneading a bread or biscuit (cookie) dough is a very slow and deliberate action, so repeat this by setting the mixer to the lowest speed. Never over-knead bread by machine, or indeed by hand.

Check the manufacturer's instructions for the appropriate attachment to use for each process, e.g. most large mixers have a whisking tool, one for creaming and a dough hook for kneading.

Any special advice on using an electric mixer is given in the introduction to the various groups of recipes

A FOOD PROCESSOR

Modern food processors, like mixers, can save a great deal of time in preparing many ingredients but it is essential to appreciate the *speed* and *power* of this electrical equipment. Various actions often take a matter of seconds, rather than minutes.

Remember that the cutting edges used are ultra sharp and handle these with the utmost care.

Use the food processor for:

Chopping nuts: watch carefully to see that the nuts are not ground to a powder, which will spoil the texture of the dish. It is best to use the pulse action if your machine has this facility.

Creaming ingredients: the processor will cream fat and sugar or make one-stage mixtures rapidly and well. Because of the speed of mixing, one does not incorporate as much air into the mixture as when doing this by hand or with an electric mixer.

It is very good for one-stage mixtures, as in the various recipes. Do read the comments on page 72.

Rubbing fat into flour for pastry and scones, etc. This is when special care must be taken that the food processor does not over-handle the mixture. Watch carefully and the moment the fat has been incorporated into the flour switch off. The results will be good. If you leave the machine running you force the mixture to bind together, resulting in a very crumbly texture, see page 110.

When making biscuits you can continue until the ingredients, including egg, or any liquid, are just blended together. Over-handling will produce a tougher mixture.

Special advice on using the processor is given in the various sections.

A MICROWAVE

A microwave oven has become a familiar piece of equipment in a large proportion of kitchens; the saving of cooking time when this is used is invaluable.

There is a selection of recipes that are especially suitable for cooking in a microwave oven on pages 176 to 178. In addition you will find a note on other recipes where microwave cooking can be applied to give an acceptable result.

Always follow the advice about the power output given in the recipe or the introduction to the section. Often a lower output (power) will result in a better result than by using full output. Comments about this are on page 107.

The microwave is an excellent appliance to use when melting chocolate or small amounts of fat, etc. It is ideal for defrosting cakes and bread, etc. Do read the special instructions on pages 176 to 178.

EQUIPMENT FOR MICROWAVE COOKING

If you have a combination microwave, i.e. one that gives both conventional plus microwave heating then follow the manufacturer's advice as to the utensils you can use. Most useful is **The Basics Basics Combination & Microwave Handbook** by Carol Bowen.

In an ordinary microwave oven you must use recommended plastic-ware or ordinary ceramic and glassware.

Always check the manufacturer's advice about the use of *foil* and *clingfilm* in that particular oven.

STANDING TIME

When you are familiar with microwave cooking you will appreciate that food needs to stand for a short time after it comes out of the microwave oven.

This applies to dishes you have baked by microwave as well as other forms of cooking.

FOLLOWING THE RECIPES

Everyone works out the best method to use when preparing various kinds of food but I have found these points extremely important and helpful.

1. Assemble all the ingredients listed in the recipe, this will enable you to check that you have everything that is required.
2. Check through the method. Do any ingredients, such as nuts or cheese need chopping or grating? If this is the case get these jobs done first before starting to assemble the dish ready for cooking. You don't want to stop halfway through, to do these processes; you may be diverted from following the correct method.
3. Gather together the tin or tins (pans) and other utensils you may need. Prepare any tins if that job needs doing. Get out the wooden spoon, measuring jug, etc. if these are required for the recipe. If you watch a good television or live demonstration you will see all the essential tools are at hand so there is no frantic looking for them. This makes it easier and time-effective in your kitchen.
4. Check the oven setting required and pre-heat the oven *at the stage given in the recipe*. In many recipes this is at stage 1 but not always.

In some recipes, such as when making bread, there is a time-lag when the dough has to stand to 'prove' (rise) so it would be a waste of fuel to heat the oven too early. The correct oven heat is at the top of each recipe.

5.   Check the timing when you put the food into the oven. It is so easy to forget exactly WHEN you started baking the dish. Invest in a timer that has a really *loud* ring that you can hear when not adjacent to the cooker. Remember though that ovens vary and it is worthwhile checking the cooking process a little early, just in case the food is ready a few minutes before the time given.

6.   Test the food, where this is possible, following the advice in the recipe but appreciate the fact that your oven may be slightly *slower* than average and a little extra cooking time may be needed. Use your timer to remind you to check again after a few minutes.

7.   When you are satisfied that the dish is perfectly cooked bring it out of the oven. Either leave it to cool for the time recommended in the recipe or lift on to the wire cooling tray.

8.   Remember that baked food, when it comes from the oven, is *very hot* so be careful where you place the dish or a tin. Check the surface is dry and suitable for hot containers.

Quantities in Recipes

Each recipe gives the approximate number of small cakes, muffins or biscuits (cookies) that the mixture will make. Do not be unduly worried if you make slightly less or more, your tins (pans) are just a little larger or smaller than those in which the food was tested.

MEASURING THE INGREDIENTS

There are three sets of measurements in the recipes.
The first is **metric**, the second **imperial** and the third **American**.

Metric Measures

Solid metric measures are given in grammes, abbreviated to g and larger amounts in kilogrammes, abbreviated to kg.

Liquid measures are given in millilitres abbreviated to ml and larger amounts to litres, this word is not abbreviated.

Sometimes a measurement of liquid or solid ingredients is given in teaspoons and tablespoons. As explained on page 16 a teaspoon is equivalent to 5 ml and a tablespoon to 15 ml. These ml measurements are not given in the recipes.

Imperial Measures

Solid imperial measures are given in ounces, abbreviated to oz and larger amounts to pounds abbreviated to lb.

Liquid measures are given in two ways, i.e. pints or proportions of pints or liquid oz. The latter is sometimes used when dealing with foods one buys, such as yoghurt and similar products.

Sometimes a teaspoon or tablespoon measure is used for some solid ingredients, such as sugar, etc. as well as for liquids.

American Measures

The most usual way of measuring in America is by the cup but this must be an accurate one. The standard American cup is 224 ml/8 fl oz capacity and sets of American cup measures can be bought from kitchenware shops. This cup is used to measure both liquid and solid ingredients, e.g. 1 American cup of flour is equivalent to 115 g/4 oz but an American cup of butter is 225 g/8 oz.

Sometimes you will find ounces (oz) and pounds (lb) under the American column for these are used when purchasing certain foods.

Tablespoons are used but these will not match the tablespoon measure under metric/imperial as the American tablespoon is slightly smaller. Where just 1 tablespoon is used no adjustment is made but for 2 metric/imperial tablespoons you need 2½ American tablespoons. An American teaspoon is the same size as the metric/imperial one.

When filling an American cup you may find you are sometimes told to 'pack tightly', this is to ensure the accurate weight of the food. In most cases though simply add the ingredients to the cup and do not press down or make any effort to pack more tightly.

Comparing Measurements

You must follow one list of measurements and not wander from one column to another. You may however like to know just WHY certain amounts are given.

The **exact** metric equivalent amounts to match the imperial ones would be difficult to weigh or measure so rounded figures are given, e.g. 28.35 g is the exact equivalent of 1 oz but this is calculated as 25 g. As the amounts get larger a certain adjustment has to made, e.g. 115 g is given as the equivalent of 4 oz and 225 g as 8 oz.

Very occasionally an **exact** metric figure is listed. This is where the very accurate amount of liquid or food is essential for the success of that particular recipe.

MADE IN MINUTES

On the next pages you will find a selection of the following recipes:

Muffins of various kinds; a selection of scones (biscuits); Popovers.

All of these are quickly made and need a short baking time. **They should be baked towards the top of the oven at the setting given in the recipe – except with a fan oven, where every shelf has the same temperature.**

Sweet and savoury muffins are ideal for any time of the day, including breakfast. Scones are regarded as a teatime delicacy but savoury ones can be used instead of bread to accompany soups or salads.

Popovers are an American speciality we might well adopt. Based on a batter, not unlike a Yorkshire Pudding, they are an ideal container for sweet or savoury ingredients. They make a change from pastry and are quicker to prepare.

MAKING MUFFINS

Until recently, if you mentioned muffins in Britain, you were talking about a yeast teacake, not unlike a thickish pancake. Nowadays we have virtually forgotten these traditional muffins in favour of the American type, which are quite different. They are infinitely versatile for you can include fruits of various kinds or cheese or bacon or base the recipe on cornmeal (or polenta) instead of flour. The basic rules for success are similar.

1. Combine the ingredients speedily but lightly. Do **NOT over-beat or over-mix**. These actions will produce a tough texture to the muffins. If there appears to be small uneven lumps do not worry they will disappear in baking. The exception to this rule is the recipe on page 30.
2. In view of the liquid consistency of the mixture you must grease muffin or patty tins (shells) well, this of course is not necessary if you buy paper cases to insert into the tins. If the tins are shallow you must use paper cases to support the mixture, for this rises quite appreciably. Supermarkets and stationers sell packs of paper cases for muffin or patty tins. Always fill tins or paper cases three-quarters full, then the muffins will rise high with rounded tops.
3. Bake the muffins as soon as they are prepared, the mixture is not improved by standing. When cooked, test by pressing on top – they should feel firm.
4. If baking in the greased tins allow the muffins to stand in the tins for 5 minutes after they come from the oven, they could break if you try to lift them out before then. If baked in paper cases they may be served or placed on a wire cooling tray immediately they come from the oven.

FOR MUFFINS YOU NEED:

1. To melt the butter or margarine, this makes it easier to mix with the milk and eggs. Either melt over a low heat in a saucepan or in a basin in the microwave on DEFROST setting. Cool before mixing with the other ingredients.
2. Adding eggs. When new to cooking it is sensible to break the first egg into a basin or cup, rather than adding it straight to the other ingredients. You can check that no shell has dropped in. After adding it to the mixture repeat with the second egg.

   In many recipes you are told to whisk the eggs before adding them to other ingredients, this step is not necessary when making muffins.

   To break the egg: have a basin or cup ready, sharply tap the shell against the rim, making a crack, then gently pull the two halves of the shell apart so allowing the egg to drop into the container.

PLAIN MUFFINS

These muffins are only slightly sweetened which makes them ideal to serve at breakfast time with marmalade, jam or honey. Before making them check the advice on the previous page.

Oven Setting: 200°C/400°F, Gas Mark 6 or 190°C with a fan oven
Baking Time: 15 minutes
Baking Equipment: 12 x 7.5 cm/3 inch patty tins (shells), preferably with paper cases. See under Variation.
Makes: 12 muffins. Eat when fresh. They freeze well, reheat for a few minutes from frozen.

Metric/Imperial	Ingredients	American
40 g/1½ oz	butter, melted	3 tablespoons
190 ml/6 fl oz	milk	¾ cup
2 small	eggs	2 small
175 g/6 oz	self-raising flour with ½ teaspoon baking powder or plain (all-purpose) flour with 2 teaspoons baking powder	1½ cups
1 pinch	salt	1 pinch
50 g/2 oz	caster sugar	¼ cup

1. Preheat the oven; insert paper cases into the patty tins or grease them well if you have no paper cases.
2. Mix the melted, but cool, butter with the milk and eggs. Sift the flour and salt, add the sugar then blend with the egg mixture.
3. Spoon into the tins or paper cases, they should be three-quarters full.
4. Bake until well risen and firm. Remove from the oven and allow to cool for 5 minutes in the tins or lift out at once if in paper cases. Place on a wire cooling tray. Serve hot, warm or cold.

Variation

- Use 8 to 9 larger muffin tins about 10 cm/4 inches in diameter and bake for 20 minutes.

To make a change

Blueberry Muffins: add 100 g/3½ oz (scant 1 cup) blueberries to the mixture at the end of stage 2. The berries should be rinsed in cold water then allowed to dry. Other fruits, such as raspberries, small strawberries, blackberries, black, red and white currants, could be added instead. If the fruit is very acid increase the sugar in the recipe above to 85 g/3 oz (⅜ cup).

Nut Muffins: chop enough pecans, walnuts or almonds to give 50 g/2 oz (½ cup). Add to the ingredients after the flour at stage 2.

Raisin Muffins: add 85 g/3 oz (scant ½ cup) raisins to the hot butter before adding the milk and egg at stage 2. This softens the raisins and makes them more succulent. Other dried fruit can be used.

HONEY AND BLUEBERRY MUFFINS

These muffins are unusual in that the mixture is handled more briskly than in other muffin recipes. This is because the honey is heavy and therefore has a tendency to fall to the bottom of the other ingredients, so use an energetic, but not prolonged, beating movement with your wooden spoon immediately before spooning the mixture into the paper cases or tins (pans).

Oven Setting:	200°C/400°F, Gas Mark 6 or 190°C with a fan oven
Baking Time:	15 to 18 minutes
Baking Equipment:	12 x 7.5 cm/3 inch patty tins (shells) preferably with paper cases. See under Variation.
Makes:	12 muffins. Eat when fresh. They freeze well, reheat for a few minutes from frozen.

Metric/Imperial	Ingredients	American
85 g/3 oz	blueberries	¾ cup
1½ tablespoons	olive or other vegetable oil	1¾ tablespoons
2 small	eggs	2 small
85 ml/3 fl oz	milk	⅜ cup
4 level tablespoons	clear (thin) honey	5 level tablespoons
1 tablespoon	caster sugar, optional	1 tablespoon
175 g/6 oz	self-raising flour with 1 level teaspoon baking powder or plain (all-purpose) flour with 2½ level teaspoons baking powder	1½ cups
1 pinch	salt	1 pinch
	To fill the muffins	
	little extra honey	

1. Preheat the oven; insert the paper cases into the muffin tins or grease the tins very well if you have no paper cases.
2. Rinse the blueberries in cold water, drain and leave on kitchen (wax) paper to dry.
3. In a good-sized basin beat the oil with the eggs, milk, honey and sugar.
4. Sift the flour, baking powder and salt into the egg mixture then stir in the blueberries. Mix thoroughly then spoon into the tins or paper cases.
5. With a teaspoon make a small well in the top of each muffin and fill with a little honey.
6. Bake until well risen and firm. Serve hot, warm or cold.

Variation

- Use 8 to 9 larger muffin tins about 10 cm/4 inches in diameter and bake for 20 to 25 minutes.

To make a change

Chocolate, Honey and Blueberry Muffins: follow the recipe above but **replace** 25 g/1 oz (¼ cup) of flour with the same amount of chocolate powder. Sift this with the flour, baking powder and salt.

Honey and Pecan Muffins: follow the directions in the recipe above but omit the blueberries and **add** 85 g/3 oz (scant ½ cup) chopped pecan nuts.

Maple Syrup and Blueberry Muffins: follow the directions in the recipe above but **replace** the honey with maple syrup.

CHEESE MUFFINS

These muffins are ideal to serve as a snack with more cheese or with a vegetable or fish soup or all kinds of salads. Like the muffins on pages 29 and 30 they should be baked in well-greased tins, even if the surface is non-stick, since cheese makes the mixture inclined to stick. Better still insert paper cases into the tins. Because the cheese contains an appreciable amount of fat do not increase the amount of butter in the recipe.

Oven Setting: 200°C/400°F, Gas Mark 6 or 190°C with a fan oven.
Baking Time: 15 to 18 minutes
Baking Equipment: 12 x 7.5 cm/3 inch patty tins (shells), preferably with paper cases. See under Variation.
Makes: 12 muffins. Eat when fresh. They freeze well, reheat from frozen.

Metric/Imperial	Ingredients	American
25 g/1 oz	**butter, melted**	2 tablespoons
190 ml/6 fl oz	**milk**	¾ cup
2 small	**eggs**	2 small

85 g/3 oz	*Cheddar or Cheshire or Double Gloucester cheese, finely grated*	*³/₄ cup*
175 g/6 oz	*self-raising flour with 1 teaspoon baking powder or plain (all-purpose) flour with 2¹/₂ teaspoons baking powder*	*1¹/₂ cups*
1 pinch	*salt*	*1 pinch*
1 pinch	*dry mustard powder*	*1 pinch*
1 shake	*cayenne or black pepper*	*1 shake*

1. Preheat the oven; insert paper cases into the patty tins or grease them well if you have no paper cases.
2. Mix the melted, but cool, butter with the milk, eggs and cheese. Sift the flour with the baking powder, salt, mustard, and pepper. Blend with the cheese mixture.
3. Spoon into the tins or paper cases, they should be three-quarters full.
4. Bake until well risen and firm. Remove from the oven but allow to cool in the tins for 5 minutes. If using paper cases lift out of the tins immediately and place on a wire cooling tray. These are better served piping hot.

Variation

• Use 8 to 9 large muffin tins about 10 cm/4 inches in diameter. Bake for 22 to 25 minutes.

To make a change

Bacon Muffins: either **omit** all the cheese and **add** 85 g/3 oz (³/₈ cup) finely chopped cooked bacon **or use** 40 g/1¹/₂ oz (¹/₆ cup) grated cheese and 50 g/2 oz (¹/₄ cup) cooked chopped bacon. Cooked ham may be used instead.

Cheese and Sesame Seed Muffins: use Cheese muffins recipe but **add** 1 teaspoon sesame seeds. Top each muffin with a sprinkling of grated cheese and sesame seeds before baking.

GLUTEN-FREE FLOUR IN MUFFINS

As some people are either intolerant to wheat, or even allergic to it, ordinary flour cannot be used for these sufferers. Fortunately all supermarkets now have good stocks of gluten-free flour of various kinds. This flour is excellent in all the muffin recipes in this book. The muffins rise well, providing you realise that the flour is the equivalent of plain (all-purpose) flour, and add the same amount of baking powder as given in each recipe with that flour.

OIL IN MUFFINS

Butter or margarine can be replaced with olive or sunflower oil. In place of each 25 g/1 oz fat (2 tablespoons) use 30 ml/1 fl oz (⅛ cup) of oil.

PERFECT SCONES

Some scones (biscuits in America) can be served instead of muffins. Scones should be very light in texture, be a good shape and have a pleasing pale golden colour. There is a wide range of flavourings, both sweet and savoury, that can be added to the plain mixture. Recipes for these are given on the following pages.

The basic ingredients for making scones have altered during the past few years. Once both bicarbonate of soda (baking soda) and cream of tartar were added to plain (all-purpose) flour. In the days when milk soured naturally this was sometimes used as the liquid to mix the dough but today's pasteurised milk tastes unpleasant as it becomes stale. Buttermilk, which can be purchased from some supermarkets, is an alternative for the liquid.

Nowadays it has been found that modern self-raising flour, or plain flour with baking powder, gives a good result. However to acquaint you with the various raising agents that can be used I list these on page 34.

A golden rule is NOT to exceed any recommended amount of raising agent; spoon measures must be level. Nothing is worse than to taste an excessive amount of baking powder or other alternatives in the cooked scones. I think some people aim for a scone that rises drastically; in my opinion it is far better to have one that rises moderately but tastes good.

Here are some of the other points to follow:

1. Make sure the dough is not too dry, it should be definitely stickier than a shortcrust (basic pie) dough. Your fingers may get a little sticky in handling it.
2. Do not spend too much time in rolling out the dough, the lighter and quicker this is handled the better. Some excellent cooks just pat out the dough.
3. The oven must be thoroughly pre-heated before the scones are placed into it. The baking time is short and the heat should be high.
4. Place the baking tray of scones towards the top of the oven, unless you have a fan oven, when all shelf positions should have the same heat.
5. Test the scones early, scones contain only a small amount of fat and they will become too dry if over-baked by even a few minutes.

To test if the scones are cooked, press the sides; they should feel firm.
6. To keep scones soft place a clean dry teacloth (dish towel) over the wire cooling tray, add the hot scones and cover with a second cloth. This creates condensation and gives soft scones. For crisp scones do not use cloths.
7. Scones freeze well, see page 34.

Alternative Raising Agents

Self-raising flour needs no extra raising agents, unless specifically mentioned. Instead of the plain (all-purpose) flour and baking powder given in the recipes you could use:-

To 225 g/8 oz (2 cups) flour add
  $\frac{1}{2}$ level teaspoon bicarbonate of soda (baking soda) and 1 level teaspoon cream of tartar or, if mixing with buttermilk or soured milk $\frac{1}{2}$ level teaspoon bicarbonate of soda and $\frac{1}{2}$ level teaspoon cream of tartar
ALWAYS sift the raising agents carefully with the flour.

BASIC PLAIN SWEET SCONES

The following recipe is made with white flour. When using wholemeal (wholewheat) flour you will need a little extra milk, see the information on page 35. The 50 g/2 oz ($\frac{1}{4}$ cup) of butter or margarine is the maximum amount of fat to use for a light scone. If you are trying to cut down on fat use 25 g/1 oz (2 tablespoons) of butter or margarine; this is quite enough to produce a good scone.

Oven Setting: 220°C/425°F, Gas Mark 7 or 210°C with a fan oven
Baking Time: 10 to 12 minutes, see stage 6
Baking Equipment: one flat baking (cookie) tray
Makes: 8 to 15, see stage 5. Eat when hot or freshly made or cool then pack and freeze. Reheat from frozen.

Metric/Imperial	Ingredients	American
225 g/8 oz	*self-raising flour or plain (all-purpose) flour with 2 teaspoons baking powder*	2 cups
pinch	salt	pinch
25 to 50 g/1 to 2 oz	**butter or margarine**	2 to 4 tablespoons
50 g/2 oz or to taste	caster sugar	$\frac{1}{4}$ cup or to taste
approx 150 ml/$\frac{1}{4}$ pint	milk	approx $\frac{2}{3}$ cup
	To glaze, optional	
1 to 2 tablespoons	milk	1 to 2$\frac{1}{2}$ tablespoons

1. Preheat the oven, with plain scones it is not necessary to grease or line the baking tray. A very light dusting of flour makes certain they do not stick to the tin.
2. Sift the flour, or flour and baking powder, and salt into a mixing bowl, rub in the butter or margarine (see advice on page 109) then add the sugar.
3. Gradually add enough milk to give a SOFT rolling consistency, i.e. the mixture can be gathered together to form a ball but in doing so your fingers will become a little sticky. Place on a lightly floured board.
4. Either roll out with a lightly floured rolling pin or pat out until a

smooth shape, no more than 2 cm/³/₄ inch in thickness. You can make them slightly thinner.

5. Select a round pastry cutter, dip the cutting edge in a very little flour, this enables you to press easily through the dough, then cut into rounds. A usual size is about 6.25 to 7.5 cm/2¹/₂ to 3 inches in diameter but smaller scones can be about 5 cm/2 inches in diameter. The size and thickness will affect the exact baking time and the quantity of scones.

6. Place the scones on the baking tray. If you want them to have a slight shine dip a pastry brush into the milk and brush over the top of each scone, do not make them too wet. Cook until firm to the touch then remove on to a wire cooling tray, see point 6 on page 33.

A SCONE ROUND

1. Instead of cutting out individual scones form the dough into a neat round at stage 4 above. Place this on to the baking tray.
2. With a knife mark the round into 6 to 8 portions, do not cut right through the dough. Brush the top with a little milk.
3. Bake at the oven setting given above and allow about 20 minutes. If the round is becoming slightly too brown at the end of 12 to 15 minutes, lower the heat to 190°C/375°F, Gas Mark 5 or 180°C with a fan oven for the rest of the cooking time.

MIXING SCONES IN AN ELECTRIC MIXER OR FOOD PROCESSOR

The fat can be rubbed into the flour with the whisk of the electric mixer. When first making scones though it is advisable to add the liquid by hand (see under pastry point 4 on page 109). The same advice applies when using a food processor, see point 2 on page 110.

WHOLEMEAL SWEET SCONES

Follow the recipe on page 34 but use wholemeal (wholewheat) self-raising or plain flour with the same amount of baking powder.

When you sift the flour you will probably find some grains of bran left in the sieve, simply tip these back into the mixing bowl. The mixture absorbs about 1 to 1¹/₄ tablespoons more milk than when using white flour. This means the scones may take 1 to 2 minutes longer cooking time.

BROWN SWEET SCONES

Use half white flour and half wholemeal flour and follow the recipe on page 34. You will find you need to add ¹/₂ to 1 tablespoon more milk than when using white flour. The baking time should be similar as for white scones.

ALMOND SWEET SCONES

Add 50 g/2 oz (¹/₂ cup) blanched and chopped almonds to the dough at the end of stage 2. Cut the rounds, brush with milk, top with a sprinkling of finely chopped blanched almonds. Bake as the recipe on page 34. Other nuts, such as walnuts and pecan nuts can be used instead.

CITRUS SWEET SCONES

Add 1 to 2 teaspoons finely grated lemon, orange or grapefruit zest to the mixture at the end of stage 2. Stir 1 tablespoon lemon or grapefruit juice or 2 (2½) tablespoons orange juice into the mixture at stage 3 and reduce the amount of milk used by this amount.

CREAM SCONES

Use 1 beaten egg and single (light) cream to mix the dough instead of milk. By using an egg you need to reduce the amount of liquid by 2 (2½) tablespoons.

DRIED FRUIT SCONES

A great variety of dried fruits can be added to the mixture at the end of stage 2. Use about 50 g/2 oz (an approximate ½ cup) of finely chopped tenderized dried apricots or glacé (candied) cherries or currants or dates or raisins or a mixture of fruits.

BASIC SAVOURY SCONES

These make an excellent accompaniment to soups and salads. There are many variations you can produce. Follow the directions for the Basic Sweet Scones as on page 34 but omit the sugar and instead sift ¼ teaspoon salt, a good shake of pepper and a pinch of dry mustard powder with the flour.

Bake as the recipe on page 34. To vary these try:

CHEESE SCONES

Add 50 g/2 oz (½ cup) finely grated Cheddar, Cheshire, Lancashire or other good cooking cheese to the mixture after rubbing in the butter or margarine.

Blue cheeses such as Stilton or Danish Blue can be crumbled finely and added instead of the grated cheese. Cheese Scones are best mixed with 1 or 2 beaten eggs and less milk. The cheese content makes these scorch easily so reduce the oven setting to 200°C/400°F, Gas Mark 6 or 190°C with a fan oven.

HERB SCONES

A variety of chopped herbs give a good flavour to a plain scone. Add 1 to 2 tablespoons of finely chopped parsley or coriander (cilantro) or snipped chives to the mixture, after rubbing in the butter or margarine. Use only 1 to 2 teaspoons of the more strongly flavoured herbs such as thyme or rosemary or basil.

VEGETABLE SCONES

Add 2 to 3 (2½ to 3¾) tablespoons finely grated raw carrot or shredded leek to the flour after rubbing in the butter or margarine. These could be combined with the cheese as in the cheese recipe above.

The same quantity of well-drained cooked or canned sweetcorn or cooked chopped mushrooms could be added. As these are moist you will find you need slightly less milk to mix the ingredients together.

POTATO SCONES

The addition of some mashed potato gives a very light texture and good flavour to scones.

Turn to the basic recipe on page 34 and use the same ingredients except:

1. Instead of 225 g/8 oz (2 cups) of flour use 115 g/4 oz (1 cup) flour. Sift this with the pinch of salt.
2. If using self-raising flour also sift with 1 teaspoon baking powder. If using plain (all-purpose) flour sift with 2 teaspoons baking powder.
3. Rub in the fat, add the sugar as the recipe then add 115 g/4 oz (1/2 cup) mashed potato. I use the pulp from a jacket potato, cooked in the oven or in the microwave.
4. Add the milk gradually and proceed as for the recipe on page 34.

GLUTEN-FREE FLOUR FOR SCONES

Until recently I would have hesitated to use gluten-free flour in scones for the light delicate texture is created by wheat flour.

Nowadays a great deal of work has been done to perfect gluten-free flours and the results in the scones in this book are very acceptable. Obviously the appearance and taste are not the same as scones made with wheat.

Use the same quantity of gluten-free flour as **plain** (all-purpose) wheat flour and add exactly the same amount of baking powder as in the recipe.

The scones take the same cooking time but do not brown as much as usual.

Variation

• Instead of gluten-free flour use half fine polenta and half buckwheat with the same amount of baking powder as for plain flour.

MICROWAVE COOKING OF SCONES

If you have a microwave that combines conventional heating with microwave, then simply follow the instructions in the manufacturer's book. If you have just an ordinary microwave oven it is possible to cook the scones in that.

Arrange the sweet or savoury scones in a circle on a suitable flat dish or plate then place just one scone in the centre of the container. Allow 1 1/2 to 2 minutes (depending upon the output of the microwave) on full output. The scones will look pale unless you are using wholemeal (wholewheat) flour but they will be cooked.

To defrost frozen scones use the DEFROST setting, a higher output would make the scones tough and dry.

TO SERVE SCONES

The simplest way to serve either sweet or savoury scones is to arrange them on a plate or in a bread basket and serve them with clotted or whipped cream and jam. Arrange these in separate dishes. It is not usual to serve butter at the same time, but that is a matter of personal taste.

Scones can be cut across the centre and topped with butter or cream cheese and garnished with slices of tomato. Sweet scones can be topped with a spoonful of whipped cream and jam or lemon curd.

CHEESE STRAWS

These are one of the most popular of British cheese savouries and deservedly so for they are delicious. The classic recipe given first produces very rich and delicate biscuits (cookies). A more economical version is given under Variation.

Oven Setting: 220°C/425°F, Gas Mark 7 or 190 to 200°C with a fan oven

Baking Time: 7 to 10 minutes; time the baking carefully in this very hot oven

Baking Equipment: two or three baking (cookie) trays

Makes: about 48 straws. Store apart from other biscuits in an airtight tin and always handle carefully.

Metric/Imperial	Ingredients	American
115 g/4 oz	plain (all-purpose) flour plus extra for rolling out the cheese pastry	1 cup
pinch	salt and cayenne pepper	pinch
1/2 to 1 teaspoon	English mustard powder	1/2 to 1 teaspoon
115 g/4 oz	butter	1/2 cup
85 g/3 oz	Parmesan cheese, finely grated	1/2 cup
1	yolk from medium egg	1
	To glaze	
1	egg white or egg	1

1. Preheat the oven and grease or line the trays with baking parchment.
2. Sift the flour with the seasonings then rub in the butter until the mixture looks like fine breadcrumbs, do not over-handle and make the dough sticky, which is very possible with such a high percentage of butter.
3. Add the cheese and mix in the egg. If the dough seems slightly sticky wrap it in clingfilm or baking parchment and chill for about 30 minutes in the refrigerator.
4. Lightly flour a pastry board and rolling pin and roll out the dough until about 6 mm/1/4 inch thick then cut into fingers about 6 mm/ 1/4 inch wide and 7.5 cm/3 inches long. Lift carefully on to the prepared trays.
5. Lightly whisk the egg white or egg and brush over the straws with a soft pastry brush. Bake just above the centre of the oven until firm and golden in colour. Cool for at least 5 minutes before lifting on to a cooling tray. When cold store in an airtight tin.

Variation

Economical Straws: use 150 g/5 oz (1¼ cups) plain flour with seasonings and 85 g/3 oz (¾ cup) butter and 85 g/3 oz (½ cup) Parmesan or other good cooking cheese. Cut into straws and glaze. Bake at 200°C/400°F, Gas Mark 6 or 180 to 190°C with a fan oven. Store as page 38. These tend to soften slightly with storage so crisp for 2 or 3 minutes in the oven before serving.

MAKING BATTERS

A batter mixture is used for pancakes and for the famous Yorkshire Pudding, but a slightly thicker batter is the basis for the recipe on page 40, which is extremely popular in America. Popovers are quickly made and they are an ideal container for sweet or savoury fillings, see suggestions below.

POPOVERS

Genuine Popovers are baked in fairly large patty tins (shells) but I have given the baking time for cooking the mixture in the type of tins you would use for small cakes. If you become a devotee of Popovers you can invest in larger tins. Make quite sure the greased tins are very hot before adding the batter.

Oven Setting: 220 to 230°C/425 to 450°C, Gas Mark 7 to 8 or 210 to 220°C with a fan oven (use the lower setting if your oven is on the fierce side) for 15 minutes then 160°C/325°F, Gas Mark 3 or 150°C with a fan oven for approximately 15 minutes
Baking Time: 30 minutes but see stage 4
Baking Equipment: approximately 9 patty tins (shells)
Serves: 4 to 6. Serve as soon as cooked.

Metric/Imperial	Ingredients	American
115 g/4 oz	**plain (all-purpose) flour**	1 cup
pinch	salt	pinch
2	eggs	2
225 ml/7½ fl oz	milk	scant 1 cup
2 teaspoons	olive or sunflower oil	2 teaspoons
	To grease the tins	
2 teaspoons	olive or sunflower oil	2 teaspoons

1. Preheat the oven. Sift the flour and salt into a large basin. Break the first egg into a cup to check there is no shell then add to the flour, repeat with the second egg.
2. Beat the mixture well with an egg whisk until smooth; it is easy to beat a thickish mixture like this without splashing. Gradually whisk in the milk. Add the oil just before cooking the batter.
3. Brush the inside of the patty tins with the oil, place in the oven for 4 to 5 minutes or until very hot. Remove carefully. Give the batter a

final whisk then spoon into the hot tins, filling them about ²/₃rds full.
4. Return to the oven and bake for 15 minutes, by this time the
    Popovers will have risen well but they must hold their shape, so
    lower the heat and cook until firm. Remove from the tins then fill
    while piping hot and serve.

Savoury Fillings: mixed vegetables in a cheese sauce; a savoury minced
meat mixture; curry, canned beans in tomato sauce.

Sweet Fillings: fruit or fruit purée, jam, lemon curd, honey, butter and
sugar.

BUCKWHEAT POPOVERS AND SCOTCH PANCAKES

If you are anxious to avoid wheat use buckwheat, which is gluten-free,
for the recipe on page 39 or Scotch Pancakes below.

SCOTCH PANCAKES

*Scotch Pancakes or Drop Scones are not baked in the oven but are cooked
on a griddle (also known as a girdle or bakestone) or a solid hotplate on
an electric cooker. If you do not possess any of these then you can cook
the pancakes in a **heavy** frying pan. A light pan is unsuitable, for the
pancakes could burn on the outside before being cooked in the centre.*
*   *Scotch Pancakes are small round thick pancakes and they are delicious
spread with butter.*

Cooking Temperature: a hot griddle or alternative
Cooking Time: approximately 4 minutes
Cooking Equipment: see above
Makes: 8 to 10 pancakes. Serve when freshly cooked;
they can be frozen.

Metric/Imperial	Ingredients	American
	To grease the griddle	
few drops	**olive or sunflower or ground nut oil**	*few drops*
	For the pancakes	
115 g/4 oz	**self-raising flour or plain (all-purpose) flour with 1 teaspoon baking powder**	*1 cup*
pinch	*salt*	*pinch*
1	*egg*	*1*
150 ml/¼ pint	*milk*	*²/₃ cup*
1 tablespoon	**olive or sunflower oil, optional**	*1 tablespoon*

1. Grease the griddle or hotplate or the bottom of the frying pan with
    the oil; preheat when the batter is made.
2. Meanwhile sift the flour, or flour and baking powder, with the salt.
3. Crack the egg and allow it to drop into the flour, then gradually add
    the milk, whisking or beating as you do so. You should have a

smooth thick batter. It is not essential to add the oil but it does make more moist pancakes. It is particularly important if you intend to freeze these, for it stops them becoming 'leathery'.

4. Preheat the cooking griddle, hotplate or frying pan. **To test the heat:** drop a teaspoonful of the batter on to the preheated appliance and check the timing. If correctly heated the tiny pancake should turn golden coloured on the base in one minute. If it is much quicker then the surface is too hot and you should reduce the heat.

5. Drop tablespoonfuls of the mixture on to the heated griddle and cook for approximately 2 minutes or until the top surface is covered with small bubbles. Do not try and cook too many pancakes at one time.

6. Insert a thin fish slice or wide-bladed spatula (palette knife) under the first pancake and turn it over. This may seem difficult to do first of all but with practise it will become quite easy.

7. Cook for approximately 2 minutes on the second side. To check that the pancakes are adequately cooked press firmly with the back of a knife. They should feel firm with no uncooked batter coming from the sides.

8. Spread a teacloth (dish towel) over the wire cooling tray, add the cooked pancakes and cover. This prevents them becoming too dry.

EMERGENCY BAKING

There may be times when you have forgotten to buy bread and have neither the time nor the ingredients to make muffins or scones or any type of bread. The following recipes are old traditional ones, which were particularly popular in East Anglia and used in times of emergency.

COBS

These must be eaten when freshly made but they are deliciously crusty and ideal for breakfast.

Oven Setting: 220°C/425°F, Gas Mark 7 or 210°C with a fan oven
Baking Time: 10 to 12 minutes, depending upon the size
Baking Equipment: one flat baking (cookie) tray
Makes: 6 to 8. It is not worth freezing these, they lose their crispness.

Metric/Imperial	Ingredients	American
225 g/8 oz	*self-raising flour or plain (all-purpose) flour with 2 teaspoons baking powder*	2 cups
good pinch	salt	good pinch
25 g/1 oz	*butter, margarine or lard (shortening), optional*	2 tablespoons
approx 150 ml/¼ pint	milk	approx ⅔ cup

1. Preheat the oven. There is no need to grease the baking tray.
2. Sift the flour, or flour and baking powder, with the salt. Rub in the

fat, although this could be omitted. Gradually add enough milk to make a sticky dough but one that can be handled with floured fingers.

3. Roll in balls with your floured fingers, place on the baking tray and cook until lightly browned and crisp. Serve while warm.

RUSKS

These make an excellent alternative to bread or even plain home-made biscuits, to serve with cheese.

1. Make up the mixture for Cobs on page 41 but include the amount of fat given. Use slightly less milk so the dough is sufficiently stiff to roll out to about 1.5 cm/½ inch in thickness.
2. Cut into rounds and bake as Cobs above but allow about 8 minutes cooking time so the rounds are only just firm.
3. Take the tray out of the oven and, when the Cobs are sufficiently cool enough to handle, cut right through the centres horizontally, so doubling the number of rounds.
4. Place the rusks, with the ridged cut surfaces downwards so touching the tray(s) – they now take up twice as much space – reduce the oven heat to 150°C/300°F, Gas Mark 2 or 140°C with a fan oven. Bake for about 30 minutes until the rusks are very crisp. Cool and serve. They keep crisp for some days in an airtight tin.

BISCUITS, COOKIES, MERINGUES AND ECLAIRS

Biscuits (cookies) are very easy to make at home. As you will see in the following recipes the method of preparation varies. In Flapjacks (page 49), for example, some of the ingredients are melted. In others such as Vanilla Shorties (below), the fat and sugar are creamed together whereas in the classic Shortbread (page 45), the fat is rubbed into the flour.

You may find the consistency of some biscuit doughs rather dry and be tempted to add liquid. Do not do this, just knead the dough very firmly and you will find the ingredients combine well to form a dough that can be handled or rolled out. Whereas one must handle pastry gently you can be quite vigorous with most biscuit mixtures.

The baking times have been carefully tested but on occasions you may find that the biscuits are not quite as crisp as they should be. In this case simply put them back into the oven at the original setting and bake for a brief period – about 4 minutes. This double cooking is an accepted technique for cooking biscuits.

British biscuits (called cookies in America) are followed on page 51 by examples of true American cookies. These give a complete change of texture, they are crisp on the outside and chewy in the centre.

Biscuits and cookies should be baked in the centre of the oven except with a fan oven, where all shelves should enjoy the same heat.

ALTERNATIVE FLOURS FOR BISCUITS
If you are making biscuits for anyone who is allergic or intolerant to wheat or gluten you can obtain good results in some of the recipes in this book by using a mixture of cornflour (cornstarch) and rice flour. I liked half cornflour and half rice flour. There is no need to alter the proportions of the other ingredients in any way.

I found this mixture of flours particularly good in the Shrewsbury Biscuits on page 46 and the Easter Biscuits on page 47.

VANILLA SHORTIES

These easy to make biscuits (cookies) are crisp and have a very attractive appearance. They are unusual in that self-raising flour, or plain (all-purpose) flour with baking powder, are used. Most biscuits are made with plain flour and no raising agent. These biscuits crack in an interesting manner as they cook.

Oven Setting: 160°C/325°F, Gas Mark 3 or 150°C with a fan oven
Baking Time: 15 minutes
Baking Equipment: two baking (cookie) trays, see stage 4

Makes: 12 to16 biscuits, see stage 4. They keep for several weeks in an airtight tin.

Metric/Imperial	Ingredients	American
85 g/3 oz	butter	3/8 cup
50 g/2 oz	caster sugar	1/4 cup
1/4 to 1/2 teaspoon	vanilla extract, or see using vanilla sugar (page 13)	1/4 to 1/2 teaspoon
115 g/4 oz	self-raising flour or plain flour with 1 teaspoon baking powder	1 cup

1. Preheat the oven. There is no need to grease the baking trays for these biscuits.
2. Cream the butter, sugar and vanilla extract together. Sift the flour, or flour and baking powder, into the creamed ingredients.
3. Mix these together with a knife, then with your fingers, until the mixture binds together quite easily. Divide into 12 to 16 equal sized portions and roll into balls. In cold weather the mixture may seem a little stiff, in which case handle it very firmly to soften. In hot weather it may seem slightly sticky. It will be easier to roll in balls if you damp your fingers in cold water, but make sure they are not too wet.
4. Place the shorties on the baking trays, allowing a good 2.5 cm/1 inch around each ball. You should be able to space 6 to 8 balls. If you have insufficient baking trays the balls of dough can stand while you bake one batch.
5. Bake until pale golden, these biscuits will still feel soft but will harden as they cool on the baking trays. When quite cold remove from the trays on to a wire cooling tray.

CHOCOLATE SHORTIES

Sift 85 g/3 oz (3/4 cup) self-raising flour with 1/4 teaspoon baking powder, or the same amount of plain flour with 1 teaspoon baking powder, and 25 g/1 oz (1/4 cup) chocolate powder (the type used to make chocolate drinks). Mix and bake as above. Retain the vanilla extract – it helps to emphasise the taste of chocolate.

GINGER SHORTIES

Omit the vanilla extract and sift 1/2 to 1 teaspoon ground ginger with the flour. A richer biscuit is made if you also add 50 g/2 oz (1/4 cup) of chopped crystallized (candied) ginger.

CHEESE SHORTIES

These are very pleasant savoury biscuits. When cooking them allow plenty of space as the small balls flatten and spread out.

1. Use the same amount of butter and flour as in the Vanilla Shorties but omit the sugar and vanilla extract.
2. Sift a good pinch of salt, a shake of white or cayenne pepper and

$^1/_4$ teaspoon dry mustard powder with the flour.

3. Cream the butter with 85 g/3 oz ($^3/_4$ cup) finely grated Cheddar or Gruyère cheese. Add the flour and proceed as the recipe on page 44. Form the mixture into 16 to 18 small balls and place on well-greased baking (cookie) trays. Instead of greasing the trays line them with baking parchment.

4. Bake at the temperature given on page 44 for about 12 minutes. Allow to cool on the baking trays. Store in an airtight tin away from other biscuits.

SHORTBREAD

Shortbread, which is traditional to Scotland, was known as Dreaming Bread in the past, as it was sometimes served at a wedding instead of a cake.

The golden rules for good shortbread are:-
a) use the best butter possible and do not add liquid to the mixture
b) bake the biscuit slowly.
Rice flour is generally used with ordinary plain (all-purpose) flour. If you have no rice flour you can substitute cornflour (cornstarch). The rice flour or cornflour helps to produce a short crisp texture.

Oven Setting: 150°C/300°F, Gas Mark 2 or 140°C with a fan oven
Baking Time: 1 hour but see stage 5 on page 46
Baking Equipment: one 20 cm/8 inch round. This keeps well in an airtight tin.

Metric/Imperial	Ingredients	American
175 g/6 oz	*plain flour*	1$^1/_2$ cups
25 g/1 oz	*rice flour or cornflour*	$^1/_4$ cup
50 g/2 oz	*caster sugar*	$^1/_4$ cup
150 g/5 oz	*butter*	$^5/_8$ cup
	To top the shortbread	
1 tablespoon	*caster sugar*	1 tablespoon

1. Preheat the oven. There is no need to grease either the baking tray or sandwich tin.
2. Sift the dry ingredients into a mixing bowl. Cut the butter into small pieces, add to the dry ingredients, rub in, then handle the dough quite firmly, to make the butter and dry ingredients blend together. Do not add liquid.
3. Turn on to a lightly floured surface and gently roll out to make a neat round about 1.25 cm/$^1/_2$ inch in thickness. Lift on to a baking tray. You can then pinch the edges of the round at regular intervals to give a scalloped effect. If preferred put into a sandwich tin, this ensures a very neat round.
4. Gently mark into sections, do NOT cut right through the biscuit. Prick at regular intervals with the tip of a fork. Sprinkle the extra sugar over the top of the shortbread.
5. Bake in the centre of the oven for about 1 hour, but check after 45

minutes to see the shortbread is not becoming too brown. If it is, lower the heat slightly. A good shortbread should retain a light colour.

6.   Cool on or in the tin then lift out and store in an airtight tin. It should be easy to cut or break the round into individual biscuits when cold.

Variations

• Use 200 g/7 oz (1¾ cups) flour and omit rice flour or cornflour.

Rich Shortbread: use 175 g/6 oz (¾ cup) butter with the ingredients given above. This mixture, or the basic recipe, can be used with the following suggestions:

Almond Shortbread: add 2 (2½) level tablespoons of finely chopped blanched almonds to the other ingredients. In this case lightly grease the tin or line it with baking parchment for the nuts may make the shortbread liable to stick.

Chopped hazelnuts, pecans or walnuts can be used.

Coconut Shortbread: add 50 g/2 oz desiccated (⅔ cup shredded) coconut to the other ingredients. Increase the sugar to 85 g/3 oz (⅜ cup).

BISCUIT DOUGHS THAT NEED ROLLING OUT

The recipes on this and the next page are examples of biscuits where the dough is rolled out then cut into the desired shapes.

You do NOT handle a biscuit dough or roll it out in the same way as for pastry (page 109). A biscuit dough can be firmly kneaded with your hands to give a mixture that is easy to roll. Try and avoid using much flour on the working surface or rolling pin, for that would spoil the basic proportions. Roll the mixture with a firm pressure.

SHREWSBURY BISCUITS

These biscuits are made from a firm mixture which is rolled out and cut into shapes. The biscuits were originally known as Shropshire Cakes and they were served on All Saints Day on November 1st each year. Traditionally the mixture included a small amount of caraway seeds but over the years these have been omitted. Shrewsbury Biscuits could be considered a good basic recipe. Do knead the dough firmly and roll it out with a strong pressure of the rolling pin. The rice flour gives an interesting texture but it can be replaced with more plain flour.

Oven Setting:	160°C/325°F, Gas Mark 3 or 150°C with a fan oven
Baking Time:	approximately 12 to 15 minutes
Baking Equipment:	flat baking (cookie) tray(s)
Makes:	12 to 18 biscuits, store in an airtight tin.

Metric/Imperial	Ingredients	American
115 g/4 oz	*plain (all-purpose) flour*	1 cup
115 g/4 oz	*rice flour or more flour*	1 cup

Metric/Imperial	Ingredients	American
115 g/4 oz	*butter*	*½ cup*
115 g/4 oz	*caster sugar*	*½ cup*
1 to 2 teaspoons	*caraway seeds, optional*	*1 to 2 teaspoons*
1	*yolk from a small egg*	*1*

1. Preheat the oven, lightly grease the baking tray(s) unless using a non-stick type.
2. Sift the two types of flour together into a mixing bowl. Cut the butter into small pieces, drop into the flours and rub it in, until the mixture looks like fine breadcrumbs.
3. Add the sugar and the caraway seeds if using these, then stir in the egg yolk and mix thoroughly.
4. Turn the dough on to a lightly floured board and roll out until the dough is about 6 mm/¼ inch in thickness.
5. Cut into rounds or any other shapes and place on the baking tray(s). Cook until firm and light gold in colour.
6. Cool for 5 minutes on the baking tray then lift on to a wire cooling tray.

LEMON BISCUITS

Follow the recipe for Shrewsbury Biscuits above but use 200 g/7 oz (1¾ cups) plain (all-purpose) flour with 25 g/1 oz cornflour (¼ cup cornstarch).

Rub in the butter, add the sugar and 2 teaspoons finely grated lemon zest then the egg yolk.

Bake as Shrewsbury Biscuits.

EASTER BISCUITS

Although this is a traditional recipe for teatime on Easter Day it makes a good basic recipe for spice and currant biscuits. Easter Biscuits are large so you can make them a smaller size for other occasions.

Oven Setting: 160°C/325°F, Gas Mark 3 or 150°C with a fan oven
Baking Time: 15 to 18 minutes but see Variation
Baking Equipment: one or two flat baking (cookie) tray(s)
Makes: 10 to 12 crisp biscuits which keep well in an airtight tin.

Metric/Imperial	Ingredients	American
150 g/5 oz	*butter or margarine*	*⅝ cup*
115 g/4 oz	*caster sugar*	*½ cup*
225 g/8 oz	*plain (all-purpose) flour*	*2 cups*
1 teaspoon	*mixed spice*	*1 teaspoon*
115 g/4 oz	*currants*	*⅔ cup*
1	*egg yolk, whisked*	*1*

1. Preheat the oven; lightly grease the baking tray(s) unless they are of

the non-stick type.

2. Cream the butter or margarine and sugar until soft and light. Sift the flour and spice and add to the creamed mixture.

3. Stir in the currants and then the egg yolk, mix well then turn out on to a lightly floured board.

4. Knead the dough until smooth then roll out until 6 to 8mm/$^1/_4$ to $^1/_3$ inch in thickness. Cut into rounds each about 8.5 to 10 cm/ 3$^1/_2$ to 4 inches in diameter.

5. Place on the baking tray(s) and cook until firm and pale gold in colour.

6. Cool for 5 minutes on the tray(s) then lift on to a wire cooling tray.

Variation

• Make about 18 smaller biscuits and bake for 12 to 15 minutes.

BISCUITS MADE BY THE MELTING METHOD

Flapjacks and Gingernuts are made by melting some of the ingredients in a saucepan. When doing this use just a low heat and stir once or twice to make sure that all the ingredients are mixed together.

Remove the pan from the heat as soon as the ingredients are melted.

GINGERNUTS

These are some of the oldest traditional biscuits (cookies) known in Britain. They are deliciously crisp and keep well in an airtight tin away from other biscuits. The best method of baking is to use two heats as given below.

Oven Setting:	200°C/400°F, Gas Mark 6 or 190°C with a fan oven for the first 5 minutes then 160°C/325°F, Gas Mark 3 or 150°C with a fan oven but read stage 6 carefully
Baking Time:	15 minutes
Baking Equipment:	two to three baking (cookie) trays, see stage 1
Makes:	about 16.

Metric/Imperial	Ingredients	American
115 g/4 oz	*plain (all-purpose) flour*	1 cup
$^1/_2$ level teaspoon	*bicarbonate of soda (baking soda)*	$^1/_2$ level teaspoon
$^1/_2$ to 1 teaspoon	*mixed spice, or to taste*	$^1/_2$ to 1 teaspoon
$^1/_2$ to 1 teaspoon	*ground cinnamon, or to taste*	$^1/_2$ to 1 teaspoon
1 teaspoon	*ground ginger, or to taste*	1 teaspoon
55 g*/2 oz	*butter*	$^1/_4$ cup
2 tablespoons	*golden (corn) syrup*	2$^1/_2$ tablespoons
25 g/1 oz	*caster sugar*	2 tablespoons

* use this metric amount

1. Preheat the oven. Grease the baking trays well. If you are short of these do not worry, the balls of uncooked dough can stand while one batch is cooked.
2. Sift the flour with the bicarbonate of soda and the spices into a basin.
3. Put the butter, syrup and sugar into a good-sized saucepan. Stir over a low heat until the ingredients have just dissolved. Remove from the heat.
4. Add the dry ingredients to the saucepan, this saves wasting any of the butter and syrup mixture, stir thoroughly, scraping the mixture from the bottom of the pan from time to time. Leave until sufficiently cool to handle.
5. Roll into about 16 balls. If they seem sticky just moisten your fingers in cold water; make sure your fingers are not over-wet.
6. Place the balls on the baking trays, allowing a good 3.5 cm/1½ inches around each. Bake for 5 minutes only at the higher setting given then immediately reduce the heat and allow 10 minutes at the lower setting. Many electric ovens retain the heat so it would be a good idea to switch the electric oven off at the end of 5 minutes then check the heat after another 5 minutes. If it is still high let the biscuits finish cooking in the retained heat. You cannot do this with a gas oven, the heat drops very quickly. Cool the biscuits on the trays for 10 minutes then remove on to a wire cooling tray.

SPICED CHOCOLATE NUTS

These are not a traditional biscuit but they are made in exactly the same way as the Gingernuts. They are a very pleasant crisp chocolate biscuit.

Use just 100 g/3½ oz (good ¾ cup) of flour plus 15 g/½ oz (2 level tablespoons) of cocoa powder. Sift these with the bicarbonate of soda, the mixed spice and cinnamon but **omit** the ground ginger.

Continue to mix the ingredients in exactly the same way as the recipe above and bake at the same settings.

FLAPJACKS

The crisp texture of these sustaining oatmeal biscuits (cookies) have made them a general favourite. It is important to follow the advice about cutting the mixture into fingers while warm, for it is difficult to do this when they are cold. Do not store these oatmeal biscuits in a tin with different kinds of biscuits; they will lose their crispness and adversely affect other biscuits too. Rolled oats are the type one uses for making quick-cooking porridge.

Oven Setting:	180°C/350°F, Gas Mark 4 or 170°C with a fan oven
Baking Time:	25 minutes
Baking Equipment:	one 18 cm/7 inch square or 20 cm/8 inch round sandwich tin (layer pan)
Makes:	about 12 fingers; store in an airtight tin (see above); tend to crumble if frozen.

Metric/Imperial	Ingredients	American
85 g/3 oz	butter	⅜ cup
50 g/2 oz	caster or light brown sugar	¼ cup
2 tablespoons	golden (corn) syrup or maple syrup	2½ tablespoons
175 g/6 oz	rolled oats	scant 2 cups

1. Preheat the oven; grease the tin thoroughly with a little olive oil or melted butter or lard. Any biscuits that include rolled oats are inclined to stick to the tin so this step is important, even if you have a non-stick tin. Lining with greaseproof (wax) paper or baking parchment is not satisfactory as you have to cut the mixture down to the base while still in the tin.
2. Put the butter, sugar and syrup into a saucepan and heat gently until the ingredients have melted, stir several times and make certain the ingredients do not overheat or burn.
3. Take the saucepan off the heat, add the rolled oats and stir briskly.
4. Spoon into the tin and spread evenly and flat on top; the back of a metal spoon or a firm palette knife (spatula) is best for this purpose.
5. Bake for approximately 25 minutes or until evenly golden brown. Remove the tin from the oven, wait for about 3 minutes then mark the mixture into the required number of fingers.
6. Leave in the tin until **nearly** cold then remove carefully on to a wire cooling tray.

To make a change

- Add a few drops of vanilla or almond extract at stage 3.

Chocolate and Walnut Flapjacks: add 50 g/2 oz (2 squares) finely chopped plain chocolate and 50 g/2 oz (½ cup) chopped walnuts to the mixture at stage 3. Continue and bake as above.

Orange Flapjacks: add 2 teaspoons finely grated orange zest to the butter and sugar at stage 2.

NOTE: if flapjacks become a little soft with storage warm them in the oven for about 5 minutes at the setting given on page 49. Let them cool on the baking tray before removing on to a plate.

Peanut butter gives an interesting flavour but you cannot use ALL peanut butter and have a good result.

Peanut Butter Flapjacks: use 50 g/2 oz (¼ cup) butter and 50 g/2 oz (¼ cup) peanut butter preferably the crunchy type. This mixture gives a slight increase in the fat content and produces very good biscuits.

Never give anyone food containing peanut butter unless you are certain they are not allergic to these nuts.

AMERICAN COOKIES

Although the term 'cookie' is used in America to describe our British biscuits, true American cookies are somewhat different. Instead of being really crisp they are slightly chewy in the middle.

CHOCOLATE CHIP COOKIES

By adjusting the baking time it is possible to make American type cookies, that are slightly soft in the centre, or really crisp British biscuits. It is better to chop the chocolate on a board, using a sharp knife, rather than put it into a food processor, for that makes some ultra-fine crumbs that darken the colour of the dough. If you can buy chocolate chips, use those. The best quality chocolate should contain nearly 70% cocoa butter.

Oven Setting:	160°C/325°F, Gas Mark 3 or 150°C with a fan oven
Baking Time:	11 to 15 minutes, see stage 5
Baking Equipment:	two flat baking (cookie) trays
Makes:	12 to 16 cookies that keep well in an airtight tin; as they contain chocolate they are better stored away from other cookies.

Metric/Imperial	Ingredients	American
50 g/2 oz	**good quality plain (semi-sweet) chocolate**	2 squares
85 g/3 oz	**butter, preferably unsalted**	³⁄₈ cup
50 g/2 oz	**caster sugar**	¼ cup
few drops	**vanilla extract* or essence**	few drops
115 g/4 oz	**self-raising flour or plain (all-purpose) flour with 1 teaspoon baking powder**	1 cup

* this gives the better flavour

1. Preheat the oven, line the trays with baking parchment or lightly grease them.
2. Cut the chocolate into very small pieces. Cream the butter with the sugar and vanilla until soft then add the sifted flour, or flour and baking powder.
3. Stir in the chocolate and mix with your fingers to form a pliable dough. Divide the mixture into 12 to 16 equal sized portions and roll into balls.
4. Place on the baking trays, allowing plenty of space for the mixture to spread out in baking.
5. Cook for 11 minutes to produce cookies that are firm on the outside but slightly soft in the centre or for about 15 minutes to give really crisp biscuits. Cool on the trays.

NOTE: if you are disappointed that the biscuits are not quite as crisp as you would wish then simply return them to the oven and bake for a few more minutes.

Variation

- For a very crisp biscuit use 85 g/3 oz (¾ cup) plain (all-purpose) flour with 25 g/1 oz cornflour (cornstarch) or rice flour and 1 teaspoon baking powder.

COCONUT OATMEAL COOKIES

The mixture of desiccated coconut and rolled oats gives cookies that are deliciously crisp on the outside and softer in the centre. It is a typical recipe which can be adapted.

Oven Setting: 180°C/350°F, Gas Mark 4 or 170°C with a fan oven
Baking Time: 10 minutes
Baking Equipment: two baking (cookie) trays
Makes: 24 to 30 cookies. These keep well in a tightly sealed airtight tin away from other cookies or biscuits.

Metric/Imperial	Ingredients	American
3	eggs	3
300 g/10 oz	caster sugar	1¼ cups
25 g/1 oz	butter, melted	2 tablespoons
½ teaspoon	vanilla extract	½ teaspoon
pinch	salt	pinch
85 g/3 oz	desiccated (shredded) coconut	1 cup
225 g/8 oz	rolled oats	good 2 cups

1. Preheat the oven; thoroughly grease the baking trays.
2. Break the eggs into a good-sized mixing bowl and whisk until they begin to thicken.
3. Gradually whisk in the sugar then stir in the remaining ingredients.
4. Drop spoonfuls on to the trays; leave plenty of room for them to spread.
5. Bake until golden coloured. Leave on the baking trays until almost cold then lift onto a wire cooling tray.

NUT AND FRUIT COOKIES

These cookies have an interestingly spicy flavour and are full of nuts and raisins.

Oven Setting: 190°C/375°F, Gas Mark 5 or 180°C with a fan oven
Baking Time: 12 to 14 minutes
Baking Equipment: two baking (cookie) trays
Makes: 24 to 30 cookies. Store in an airtight tin.

Metric/Imperial	Ingredients	American
115 g/4 oz	butter	½ cup
175 g/6 oz	soft brown sugar	¾ cup
2	eggs, whisked	2
175 g/6 oz	plain (all-purpose) flour	1½ cups
½ teaspoon	bicarbonate of soda (baking soda)	½ teaspoon
½ teaspoon	ground cinnamon	½ teaspoon
¼ teaspoon	grated or ground cloves	¼ teaspoon

½ teaspoon	*ground ginger*	½ teaspoon
150 g/5 oz	*pecans or walnuts, finely chopped*	1 cup
150 g/5 oz	*raisins, coarsely chopped*	scant 1 cup

1. Preheat the oven. Grease the baking trays. Cream the butter then gradually beat in the sugar.
2. Gradually beat in the eggs. Sift the flour with the bicarbonate of soda and the spices into the creamed mixture then stir in the nuts and the raisins.
3. Drop spoonfuls of the mixture on to the baking tray and bake until golden in colour. Cool on the trays then lift on to a wire cooling tray.

ADAPTATION TO NUT AND FRUIT COOKIES

There are various ways in which the cookies above can be adapted.

If allergic to nuts: these can be replaced by crisp breadcrumbs. Use the same amount of crumbs, i.e. 150 g/5 oz (1¼ cups). Add these at stage 2.

On page 56 you will find directions for making crisp breadcrumbs from bread. You could alter the flavour of the cookies by the kind of bread used.

If intolerant or allergic to wheat flour: this can be replaced in several ways:

a) Use rice flour instead of plain (all-purpose) flour and allow exactly the same amount, i.e. 175 g/6 oz (1½ cups).

b) Use cornmeal, which is generally sold as polenta. Allow the same amount, i.e. 175 g/6 oz (1½ cups). If by chance you can only obtain the coarser polenta make this finer in a food processor or liquidizer (blender). If using the latter it is advisable to add the polenta in small batches.

c) Use a mixture of ordinary cornflour (cornstarch) and rice flour. I like to use rather more rice flour than cornflour, i.e. 50 g/2 oz (½ cup) cornflour and 115 g/4 oz (1 cup) rice flour.

WHISKING METHOD OF INCORPORATING INGREDIENTS

In the Coconut Oatmeal Cookies on page 52 the eggs and sugar are whisked together (see stages 2 and 3).

The delicious biscuit-type cakes that follow, i.e. Almond Macaroons, Coconut Pyramids and Meringues are made by the whisking method. In the case of the first two recipes the egg whites are only lightly whisked until frothy, not stiff. It would be a mistake to over-whisk them for it would make the result much too solid.

In Meringues it is essential to whisk the egg whites very well indeed but not to over-whisk them. Full details for making Meringues are given on pages 56 and 57.

Almond Macaroons, Coconut Pyramids and Meringues do not contain any flour so they are ideal for anyone who is intolerant to wheat. Although these recipes are high in sugar content and therefore have a generous amount of calories, they do not have any added fat.

ALMOND MACAROONS

These delicious small cakes or biscuits (cookies) are ideal at teatime.
If you like a macaroon that is slightly sticky in the centre then follow the
advice in stage 1. Rice paper is obtainable from supermarkets and some
stationers. You can however make macaroons without using this, see stage
1. Advice on adding drops of flavouring is on page 185.

Oven Setting: 180°C/350°F, Gas Mark 4 or 170°C with a fan oven
Baking Time: 15 to 20 minutes depending upon the size
Baking Equipment: one or two baking (cookie) tray(s)
Makes: 12 to 18 macaroons. These are better eaten the day
                         they are baked. They tend to dry out and crumble
                         if stored for too long or frozen.

Metric/Imperial	Ingredients	American
few sheets	rice paper	few sheets
2	whites from small eggs	2
few drops	almond extract* or essence	few drops
175 g/6 oz	caster sugar	¾ cup
150 g/5 oz	ground almonds	1¼ cups
1 teaspoon	rice flour or cornflour (cornstarch) optional	1 teaspoon
	To decorate	
12 to 18	almonds, blanched	12 to 18

* this gives the better flavour

1. Place a small container of cold water into the oven, make sure this is
    on a shelf below the one on which you will bake the macaroons.
    These should be cooked in the centre of the oven, except when using
    a fan oven when all the shelves have the same heat.
2. Preheat the oven, lay rice paper on the tray(s) or line these with
    baking parchment.
3. Whisk the egg whites until just frothy, do not try and make them
    stiff. Add the rest of the ingredients. The mixture should be of a
    consistency that you can just roll into balls. The rice flour or
    cornflour makes this a little easier to do. The size of egg whites varies
    so if you find the mixture is a little stiff add water, drop by drop.
    If you find it too soft add a very little more rice flour or cornflour or
    ground almonds.
4. Place the balls on the prepared trays allowing 3.75 to 5 cm/1½ to 2
    inches around the larger balls but slightly less around the smaller ones.
    If you only have one baking tray you can bake one batch at a time.
5. Place an almond in the centre of each ball. Bake smaller macaroons
    for about 15 minutes or larger ones for 20 minutes or until golden
    coloured.
6. Remove the trays from the oven, let the macaroons cool then remove
    and cut around the rice paper, if using this. Remove the macaroons
    from the trays.

Variations

- Some recipes recommend ratafia essence. This is made from the stones of peaches or cherries and is more delicate in taste than almond.

Chocolate Macaroons: use 85 g/3 oz (¾ cup) ground almonds, 25 g/1 oz (¼ cup) rice flour or cornflour and 50 g/2 oz (½ cup) chocolate powder.

Coconut Macaroons: use 85 g/3 oz (¾ cup) almonds and 50 g/2 oz desiccated (⅔ cup shredded) coconut. Prepare and bake as page 54.

COCONUT PYRAMIDS

These small sweet cakes have always been very popular. The baking time is short, just enough to brown the tips of the pyramids and make the mixture firmer in texture. If you have no rice paper line the tray with baking parchment. Rice paper is obtainable from supermarkets and stationers.

Oven Setting:	160°C/325°F, Gas Mark 3 or 150°C with a fan oven
Baking Time:	10 to 15 minutes
Baking Equipment:	one baking (cookie) tray
Makes:	about 15 small pyramids. These keep in an airtight tin for about 3 days after which they tend to dry out and crumble. They are not suitable for freezing.

Metric/Imperial	Ingredients	American
few sheets	rice paper	few sheets
2	whites from small eggs	2
115 g/4 oz	caster sugar	½ cup
175 g/6 oz	desiccated (shredded) coconut	2 cups
2 teaspoons	cornflour (cornstarch), or as required, see stage 2	2 teaspoons

1. Preheat the oven. Place the rice paper on the baking tray.
2. Whisk the egg whites until just frothy. Add the sugar and coconut and mix well. The mixture should be a consistency that can be formed into pyramid shapes. Add the cornflour slowly to give the right degree of stiffness.
3. Divide the mixture into portions then mould these with your fingers and place on the rice paper. You will find shaping the mixture easier if you just damp your fingers.
4. Bake in the centre of the oven, except with a fan oven, where all shelves should be of the same heat. The pyramids are ready when the tips are golden brown. Remove from the oven but allow to cool on the tray until firm enough to handle.
5. Cut around the rice paper or simply lift from the tray.

Variation

- Some of the mixture can be tinted with a few drops of culinary colouring; page 185 gives hints on adding colourings.

NOTE: desiccated coconut does deteriorate with storage in a cupboard, so when a packet is opened it is wise to store the remainder in the refrigerator.

BAKING BREADCRUMBS

Many recipes state that crisp breadcrumbs are needed for coating the food. If you have some bread left over it is a wise, and economical, idea to make crumbs from the bread then crisp these. They keep for weeks in an airtight container.

Make the bread into fine crumbs in a food processor, place on a baking (cookie) tray in a flat layer.

Preheat the oven to 120°C/250°F, Gas Mark 1 or as low as possible with a fan oven. Bake the crumbs for about 1 hour or until crisp and only very lightly coloured. Cool then store. If the crumbs do not appear very fine they can be put into the food processor once again after baking.

MAKING MERINGUES

Meringues are not difficult to make, but there are certain points to observe.

1. Do not use whites from eggs that have just been laid; they should be at least 24 hours old.
2. Caster sugar is usual but you can use half caster and half well sifted icing (confectioners) sugar or even brown sugar.
3. When whisking the egg whites, whether by hand or with an electric mixer, make sure the bowl is absolutely dry and free from any trace of grease.
4. Separate the egg whites, as described on page 12. Left over egg yolks could be used to mix stuffings, add to sauces or even frozen.
    If storing to use later make sure they are covered with cold water to prevent a skin forming, store in the refrigerator and use within 2 days.
    To freeze egg yolks: whisk and either add a good pinch of salt or 1 teaspoon caster sugar to each egg yolk. Pour into a container and label these clearly as to how many yolks are there and whether they are salted or sweetened. Use within 3 months.
5. **Whisk the egg whites until very stiff, they should stand in firm peaks but they should not be over-whisked for they become dry and crumbly.** Vanilla or other flavouring can be added, see the recipes following.
6. There are several ways of adding the sugar to the egg whites but the most satisfactory is to add it **gradually, whisking as you do so.** You should keep the electric mixer running on a slow speed as you do this.
7. When the sugar has been incorporated into the egg whites you are then ready to put the mixture on to the baking tray, which must be carefully prepared. Even if this is labelled 'non-stick' it is worthwhile either brushing it with a few drops of oil or melted butter or lard (not margarine) or lining it with greased greaseproof (wax) paper or better still with baking parchment. This prevents any possibility of the meringues sticking.

8. Use the meringue mixture as soon as it is mixed. If by any chance you are hindered cover the bowl with a plate to exclude any air. This should prevent it becoming 'watery' for up to 10 minutes. You may have to whisk a little again.
9. The meringue mixture can be spooned on to the tin as follows:
   a) fill a tablespoon with the meringue mixture.
   b) take a second spoon of the size you want the meringues to be, i.e. either a teaspoon for 'baby' meringues or a dessertspoon for medium sized ones or another tablespoon for larger ones.
   c) spoon the mixture from the original spoon, then, in a rolling movement, place on the baking tray. With a little practise you will achieve a good and uniform shape.
   If you intend making meringues frequently it is worthwhile investing in a piping bag (see page 27) and a rose pipe. The diameter of this will depend upon the size you want the meringues to be. Spoon the meringue mixture into the piping bag and gently squeeze this to get the required amount of mixture on to the tray.
10. Bake as the timing in the recipe which follows. You can tell if the meringues are adequately dried out if they are easy to remove from the tray or paper or parchment. In the unlikely event of their looking firm but still sticking, dip a flat-bladed knife into hot water, shake hard to remove the surplus moisture then carefully lift them with the knife.

MERINGUES

An old name for these was 'whispers' for they are so very light and delicate. Do read the previous page before following this recipe, for the points given there will make sure you have great success. Meringues are inclined to stick to a surface so follow the advice in point 7, opposite.

Oven Setting: 90 to 110°C/200 to 225°F, Gas Mark 0 or (S) to ½. Fan ovens at the lowest setting possible.
Baking Time: see stage 5 below
Baking Equipment: one or two baking (cookie) tray(s)
Makes: see stage 5.

Metric/Imperial	Ingredients	American
2	**whites from medium sized eggs**	2
few drops	**vanilla extract**	few drops
115 g/4 oz	**caster sugar but see stage 2 above**	½ cup

1. Preheat the oven, although the temperature is very low you must be certain the oven has reached the correct heat before baking.
2. Prepare the baking tray(s) as stage 7 above. Put the egg whites into a basin or mixing bowl; choose one sufficiently large to enable you to use the whisk efficiently in it.
3. Whisk the egg whites with the vanilla until stiff. Use the whisk attachment with a large electric mixer or use a small electric mixer or a hand whisk. Do not use too high a speed at first for this tends to throw the light egg whites too much to the sides of the container.

4. Check to see that the whites are evenly whisked, sometimes they appear stiff on the top surface but there is still a little liquid egg white below, so use a stirring movement from time to time.

5. When the whites stand in firm peaks then start to add the sugar. If using an electric mixer make sure this is set to a low speed. Add the sugar gradually to the egg whites whisking all the time. When it is all incorporated spoon or pipe the mixture on to the prepared baking tray(s) as stage 9 above. The quantity and baking times are as follows:

8 to 12 medium meringues   –   2 to 3 hours baking
18 to 24 finger shaped meringues   –   1½ to 2 hours baking
50 to 60 'bite-sized' meringues for small children – 1 to 1¼ hours baking

6. Check as point 10 left, then remove the meringues on to a wire cooling tray. When quite cold store in an airtight container.

FILLING MERINGUES

Meringues are generally sandwiched together with whipped cream. As this will gradually soften the crisp mixture do not add it too soon before serving.

Spread the cream over the flat side of half the meringues then top the remaining ones.

Instead of whipped cream you could use thick lemon curd or a mixture of whipped cream and lemon curd. To avoid the fat content of whipped cream use fromage frais instead.

You can serve tiny meringues without any filling, for small children tend to prefer to eat them plain.

The meringue mixture can be tinted, see hints of adding colour on page 185.

CHOUX PASTRY

There is a belief that this pastry is difficult to make. That is not true but there are certain important steps you should follow; these are defined in the recipe below. The ingredients must be measured very accurately.

Oven Setting: as recipe
Baking Time: as recipe
Baking Equipment: flat baking (cookie) trays (pans)
Makes: see recipes. Uncooked or cooked Choux pastry can be frozen, see under Cream Buns.

Metric/Imperial	Ingredients	American
150 ml/¼ pint	water	⅔ cup
50 g/2 oz	butter or margarine	¼ cup
65 g/2½ oz	plain (all-purpose) flour (firmly packed)	½ cup plus 1 tablespoon
pinch	salt	pinch
2 small or medium	eggs	2 small or medium

1. Pour the water into a medium sized saucepan, add the butter or margarine; heat until this has melted, remove from the heat.
2. Sift the flour and salt, add to the pan; make sure all the flour is added at once. It is easier to do this if it is placed into a bag or in a funnel made from greaseproof (wax) paper. Stir briskly to incorporate the flour into the liquid then return to a **low** heat.
3. Stir continually until the mixture forms a ball and leaves the sides of the pan clean. Take the pan off the heat again and leave the mixture to cool.
4. Whisk the eggs then add a little to the pan; stir into the mixture and continue like this, add the beaten eggs gradually, until you have a sticky mixture that stands in soft peaks when tested with a knife. You may find you do not use quite all the egg. The choux pastry is then ready to use.

Variations

- For a more economical choux pastry use half the amount of fat given above.
- You can add a teaspoon of caster sugar to the flour.

CREAM BUNS

1. Lightly grease one or two baking trays. Preheat the oven to 220°C/ 425°F, Gas Mark 7 or 190 to 200°C with a fan oven. Reduce the heat to 200°C/400°F or Gas Mark 6 when the buns have been baking for 5 minutes. Do NOT open the oven door when you do this.
2. It is easy to spoon the mixture into 10 to 12 round balls or pipe them using a 1.25 cm/½ inch plain pipe in a piping bag. In a conventional oven it is an advantage to use just one baking tray, so the pastry is cooked in the ideal position in the oven but do not over-crowd the buns for the pastry spreads out as it rises. In a fan oven it does not matter if two trays are used.
3. Bake just above the centre of the oven for 30 to 35 minutes or until the buns have risen well, are pale gold in colour and are firm and crisp. If you want to check on the baking process do not open the oven door too wide.
4. Leave the buns on the baking tray to cool **away from a draught or open window**.
5. When nearly cold make a small slit at the side of the buns and check they are hollow inside. If a little uncooked mixture is left scoop this out gently and carefully and return the buns to the oven for another 5 or 6 minutes to dry out.

To Complete Cream Buns
When the buns are quite cold fill with whipped and slightly sweetened cream or with dessert fruit, such as raspberries, and whipped cream. Top with sifted icing (confectioners) sugar.
For savoury buns fill with soft cream cheese mixed with chopped parsley or your favourite herbs or with chopped prawns (shrimp) in fromage frais or crème fraîche.

Freezing – uncooked pastry: make shapes on baking trays. **Open-freeze**

then pack; return to baking trays and bake from frozen. Use within 2 months.

Cooked pastry: bake and cool, split as stage 5 above. **Open-freeze** then pack. Defrost at room temperature then warm to crisp if necessary. Fill after defrosting. Use within 3 months.

ECLAIRS

1. Lightly grease the baking tray(s) and dust with a little flour. With the handle of a wooden spoon mark lines in the flour; this will help you pipe the mixture to form straight fingers. Preheat the oven as under **Cream Buns**, stage 1.
2. While you can make about 16 lines of approximately 10 cm/4 inches in length by spooning the mixture over the marks on the baking tray it is easier to do this by piping it. Use a disposable or nylon piping bag. Insert a 6 mm to 1.25 cm/¼ to ½ inch plain pipe into the bag. Fill the bag about three-quarters full with the mixture, grasp the top of the bag and press down firmly so the mixture flows at a steady pace. Pipe out lines over the marks made on the baking trays. I find it easier to snip off the mixture at the required length with kitchen scissors.
3. Bake as stage 3 under **Cream Buns** but allow approximately 20 to 25 minutes cooking. Continue as stages 4 and 5 under **Cream Buns**.

To complete Eclairs
Fill as described under **Cream Buns**. For sweet Eclairs top with:

Chocolate Glacé Icing
Melt 50 g/2 oz plain (2 squares semi-sweet) chocolate with 2 teaspoons water in a basin over hot water or in the microwave. Sift 175 g/6 oz (scant 1½ cups) icing sugar into the chocolate, mix well then add a few drops more water to make a spreading consistency.

Dip a flat-bladed knife into hot water, shake dry but use while warm, dip into the icing and coat just the top of each éclair. Leave for a short time to set before serving.

Variation

- Sift 225 g/8 oz (scant 2 cups) icing sugar with 2 to 3 teaspoons cocoa powder then slowly add enough warm water to make a spreading consistency.

PERFECT CAKES

Cake making is undoubtedly one of the most ambitious forms of baking; its success depends on the various factors described on pages 62 to 107.

When you decide to make a cake check that you have all the ingredients listed in the recipe and that the tins (pans) you have are the right size. If you have doubts about this see page 182 on adapting tin sizes. Preheat the oven at the correct setting.

Cakes are mixed by various methods.

Plain cakes are often made by **rubbing the fat (shortening) into the flour**. This process is described under Pastry on page 109, it is similar for cakes. You can do this by hand or use an electric mixer or food processor. Never use the processor when adding dried fruit or similar ingredients – it will process them into tiny particles.

Another method of mixing cakes is by **melting some of the ingredients** in a saucepan over a gentle heat or in a suitable container in the microwave on a low setting. Always check whether the ingredients must be cooled before proceeding with the recipe.

The majority of cakes are prepared by **creaming the fat with the sugar** before adding any extra ingredients. Because this is such an important stage it is described in detail on pages 70 and 72.

Whisking egg whites or whole eggs produces mixtures with ultra light textures, see Meringues on page 57 and the cakes on page 97 and 101.

CONSISTENCY OF CAKE MIXTURES

The word 'consistency' is used to describe the softness or stiffness of a cake mixture (batter). This is very important, for it makes a great difference in the texture and appearance of cakes both large and small.

Rock Buns (page 62) have a **stiff** or, as sometimes described, a **sticky** consistency and this is clearly explained in stage 4 of the recipe.

The mixture for Cup Cakes (page 64) must be a **soft** or **slow** dropping consistency. It falls from the spoon easily. This consistency should ensure that the mixture rises quite flat, so you can ice the cakes.

Queen Cakes (page 66) are almost, but not quite, the same as there is a slightly higher proportion of flour to fat so they rise in a peak.

Removing Cakes from the Tins

If you need to loosen a cake from a 'non-stick' tin use a plastic or coated knife or spatula not a sharp metal knife.

To help a cake come out of the tin give this a gentle tap on the base, this loosens the cake.

Do not try and bring the cake out of the tin too soon, allow a minute or so, or the time given in the recipe, for the cake to cook slightly and contract.

Greasing and Flouring Tins
Brush the base and sides of the tin with a few drops of melted butter, lard or margarine or olive oil. The tin should just look shiny. Shake a little flour into the tin. Turn this around so the flour sticks to the greased surface. Give the tin a sharp tap and invert it so surplus flour falls out.

SMALL CAKES

When you begin making cakes it is a good idea to start by preparing small ones. The cakes chosen for this book are easily prepared and are quickly cooked. The first recipes illustrate two distinct methods of mixing, i.e. rubbing the fat into the flour and after that creaming fat with the sugar. The recipes also stress the importance of the right consistency, i.e. degree of stiffness of the mixture, so you become accustomed to the correct terms.

Bake small cakes above the centre of the oven, unless you have a fan oven when all shelves should have the same heat.

Small cakes tend to dry out fairly quickly, so it is wise to freeze any surplus the day they are made. Always allow them to become quite cold before wrapping or packing and putting them into the freezer.

Allow the frozen cakes to thaw out at room temperature or use a very low setting in the oven or in the microwave if you are hastening this process. Too high a temperature in the oven darkens the outside before the centres are defrosted and a high setting in the microwave produces a toughened cake.

ROCK CAKES

Rock Cakes or Rock Buns are some of the easiest of all cakes to prepare and if they are made correctly and eaten when freshly baked they are delicious.It is very important to achieve the correct consistency of the mixture. If too stiff the cakes will be unpleasantly dry and if too soft the mixture will spread too much and will not keep a good shape.

Oven Setting:	200°C/400°F, Gas Mark 6 or 190°C with a fan oven
Baking Time:	15 minutes
Baking Equipment:	one or two baking (cookie) tray(s)
Makes:	10 to 12. These become dry quickly but can be freshened on a second day by being heated for just 5 minutes in a preheated oven, set to 180°C/350°F, Gas Mark 4 or 170°C with a fan oven. Rock Cakes are quite brittle when cold so pack carefully before freezing or 'open-freeze' on a flat tin and pack when frozen.

Metric/Imperial	Ingredients	American
225 g/8 oz	*self-raising flour or plain (all-purpose) flour with 2 teaspoons baking powder*	2 cups
115 g/4 oz	*butter or margarine*	½ cup

115 g/4 oz	caster sugar	1/2 cup
1	egg	1
115 g/4 oz	mixed dried fruit	2/3 cup
approx 2 tablespoons	milk	approx 2 1/2 tablespoons
	Glaze	
2 tablespoons	caster sugar	2 1/2 tablespoons

1. Preheat the oven. Grease and flour the baking tray(s) or line them with baking parchment.
2. Sift the flour, or flour and baking powder, into a mixing bowl. Cut the butter or margarine into smaller pieces, drop into the flour and rub in until the mixture looks like fine breadcrumbs. Page 109 under Pastry gives detailed instructions about rubbing fat into flour.
3. Add the sugar then break the egg into a cup, to ensure you have no shell, add to the cake mixture and mix thoroughly with a flat-bladed knife.
4. Slowly and carefully add the dried fruit and the milk and continue mixing to ascertain the consistency. Different brands of flour absorb more or less milk. You have the right **stiff consistency** if the mixture stand in peaks when you pull a knife thorough it.
5. Put spoonfuls of the mixture on to the baking trays. Even with the right consistency the cakes tend to spread out as well as rise, so do not crowd them too much. Make sure the mixture is not too flat on top; the buns look better if the mixture is swept up slightly into peaks. Sprinkle a little of the sugar over each uncooked cake.
6. Place in the oven and bake until firm and golden. To test if cooked press the sides of the cakes, they should be pleasantly firm. Remove from the oven and lift on to a wire cooling tray.

Variations

- If using wholemeal (wholewheat) flour you may find you need almost 1 tablespoon more milk to mix and the cakes will take 1 or 2 minutes longer cooking time.

Gluten-Free Rock Cakes: use half rice flour and half gluten-free flour with the same amounts of baking powder as given for plain flour above.

Using Oil in Rock Cakes
Oil as a substitute for butter or margarine is not successful in Rock Cakes for it is difficult to obtain the right consistency to the buns.

BASED ON ROCK CAKES

The following cakes all have the same consistency as the Rock Cakes.

JAM BUNS

Omit the dried fruit from the recipe above. Put the plain cake mixture on to the baking trays then make a fairly deep indentation in the centre of each cake with the back of a teaspoon. Fill this 'hole' with jam (jelly) then, using a small knife, bring the cake mixture closer to the jam to protect it in baking. Cook as the cakes above.

ORANGE BUNS

Add 1 or 2 teaspoons finely grated orange zest to the mixture after rubbing in the butter or margarine. Instead of mixed dried fruit use finely chopped candied peel and mix the buns with orange juice instead of milk.

Variation

Chocolate Orange Buns: instead of using all flour use 200 g/7 oz (1¾ cups) self-raising flour sifted with 25 g/1 oz (¼ cup) cocoa powder and ¼ teaspoon baking powder. If using plain flour then use the same amount of baking powder as given above.

CUP CAKES

Oven Setting:	190°C/375°F, Gas Mark 5 or 180°C with a fan oven
Baking Time:	10 to 12 minutes
Baking Equipment:	about 18 patty tins (shells) plus paper cases
Makes:	about 18 small cakes. These should be eaten when fresh. They freeze well.

Metric/Imperial	Ingredients	American
115 g/4 oz	*butter or margarine*	*½ cup*
115 g/4 oz	*caster sugar*	*½ cup*
2 large	*eggs, whisked*	*2 large*
115 g/4 oz	*self-raising flour or plain (all-purpose) flour with 1 level teaspoon baking powder*	*1 cup*

1. Preheat the oven. Insert the paper cases into the patty tins, these will support the paper cases and keep them a good shape as the cake mixture rises.
2. Cream the butter or margarine and sugar until soft and light. If you are doing this by hand with a wooden spoon, place a folded teacloth (dish towel) under the bowl, this stops it 'wobbling' and gives you better control.
3. Gradually beat in the eggs, if the mixture shows signs of curdling add a little of the flour.
4. Sift the flour, or flour and baking powder, into the creamed mixture, then fold the ingredients together.
5. Spoon into the paper cases, you may find a teaspoon is ideal for this purpose. Put in enough mixture to come just over half way up the paper cases.
6. Bake until firm. Because of the smaller amount of mixture these cakes can be baked at a slightly higher setting than Queen Cakes, opposite.
7. Lift the paper cases out of the tins and allow the cakes to become

quite cold before icing them. Do not remove the cakes from the paper cases. Top each with Glacé Icing.

Variations

- Flavour the mixture with a few drops of vanilla or almond extract.

Chocolate Cup Cakes: omit 25 g/1 oz (¼ cup) flour and substitute the same amount of chocolate powder. Sift this with the flour. There is no need to adjust the amount of baking powder for these cakes.

GLACÉ ICING

This soft icing is also known as Water Icing for the icing (confectioners) sugar is blended with enough water. Add the water very gradually. While you can use cold water, hot water tends to give a better shine to the icing. Always sift icing sugar before using it. To give a good coating to cover the Cup Cakes you need:

300 g/10 oz (2¼ cups) icing (confectioners) sugar.

1. Sift the icing sugar into a basin.
2. Stir in the water, using a teaspoon for this, as the icing sugar becomes moist very quickly. For Cup Cakes the icing should be a fairly soft consistency that you can spoon, then spread, over each cake, giving a smooth layer. You should find you need about 1½ (1¾) tablespoons of liquid.
3. When the cakes are covered leave them for several hours for the icing to stiffen.

Variations

- The icing can be tinted with a few drops of culinary colouring. Instead of water you could use orange juice or lemon juice.

Chocolate Glacé Icing: sift 2 (2½) level tablespoons chocolate powder with the icing sugar or just a scant 1 tablespoon of cocoa powder.

Coffee Glacé Icing: mix the icing sugar with fairly strong liquid coffee instead of water.

QUEEN CAKES

These have long been favourite small cakes. They are cooked in small patty tins (shells). It is important that the cake mixture should be of a slow dropping consistency so the little cakes rise to a peak.

Oven Setting: 190°C/375°F, Gas Mark 5 or 180°C with a fan oven
Baking Time: 12 to 15 minutes
Baking Equipment: 12 patty tins
Makes: 12 cakes. These should be eaten when fresh. They freeze well.

Metric/Imperial	Ingredients	American
85 g/3 oz	**butter or margarine**	⅜ cup
85 g/3 oz	**caster sugar**	⅜ cup
2	**eggs, whisked**	2
115 g/4 oz	**self-raising flour or plain (all-purpose) flour with 1 teaspoon baking powder**	1 cup
85 g/3 oz	**sultanas (light seedless raisins) or currants**	good ½ cup

1. Preheat the oven. Grease and flour the patty tins or place paper cases in the tins.
2. Cream the butter and sugar until soft and light then gradually beat in the eggs. If the mixture shows any signs of curdling add a little of the flour.
3. Sift the flour, or flour and baking powder, and fold into the creamed mixture then gently fold in the dried fruit.
4. Spoon the mixture into the tins, take care not to fill these to the very top, you must leave a space for the cakes to rise. Bake until firm to the touch.
5. When you bring the tray(s) of patty tins out of the oven allow the cakes to cool in the tins for 3 or 4 minutes then give the tray a sharp tap. This helps to loosen the cakes so they are easy to remove on to a wire cooling tray.

Variations

- Use chopped glacé cherries instead of dried fruit.
- Flavour the cake mixture with 1 to 2 teaspoons finely grated orange or lemon zest; cream this with the butter or margarine and sugar.

Butterfly Cakes: make the Queen Cake mixture, without the dried fruit. The small cakes will rise well so it easy, when the cakes are cooked and cold, to cut a slice from the top of each. Spread the cakes with a little jam (jelly) then top with whipped cream. Cut the slices removed into halves and perch these over the cream, in the form of butterfly wings. Dust the cakes with sifted icing (confectioners) sugar.

Cornflour Queen Cakes: as explained on page 92 cornflour (cornstarch) can be substituted for plain (all-purpose) flour for anyone who cannot tolerate wheat in certain cakes. It could be used in these cakes and the Cup Cakes on page 64. Sift the baking powder with the cornflour and proceed as the recipe.

These cakes do tend to dry more quickly than when ordinary flour is used.

TRAYBAKES

Tray cakes, or 'traybakes' as they are known, are prepared in a quick way when you need small cakes but do not want to use individual patty (shell) tins.

When choosing a recipe for this purpose look for one with a fairly soft texture. A mixture that becomes crisp and very firm, like the Rock Cakes on page 62, would be difficult to cut into portions.

Sometimes the mixture is baked in an ordinary cake tin, such as the Brownies on page 69 then cut into the desired shapes. Another way is to use a larger shallow tin, so giving a greater number of cakes, see the recipe below and those on pages 68 and 69.

An oblong tin of sufficient depth is excellent but you could manage with a more shallow one as that used for a small Swiss Roll (see page 104), if you line it correctly first. The deep lining supports the cake mixture as it rises.

To cut Traybakes

Put the cold cake on a firm board. Work out the number of equal sized portions then cut these with a sharp knife.

ORANGE CAKES

A mixture of orange zest and juice plus marmalade make these cakes deliciously full of flavour and moist in texture.

Oven Setting: 160°C/325°F, Gas Mark 3 or 150°C with a fan oven
Baking Time: 35 minutes
Baking Equipment: one oblong baking (cookie) tray approximately
25 x 18 cm/10 x 7 inches and nearly 7.5 cm/
3 inches in depth but see stage 1
Makes: 12 to 16 cakes

Metric/Imperial	Ingredients	American
115 g/4 oz	marmalade, see stage 2	2/3 cup
1 teaspoon	finely grated orange zest	1 teaspoon
115 g/4 oz	butter or margarine	1/2 cup
115 g/4 oz	caster sugar	1/2 cup
225 g/8 oz	self-raising flour or plain (all-purpose) flour with 2 teaspoons baking powder	2 cups
2	eggs, whisked	2
4 tablespoons	orange juice	5 tablespoons

1. Preheat the oven. Prepare an oblong tin, lining it with greased greaseproof (wax) paper or baking parchment. If the tin you use is shallower than the measurements above make certain the paper or parchment stands well above the tin to give the correct depth.
2. If the peel in the marmalade is rather chunky then cut this into smaller pieces. Put the marmalade, orange zest (just the top coloured part of the fruit), the butter or margarine and sugar into a saucepan and melt over a low heat. Cool slightly.
3. Sift the flour, or flour and baking powder, into a mixing bowl, add the marmalade mixture and beat well then stir in the eggs.

4. Pour the orange juice into the saucepan used for melting the marmalade, bring just to boiling point; cool for 2 or 3 minutes then add to the other ingredients and mix thoroughly.
5. Spoon into the baking tin and bake just above the centre of the oven until firm to the touch. Cool for 10 minutes in the tin then turn out on to a wire cooling tray.
6. When nearly cold remove the paper or parchment. Leave until quite cold then cut into neat portions.

Variations

Date and Orange Cakes: add 115 g/4 oz (⅔ cup) chopped dates to the other ingredients in the saucepan at stage 2 above.

Top the cooked cake with a thin layer of heated then sieved marmalade (to remove the pieces of peel) before cutting into portions. You will need approximately 4 (5) tablespoons of preserve before sieving. If using a jelly type marmalade, or one with fine pieces of peel, simply melt the preserve then spread or brush over the top of the cake. Allow the glaze to cool and stiffen again. You could top the cake with icing instead, as below.

ORANGE GLACÉ ICING

Sift 225 g/8 oz icing (2 cups confectioners) sugar into a basin, mix with 1 tablespoon orange juice. Spread over the cake with a flat-bladed knife. Allow to stiffen then cut the cake into the required number of portions.

CHOCOLATE RAISIN CAKES

In this traybake you will enjoy pieces of firm chocolate and juicy raisins.

Oven Setting: 180°C/350°F, Gas Mark 4 or 170°C with a fan oven.
Baking Time: 35 minutes
Baking Equipment: one oblong baking (cookie) tray measuring approximately 25 x 18 cm/10 x 7 inches and nearly 7.5 cm/3 inches in depth but see stage 1
Makes: 12 to 16 cakes

Metric/Imperial	Ingredients	American
85 g/3 oz	raisins	½ cup
2 tablespoons	milk	2½ tablespoons
175 g/6 oz	butter or margarine	¾ cup
175 g/6 oz	caster sugar	¾ cup
3 large	eggs, whisked	3 large
225 g/8 oz	self-raising flour or plain (all-purpose) flour with 2 teaspoons baking powder	2 cups
85 g/3 oz	plain (semi-sweet) chocolate chips	½ cup

1. Preheat the oven. Prepare the oblong tray, lining it with greaseproof (wax) paper or baking parchment. If the tin you use is shallower than the measurements above make certain that the paper or parchment

stands well above the tin to give the correct depth.

2. Put the raisins with the milk to soak in a small basin while preparing the mixture.

3. Cream the butter or margarine and sugar until soft and light, see pages 70 and 71. Gradually beat in the eggs.

4. Sift the flour, or flour and baking powder, add to the creamed mixture with the chocolate chips, the raisins and any milk still not absorbed by them. Fold the ingredients gently together.

5. Spoon into the prepared tin, spreading the mixture evenly. Bake just above the centre of the oven until firm to the touch.

6. Cool in the tin for 5 minutes then carefully turn out on to a wire cooling tray, remove the greaseproof paper or parchment. When cold ice.

Variation

- Instead of using milk in stage 1 soak the raisins in 2 (2½) tablespoons of moderately strong coffee.

CHOCOLATE ICING

The cake can be topped with chocolate icing. Break 50 g/2 oz (¹/₃ cup) plain chocolate into pieces. Put into a basin and melt over a saucepan of hot, but not boiling, water or in the microwave on a low setting.

Allow the chocolate to cool, but not to set again. Add 50 g/2 oz (¹/₄ cup) butter and mix well with the chocolate then stir in 175 g/6 oz sifted icing (1½ cups confectioners) sugar. Beat together until smooth. Spread over the top of the cold cake. Produce a ridged effect by drawing the prongs of a fork down the icing.

Leave to become firmer then cut the cake into the required number of portions.

BROWNIES

There are many versions of these chocolate cakes but this is my favourite one. The cake should be pleasantly moist with a good chocolate flavour. Take care not to over-bake the cake and when cut into squares or fingers do not leave exposed to the air for too long, put into an airtight container.

Oven Setting: 180°C/350°F, Gas Mark or 170°C with a fan oven
Baking Time: 30 minutes
Baking Equipment: one 20 cm/8 inch square tin (pan) or a deep sandwich tin (layer pan)
Makes: 12 to 16 squares or fingers. These keep for several days and they can be frozen.

Metric/Imperial	Ingredients	American
85 g/3 oz	walnuts	¾ cup
115 g/4 oz	plain (semi-sweet) chocolate	¼ lb
115 g/4 oz	butter	½ cup
115 g/4 oz	soft brown sugar	⅔ cup
2 large	eggs, whisked	2 large

115 g/4 oz	self-raising flour or plain (all-purpose) flour with 1 teaspoon baking powder	1 cup
3 tablespoons	raisins	3¾ tablespoons
2 tablespoons	milk	2½ tablespoons

1. Preheat the oven. Grease and flour the tin or line it with greased greaseproof (wax) paper or baking parchment.
2. Chop the walnuts evenly but not too finely, you need to see quite definite pieces in the cake.
3. Chop the chocolate into a few smaller pieces so these melt easily and place in a large basin over hot, but not boiling, water and heat until melted. If more convenient melt in the microwave on a low setting. Allow the chocolate to cool but do not let it set again.
4. Add the butter and the sugar and cream until a soft light mixture. Then gradually stir in the eggs. If the mixture shows signs of curdling add a little of the flour.
5. Sift the flour, or flour and baking powder, into the creamed ingredients then add the walnuts and the raisins. Fold all the ingredients together; lastly stir in the milk. You should have a soft consistency that falls easily from a wooden spoon or from a beater if using the electric mixer.
6. Spoon the mixture into the prepared tin and bake until JUST firm to the touch. Allow to cool in the tin for 10 minutes then turn out, remove the greaseproof paper or parchment. Place the cake on a wire cooling tray and allow to cool.
7. When quite cold cut into squares or fingers with a sharp knife.

Variations

- Instead of using milk in the above recipe use 2 (2½) tablespoons of very strong liquid coffee.
- Although it is not usual to add other fruit you could use half sultanas (white seedless raisins) and half raisins.
- Pecan nuts can be substituted for walnuts.
- Add 1 to 2 teaspoons finely grated orange zest to the butter and sugar and moisten the mixture with 2 (2½) tablespoons orange juice instead of milk.

CREAMING METHOD

The creaming method of blending fat (shortening) and sugar, then incorporating the rest of the ingredients correctly, is very important. It is used to prepare a wide range of cakes as well as a limited number of other recipes.

The purpose of the initial creaming (beating) is to:

a) soften the mixture, so it is the right texture to blend in the eggs, flour and any other ingredients.
b) aerate the fat and sugar, so helping to make the mixture light. This is particularly important with sponge-type cakes, such as the Victoria Sandwich on page 83 and similar cakes – where lightness of

texture is so essential. It is important that the fat is not even slightly melted in this classic method, for that would prevent you aerating the mixture.

Modern soft type butters and margarines are much easier to cream than the harder types, although these become soft and manageable if left at room temperature for a time. See also one-stage mixing on page 72.

c) soften the sugar grains. This is helped by using caster (a fine grained sugar) in the mixture.

STAGE 1 – CREAMING BY THE CLASSIC METHOD

By hand: choose a good-sized mixing bowl so you have plenty of room for the brisk action and space to incorporate all the additional ingredients. Most people like to use a wooden spoon for creaming. This is sufficiently strong to enable you to mix the ingredients with good energetic movements.

Firstly stir fairly gently to mix the sugar into the fat. When this has been done start a brisk beating action, making sure all the fat and sugar mixture are being evenly beaten. You may find it easier to do this if you slightly tilt the bowl. Other people like to keep the bowl flat on a working surface. The action of creaming is inclined to make the bowl 'wobble', which makes it more difficult to beat the ingredients. If you place a folded teacloth (dish towel) under the bowl this will hold it steady.

The mixture has been sufficiently creamed when it becomes much lighter in colour and has the consistency of thick whipped cream.

Many professional cooks and chefs prefer to cream the butter and sugar with one hand. This has the great advantage of softening fairly hard butter or margarine more quickly.

If using a small hand electric mixer: use the lowest speed until you have mixed the sugar and fat together. If you use a high speed at this stage the light sugar would splash to the upper sides of the bowl. You can increase the speed slightly after this stage and cream in a steady, rather than a fast, action. From time to time check that the two whisks do not become coated with uncreamed mixture. You may need to stop once or twice to remove any rather solid fat and sugar from the blades and return the mixture to the bowl.

If using a large electric mixer: choose the beating attachment, not the whisk. Use the lowest speed until the sugar and fat have been blended together. Next turn to a moderate speed, too fast an action throws the fat and sugar high up the bowl and you do not get even creaming. Continue until the ingredients are lighter in colour and the consistency of thick whipped cream.

If using a food processor: this is more suitable for the quick one-stage method, given on the next page, for the speed of operation and the fact the bowl is covered by a lid means you do not get the same degree of aeration as when mixing by hand or with a small or large electric mixer.

I have found when I cream the fat and sugar, as the stage described above, I get a better result if I leave the feeder tube out, so making sure I do get a limited amount of air into the processor bowl. After this I continue as the one-stage method. This initial creaming – even though short – does make an improvement to the texture.

STAGE 2 – ADDING THE EGGS

Many people happily drop the eggs one by one into the creamed mixture. You will increase the aeration if you first break the eggs, one by one, into a separate bowl and whisk them well before adding to the creamed fat and sugar. This also means you control the speed with which the eggs are added and this is important. When you first begin baking it may seem alarming if the mixture starts to separate – 'curdle' is the right word. Do not be unduly worried, simply beat in – quite briskly – a good tablespoon of the weighed out flour. This should solve the problem.

You can continue beating very briskly as the eggs are mixed in.

STAGE 3 – ADDING THE FLOUR

As you will read, all methods state 'sift the flour' or 'flour and baking powder'. Sometimes you need a pinch of salt or spices and these should be sifted with the flour. Rubbing the flour through a sieve does two things:

a) makes sure there are no lumps
b) aerates it, again helping to make the cake light.

When you add the flour by hand to the fat, sugar and egg mixture it is essential that you no longer use a brisk beating movement. You **stir** or better still, **fold**, it in gently, carefully and thoroughly. A wooden spoon is no longer suitable for this purpose. Use a metal spoon or a flat bladed spatula.

If using a small or large electric mixer turn to the lowest speed so you emulate the action you would use if mixing the cake by hand.

Over-beating of the flour in this kind of cake can give uneven air holes and result in a close, not so light, texture.

Additional ingredients, such as dried fruit should also be folded in gently.

One-stage Mixing

The soft fats of today mean you can put all the ingredients required for a plain cake into a mixing bowl and beat them together. This can be done by hand, with an electric mixer or with a food processor. The result is quite acceptable but not as perfect as when using the classic method of adding ingredients.

You cannot include dried fruits or glacé (candied) cherries or similar ingredients if mixing with a food processor for these would be chopped so finely that they would be absorbed by the cake mixture. Fruits, cherries, etc. will not be chopped when mixing by hand or with an electric mixer.

Some cooks like to add extra baking powder to compensate for the lack of air. Personally I do not do this, for extra baking powder is inclined to taste. You may not get quite such a risen mixture but you will have one that tastes very good. All plain cakes in this book could be made by the one-stage method.

In some cakes it is possible to substitute oil for butter or margarine; this will be stated in the recipe. I do not use oil in very light cakes, such as the Victoria Sandwich.

LARGE CAKES

All the information at the front of this book and from pages 6 to 8
will help you make a great success of preparing and baking large cakes.
Each group of cakes varies in the way the ingredients are put together.

The first group of cakes are made by the **rubbing-in method**, they are
quick to prepare by hand or with an electric mixer. The instructions
under Pastry on page 109 give hints on rubbing fat into flour. Do NOT
use a food processor for any of the cakes that contain dried fruit or peel,
etc., the efficient machine would chop these into ultra small pieces and
spoil the mixture. Cakes in this section often come under the heading of
'cut and come again cakes' for they are the type that are economical and
baked to fill-up hungry people. They are ideal for packed meals and
picnics, for they are fairly robust. If you want to replace the butter or
margarine with oil, you can do in some cases. Oil is not suitable in every
cake in this group. Where oil gives good results you will find it
mentioned in the individual recipe.

Next come Gingerbreads and similar mixtures, made by the **melting
method**. Oil could be used in these, see pages 78 and 80.

The third group of cakes, which is the largest, varies from the
comparatively plain, but deliciously light, Victoria Sandwich on page 83,
to the more elaborate, but still easy-to-make cakes that follow. All are
prepared by the **creaming method**, so do read the advice on pages 71 to
72. The mixture for the Victoria Sandwich and several other cakes, is
baked in two sandwich tins, so the cooking time is comparatively short.
The two shallow cakes are then put together to form a large cake.

In this group of cakes the creaming action, and the steps that follow,
play an important part in creating the lightness of the baked cake. I prefer
NOT to use oil in place of butter or margarine, for it is difficult to create
the same light texture. As you will read on page 71 both an electric mixer
or food processor can be used for preparing a creamed mixture.

The last cakes are made by the **whisking method**. This enables you to
produce a wonderfully light sponge and Swiss Roll. Whisking eggs and
sugar can be done by hand or with an electric mixer.

Cakes made with yeast as a raising agent will be found on page 153
onwards.

BAKING LARGE CAKES

The baking time and oven setting is given in all recipes. These have been
tested carefully but remember that ovens vary slightly, so check the advice
against YOUR knowledge of YOUR cooker and the manufacturer's
instructions. This is particularly important with a fan oven.

Large cakes should be placed in the centre of the oven; more shallow
sandwich cakes just above the centre of the oven. In a fan oven every
shelf should give the same temperature so position is not important.

You should find the baking times absolutely correct for your oven but
just in case you have an oven which is slightly **above** average heat check a
little earlier than the time given. If on the other hand the oven is on the
slower side you may need a little longer cooking time. In either of these
cases it would be a good idea to pencil in any changes against the recipe,
so you know for future reference.

SPICED-TOPPED NUT CAKE

This is an interesting cake for it has a spiced nut filling and topping which adds interest to a plain cake. Make the filling first, for half has to be put into the cake mixture. Unless you are very fond of spices it is wise to use the smaller amounts the first time you make the cake.

Oven Setting:	190°C/375°F, Gas Mark 5 or 180°C with a fan oven
Baking Time:	35 to 40 minutes
Baking Equipment:	one 18 cm/7 inch square cake tin (pan) or a 20 cm/ 8 inch round tin
Makes:	one rather shallow cake that should be eaten when fresh or even slightly warm. Freezing does tend to soften the topping.

Metric/Imperial	Ingredients	American
	Topping	
40 g/1½ oz	butter, melted	3 tablespoons
25 g/1 oz	plain (all-purpose) flour	¼ cup
½ to 1 teaspoon	ground cinnamon	½ to 1 teaspoon
½ to 1 teaspoon	ground ginger	½ to 1 teaspoon
25 g/1 oz	semolina or fine polenta	⅙ cup
50 g/2 oz	Demerara (raw) sugar	scant ¼ cup
50 g/2 oz	walnuts or other nuts, chopped	½ cup
	Cake	
85 g/3 oz	self-raising flour with ¾ level teaspoon baking powder or plain flour with 2½ level teaspoons baking powder	¾ cup
pinch	salt	pinch
½ to 1 teaspoon	ground cinnamon	½ to 1 teaspoon
½ to 1 teaspoon	ground ginger	½ to 1 teaspoon
85 g/3 oz	semolina or fine polenta	½ cup
85 g/3 oz	butter or margarine	⅜ cup
115 g/4 oz	caster sugar	½ cup
1 large	egg	1 large
6 tablespoons	milk	7½ tablespoons

1. Preheat the oven. Grease and flour the cake tin or line it with greased greaseproof (wax) paper or baking parchment. With a cake with a crumbly topping like this it is wise to choose a cake tin with a loose base that you can push up from the bottom so making it unnecessary to invert the cake tin.
2. Allow the melted butter to cool slightly. Sift the flour with the spices then mix it with all the ingredients for the topping.
3. Sift the flour, baking powder, salt and spices together into a mixing

bowl, add the semolina or polenta then rub in the butter or margarine.

4. Stir in the sugar, then add the egg, mix well then gradually stir in the milk. Spoon **half** this mixture into the cake tin. Smooth flat. Sprinkle over **half** the topping ingredients.
5. Add the rest of the cake mixture, smooth flat on top then sprinkle the last of the topping ingredients evenly over the cake.
6. Bake until firm to the touch or until a fine skewer inserted into the centre of the cake comes out clean.
7. Cool in the tin for 5 minutes then carefully remove on to a wire cooling tray.

NOTE: do NOT use oil in this cake. It would make the mixture too moist and it would be difficult for the filling and topping to remain intact. This would blend too easily with the cake mixture.

STREUSEL FRUIT CAKE

A Streusel Cake is one with a crunchy topping. This is put over the uncooked cake mixture and baked with it. The topping looks most attractive. It is advisable to bake this type of cake in a tin (pan) with a loose base so that when the cake is cooked you simply push up the base, so saving the necessity of turning the cake tin upside down, to remove the cake. If you invert the tin some of the crumbly topping is inclined to fall off.

Oven Setting: 180°C/350°F, Gas Mark 4 or 170°C with a fan oven
Baking Time: 1 hour
Baking Equipment: one 18 cm/7 inch cake tin (pan)
Makes: one 18 cm/7 inch cake. The cake is a reasonably plain one, so should be eaten when freshly baked. It freezes well although the streusel topping tends to soften slightly.

Metric/Imperial	Ingredients	American
	Cake ingredients	
225 g/8 oz	*self-raising flour or plain (all-purpose) flour with 2 teaspoons baking powder*	2 cups
1 teaspoon	*mixed spice*	1 teaspoon
150 g/5 oz	*butter or margarine*	5/8 cup
150 g/5 oz	*caster sugar*	5/8 cup
3	*eggs, whisked*	3
1 tablespoon	*golden (corn) syrup*	1 tablespoon
225 g/8 oz	*mixed dried fruit*	1¼ cups
approx 2 tablespoons	*milk*	approx 2½ tablespoons
	Streusel topping	
50 g/2 oz	*plain flour*	½ cup

½ teaspoon	mixed spice	½ teaspoon
25 g/1 oz	butter or margarine	2 tablespoons
50 g/2 oz	caster sugar	¼ cup
4 tablespoons	finely chopped walnuts	5 tablespoons

1. Preheat the oven; grease and flour the tin or line with greased greaseproof (wax) paper or baking parchment.
2. Sift the flour, or flour and baking powder, with the spice into a mixing bowl.
3. Cut the butter or margarine into small pieces, add to the flour and then rub in until like fine breadcrumbs. Details of rubbing fat into flour are given on page 109 under Pastry.
4. Add the sugar, then gradually stir in the eggs then the golden syrup. Mix well.
5. Stir in the dried fruit then gradually add enough milk to give a **sticky consistency**. This means that the mixture should stand in peaks if a knife is pulled through it.
6. Spoon the mixture into the cake tin and smooth flat on top.
7. **Streusel topping:** sift the flour and spice into a bowl; rub in the butter or margarine. Add the sugar and walnuts and mix the ingredients together.
8. Sprinkle carefully and evenly over the top of the cake and bake until golden in colour. It is difficult to tell if this cake is cooked by pressing the top so insert a wooden skewer into the cake, withdraw it carefully. If the skewer is clean, with no vestige of uncooked cake mixture adhering to it, the cake is cooked.
9. Cool in the tin for 5 minutes then raise the cake out of the sides of the tin – do not attempt to remove the base of the tin at this moment. Place on a wire cooling tray and leave until cold then carefully lift the cake, take away the base of the tin and the greaseproof paper or parchment.

APPLE CAKE

*Every fruit growing area in Britain boasts that their apple cake is best. This recipe comes from the West Country and the cake is full of good flavour. **Choosing apples:** the apples used in this cake are a good cooking type (a Bramley); you could however select the kind that is both good as a dessert or cooking fruit. In this case the pieces of apple will stay firmer in the cake.*

Oven Setting: 180°C/350°F, Gas Mark 4 or 170°C with a fan oven
Baking Time: 1¼ hours
Equipment: one 20 cm/8 inch cake tin (pan)
Makes: one cake; serve freshly baked; freezes moderately well, the apple pieces tend to soften.

Metric/Imperial	Ingredients	American
225 g/8 oz	self-raising flour or plain flour with 2 teaspoons baking powder	2 cups

150 g/5 oz	*butter*	⅝ cup
175 g/6 oz	*caster or light brown sugar*	¾ cup
2	*medium cooking apples*	2
25 g/1 oz	*Demerara (raw) sugar*	2 tablespoons
½ to 1 teaspoon	*ground cinnamon*	½ to 1 teaspoon
1	*egg*	1
1 tablespoon	*milk*	1¼ tablespoons
	For the topping	
2 tablespoons	*caster sugar*	2½ tablespoons
¼ teaspoon	*ground cinnamon*	¼ teaspoon

1. Preheat the oven. Grease and flour or line the cake tin (pan).
2. Sift the flour, or flour and baking powder, into a bowl, rub in the butter, add the caster or light brown sugar.
3. Peel and core the apples, cut the flesh into 2 cm/¾ inch dice. Blend the Demerara sugar with the cinnamon and roll the apples in this mixture. Add to the flour and other ingredients.
4. Blend with the egg and milk. Do not exceed the amount of liquid as the juice from the apples flows during baking. Spoon into the cake tin and top with the caster sugar and cinnamon.
5. Bake until firm. Check after 50 minutes to 1 hour and if the cake is becoming too brown lower the heat to 150°C/300°F, Gas Mark 2 or 140°C with a fan oven.

To make a change

Apple and Orange Cake: follow the basic recipe but add 2 teaspoons finely grated orange zest after rubbing in the butter. Use orange juice instead of milk to moisten the mixture. Instead of sugar and cinnamon on top of the cake you could use the 2 (2½) tablespoons sugar plus 2 teaspoons finely grated orange zest.

Apple and Raisin Cake: follow the basic recipe but add 100 g/4 oz (generous ½ cup) raisins to the mixture with the apples.

Apricot and Apple Cake: follow the basic recipe but cut 100 g/3½ oz (⅔ cup) ready-to-eat dried apricots into small pieces, add to the mixture with the apples.

APPLE AND SULTANA CAKE

This is a cake to make if you are short of eggs, or if anyone is allergic to these. Even one slice of cake containing an egg could cause the person to have a reaction. The vinegar sounds surprising but it does not spoil the cake.

Oven Setting: 190°C/375°F, Gas Mark 5 or 180°C with a fan oven
Baking Time: 1 hour and 5 minutes
Baking Equipment: one 18 cm/7 inch round cake tin (pan)
Makes: one cake that keeps for several days. It can be frozen.

Metric/Imperial	Ingredients	American
4 tablespoons	*apple juice*	5 tablespoons
150 g/5 oz	*sultanas (seedless white raisins)*	scant 1 cup
225 g/8 oz	*self-raising flour or plain (all-purpose) flour with 2 teaspoons baking powder*	2 cups
115 g/4 oz	*butter or margarine*	½ cup
150 g/5 oz	*soft light brown or caster sugar*	good ½ cup
1½ tablespoons	*white or brown malt vinegar*	scant 2 tablespoons
2 tablespoons	*milk*	2½ tablespoons
	Topping	
1 to 1½ tablespoons	*soft light or caster sugar*	1 to 1¾ tablespoons

1. Preheat the oven. Grease and flour the cake tin or line it with greaseproof (wax) paper or baking parchment.
2. Put the apple juice and sultanas into a basin to soak for 10 minutes while preparing the cake mixture.
3. Sift the flour, or flour and baking powder, into a mixing bowl. Rub in the butter or margarine, add the sugar. Mix the vinegar with the apple juice and sultanas and stir gradually into the cake mixture.
4. Lastly stir in the milk. Spoon into the cake tin. Smooth flat then sprinkle the sugar evenly over the top of the mixture.
5. Bake until firm to the touch and the cake has shrunk away from the sides of the tin. Cool in the tin for 5 minutes then turn out on to a wire cooling tray.

In each of the recipes for the cakes made by the **rubbing-in method** you could use gluten-free flour. This does not alter the amount of raising agent – remember it is the equivalent of plain (all-purpose) flour – or the amount of liquid or the baking time in the recipe.

Cakes Without Eggs

The recipe above is made without using eggs. It is not easy to replace them in cake making. The light types of cakes **need eggs** to give the right texture and flavour but the cakes made by the rubbing in method, from pages 74 to 78 could be made without eggs if it was necessary to do so.

Follow the recipe but for every egg omitted add 2 (2½) tablespoons milk. The cakes tend to be more brittle, so must be handled with care when hot.

RICH GINGERBREAD

This is a large gingerbread for special occasions, it is rich and dark being made with a generous amount of black treacle (molasses) and golden (corn) syrup, together with a rich dark sugar, Barbados sugar is an excellent choice. Always line the tin (pan) when making gingerbreads since the mixture is inclined to stick. As the mixture is rather liquid you must make sure the lining paper or parchment covers any joins if you are using a cake tin with a loose base.

Oven Setting:	150°C/300°F, Gas Mark 2 or 140°C with a fan oven	
Baking Time:	1 hour 15 minutes	
Baking Equipment:	one 20 cm/8 inch square or 23 cm/9 inch round cake tin (pan)	
Makes:	one cake that should be kept for 2 or 3 days before cutting, so the flavour can mature. It freezes well.	

Metric/Imperial	Ingredients	American
175 g/6 oz	**butter or lard (shortening)**	¾ cup
115 g/4 oz	**moist dark brown sugar**	⅔ cup
225 g/8 oz	**black treacle**	⅔ cup
115 g/4 oz	**golden syrup**	⅓ cup
350 g/12 oz	**plain (all-purpose) flour**	3 cups
1 teaspoon	**bicarbonate of soda (baking soda)**	1 teaspoon
½ to 1 teaspoon	**allspice, or to taste**	½ to 1 teaspoon
2 teaspoons	**ground ginger, or to taste**	2 teaspoons
2 large	**eggs, whisked**	2 large
2 tablespoons	**milk**	2½ tablespoons
150 ml/¼ pint	**water**	⅔ cup

1. Preheat the oven and line the cake tin with greased greaseproof (wax) paper or baking parchment.
2. Put the butter or lard, sugar, treacle and golden syrup into a saucepan, stir over a moderate heat until the ingredients have melted; remove from the heat. If more convenient melt in a suitable bowl in the microwave. Allow the mixture to cool slightly before proceeding to the next stage.
3. Sift the flour, bicarbonate of soda, allspice and ginger into a mixing bowl, add the melted ingredients and stir well to blend.
4. Add the eggs and milk and stir again. With this recipe and most gingerbreads, vigorous mixing is quite correct.
5. Pour the water into the saucepan or bowl in which the ingredients were melted, stir well as it heats, so it absorbs any mixture left in the container. When the water is warm pour it onto the other ingredients and mix together to make a smooth **soft** consistency.
6. Pour or spoon into the prepared tin and bake for 1 hour 15 minutes, or until quite firm to a **gentle** pressure or until a fine skewer inserted into the centre of the gingerbread comes out clean. Do not be upset if the gingerbread has sunk slightly, that is quite permissible.
7. Cool in the tin then remove the greaseproof paper or parchment. Store in an airtight tin away from other cakes.

Measuring and Weighing Syrups

Treacle (molasses), golden (corn), syrup, maple syrup and honey are not easy to weigh or measure. Here are some suggestions.

1. **If the ingredients are melted:** weigh the empty saucepan or bowl (if using the microwave) then add a weight of the amount of treacle or

syrup that is required. Gradually spoon in the quantity of treacle or syrup needed in the recipe.

2. **If not melting the ingredients:** put a layer of flour or a piece of baking parchment on the scale then add the required amount of treacle or other syrup. You will find that the flour or parchment makes it easy to tip the treacle or syrup into the other ingredients.

3. **If required to measure treacle or syrup:** shake a dusting of flour over the bowl of the spoon then add the treacle or syrup. It will run off easily. If a recipe stresses 1 level tablespoon dip a second spoon into boiling water, so you measure the treacle or syrup more accurately.

FAMILY GINGERBREAD

Although this is a far more economical cake than the Rich Gingerbread it is still a very tasty cake that keeps well for several days. The remarks in the Rich Gingerbread recipe about lining the tin (page 78) are just as important in this recipe.

Oven Setting: 160°C/325°F, Gas Mark 3 or 150°C with a fan oven
Baking Time: 45 minutes in an oblong tin or 55 minutes in a square cake tin (pan)
Baking Equipment: one 20 x 15 cm/8 x 6 inch oblong tin or an 18 cm/ 7 inch square tin.
Makes: one cake that is best kept for 24 hours before serving. It freezes well.

Metric/Imperial	Ingredients	American
85 g/3 oz	butter or margarine or lard (shortening)	3/8 cup
85 g/3 oz	moist brown sugar	1/2 cup
85 g/3 oz	black treacle (molasses) or golden (corn) syrup	1/4 cup
225 g/8 oz	plain (all-purpose) flour	2 cups
1 level teaspoon	bicarbonate of soda (baking soda)	1 level teaspoon
1 to 1 1/2 teaspoons	ground ginger, or to taste	1 to 1 1/2 teaspoons
1 large	egg, whisked	1 large
5 tablespoons	milk	6 1/4 tablespoons

1. Preheat the oven. Line the cake tin with greased greaseproof (wax) paper or baking parchment.

2. Put the butter or margarine or lard with the sugar and treacle or golden syrup into a saucepan and stir over a moderate heat until melted. Remove from the heat. The ingredients could be melted in a suitable bowl in the microwave. Allow to cool slightly.

3. Sift the flour with the bicarbonate of soda and ginger into a mixing bowl, add the melted ingredients and stir briskly then beat in the egg.

4. Pour the milk into the saucepan or bowl in which the ingredients

were melted, stir well as it heats. When warm pour on to the rest of the ingredients and mix thoroughly.

5. Spoon into the prepared tin and bake as the times given above. Test as stage 6 on page 79. Allow to cool in the tin then turn out and remove the greaseproof paper or parchment.

Using Oil in Gingerbreads

In the Rich Gingerbread add 180 ml/6 fl oz (¾ cup) olive, corn or sunflower oil. In Family Gingerbread use 90 ml/3 fl oz (⅜ cup).

In either instance add the oil to the melted ingredients when the pan has been removed from the heat.

PARKIN

This is a special kind of gingerbread which contains oatmeal, so has a somewhat nutty texture. It is a particular favourite in Yorkshire and Lancashire. Many old recipes suggest baking the Parkin in the roasting tin. In the past people obviously baked a very large cake.

Recipes vary in the proportions of flour and oatmeal used and black treacle (molasses) could replace all or some of the syrup. This particular recipe does not include eggs, so it would be a good choice for anyone allergic to these.

Oven Setting:	180°C/350°F, Gas Mark 4 or 170°C with a fan oven
Baking Time:	45 minutes
Baking Equipment:	one oblong baking (cookie) tray approximately 25 x 18 cm/10 x 7 inches and nearly 7.5 cm/ 3 inches in depth, but see stage 1
Makes:	one cake that is cut into squares. Parkin keeps for several days. It can be spread with butter and served with cheese. It freezes well.

Metric/Imperial	Ingredients	American
115 g/4 oz	golden (corn) syrup	good ⅓ cup
115 g/4 oz	lard (shortening) or butter	½ cup
225 g/8 oz	plain (all-purpose) flour	2 cups
pinch	salt	pinch
1 level teaspoon	bicarbonate of soda (baking soda)	1 level teaspoon
1 teaspoon	mixed spice or ground ginger	1 teaspoon
115 g/4 oz	fine or medium oatmeal	¼ lb
175 g/6 oz	soft brown sugar	good ¾ cup
150 ml/¼ pint	milk	⅔ cup

1. Preheat the oven. Line the tin with greased greaseproof (wax) paper or baking parchment. If the tin is more shallow than the one above then let the paper or parchment stand well above the rim.
2. Weigh the syrup (see page 79) then add the lard or butter and melt these together in a saucepan over a low heat or in a bowl in the

microwave on a low setting. Allow to cool slightly.
3.   Sift the flour with the salt, bicarbonate of soda and the spice. Add the oatmeal, sugar and the melted ingredients. Beat well.
4.   Warm the milk in the pan or bowl in which the syrup and fat were melted, stir into the ingredients. Beat thoroughly then spoon into the tin.
5.   Bake until firm to the touch. Leave in the tin until almost cold then turn out and remove the paper or parchment and place on a wire cooling tray.

Variations

- You could use olive, corn or sunflower oil in this recipe in place of lard or butter. Add 120 ml/4 fl oz (½ cup) to the melted syrup after removing the pan from the heat then proceed as the recipe.

Glacé Ginger Parkin: flavour the cake with the ground ginger, not mixed spice. Add 4 (5) tablespoons finely chopped crystallized (glacé) ginger at stage 3.

Orange Parkin: add 2 teaspoons finely grated orange zest to the flour and add 4 (5) tablespoons finely chopped crystallized (glacé) orange peel at stage 3.

AUSTRIAN CHOCOLATE CAKE

This is a delicious cake that is soaked in a coffee and rum syrup, so it is suitable for a dessert as well as to serve with tea or coffee.

Oven Setting: 180°C/350°F, Gas Mark 4 or 170°C with a fan oven
Baking Time: 40 minutes or see stage 5
Baking Equipment: one 20 to 23 cm/8 to 9 inch cake tin (pan)
Makes: one cake that must be eaten when freshly made.

Metric/Imperial	Ingredients	American
100 g/3½ oz	butter	scant ½ cup
105 ml/3½ fl oz	milk	scant ½ cup
25 g/1 oz	cocoa powder	2 tablespoons
½ teaspoon	vanilla extract* or essence	½ teaspoon
150 g/5 oz	self-raising flour with ½ teaspoon baking powder or plain (all-purpose) flour with 2 level teaspoons baking powder	1¼ cups
150 g/5 oz	caster sugar	⅝ cup
2 large	eggs	2 large
	For the syrup	
150 ml/¼ pint	moderately strong coffee	⅔ cup
100 g/3½ oz	granulated or caster sugar	scant ½ cup
2 tablespoons	rum	2½ tablespoons

Topping

2 tablespoons	***icing (confectioners) sugar, sifted***	*2½ tablespoons*

* this gives the better flavour

1. Put the butter, milk and cocoa powder into a saucepan with the vanilla and stir over a low heat until the butter has melted and the cocoa powder has dissolved. Remove from the heat immediately and allow to become quite cold. This stage could be done in a bowl in the microwave on a low setting.
2. Preheat the oven then line the cake tin carefully with greased greaseproof (wax) paper or baking parchment.
3. Sift the flour and baking powder together, add the sugar then beat in the cold melted ingredients. Separate the eggs, drop the whites into a good sized bowl, add the yolks to the cocoa mixture and beat thoroughly.
4. Whisk the egg whites until they stand in soft peaks. Take a tablespoonful of the whites and beat this into the other ingredients. Fold in the remainder of the whites with a spatula or metal spoon.
5. Spoon into the tin and bake for 40 minutes or until firm to the touch. If the tin is only just 20 cm/8 inches in size the cake may take a few minutes longer. Cool in the tin for 3 or 4 minutes.
6. Turn the cake out carefully on to a large serving plate or dish and remove the paper or parchment while the cake is hot. Allow to become quite cold.
7. Put the coffee and sugar into a saucepan, stir over a low heat until the sugar has dissolved then boil briskly for 4 or 5 minutes until the mixture is beginning to look syrupy. Stir in the rum then immediately remove the pan from the heat. Do not do this in a microwave.
8. Spoon the syrup evenly over the cake. Leave for several hours then top with the icing sugar and serve.

Variations

- Instead of coffee for the syrup use water.
- To emphasise the chocolate flavour of the cake make the syrup as stage 7 with water and sugar. Omit the rum but stir 1 tablespoon cocoa powder into the hot syrup and stir until dissolved then pour over the cake.

VICTORIA SANDWICH

A Victoria Sandwich or Butter Sponge as known in America, is one of the great classic light cakes. It is assumed that it was given this name in honour of Queen Victoria, although there are no records to say she enjoyed it.

When correctly made it should be light with a smooth texture. Today it may seem old-fashioned but if you can make it correctly you have learned the secret of a delicate sponge-like cake made by the creaming method; see details on page 71. It is the basis for many different flavoured light sponge-type gâteaux, see the following pages. In the past the ingredients were listed 'as the weight of eggs in fat, sugar and flour'.

You can still use this method of weighing, put the eggs on the scale in place of the weight and then each of the ingredients in turn. It is probably easier to assume that an egg weighs 50 g/2 oz and prepare the ingredients accordingly.

The golden rules for a perfect Victoria Sandwich are:

a) correct weight of ingredients
b) efficient creaming of the fat and sugar and whisking of the eggs and
c) gentle folding when adding the flour; this should be sifted before use.

Oven Setting:	180°C/350°F, Gas Mark 4 or 170°C with a fan oven but see stage 1	
Baking Time:	20 to 23 minutes, see stage 5	
Baking Equipment:	two 18 to 19 cm/7 to 7½ inch round sandwich tins (layer pans)	
Makes:	two sponge sandwiches, which make one large cake when put together. They keep well for several days and freeze well.	

Metric/Imperial	Ingredients	American
175 g/6 oz	**butter or margarine**	¾ cup
175 g/6 oz	**caster sugar**	¾ cup
¼ teaspoon	**vanilla extract*** **or essence, optional**	¼ teaspoon
175 g/6 oz	**self-raising flour or plain (all-purpose) flour with 1½ teaspoons baking powder**	1½ cups
	Filling and topping	
3 to 4 tablespoons	**jam (jelly)**	3¾ to 5 level tablespoons
2 tablespoons	**caster sugar**	2½ tablespoons

* this gives the better flavour

1. Arrange the shelf for the sponge tins just above the centre except with a fan oven where they can be placed anywhere to suit yourself. Preheat the oven, the recipe gives the recommended setting but in a few ovens a better result is given if the sponges are baked at 190°C/375°F, Gas Mark 5 or 180°C. If your oven is on the fierce side use 160°C/325°F, Gas Mark 3 or 140 to 150°C with a fan oven. Grease and flour the sandwich tins or do this to the sides of the tins and place rounds of greased greaseproof (wax) paper or baking parchment on the base of the tins.
2. Cream the butter or margarine and caster sugar with the vanilla extract until soft and light, as described on page 71.
3. Gradually add the eggs, together with a little of the flour, if the

mixture shows any signs of curdling (see page 72).

4. Sift the flour, or flour and baking powder, and fold it gently into the creamed mixture. Page 72 gives advice on folding ingredients together.

5. Spoon the mixture into the two tins, giving an equal amount in each and smooth flat on top. Bake until firm to a gentle touch (page 183 describes the technique of testing) and the sponge has shrunk away from the sides of the tins.

6. Cool for 2 minutes then turn out the first sponge as the instructions given below and place on a wire cooling tray.

7. When cold spread the one sponge with the jam, add the second sponge and top with caster sugar.

Variations

- Many are given on page 86.
- Use two 15 to 16.5 cm/6 to 6½ inch square sandwich tins and bake as above.

TO TURN OUT THE VICTORIA SANDWICH

With most cakes that are firm in texture you can turn the cake upside down on to the wire cooling tray for a few seconds then turn it back again, so the top is upright. The wires on the cooling tray will not mark the cake.

In the case of the more delicate Victoria Sandwich, and similar mixtures, you will find that if you turn the cake upside down on to the wire cooling tray for even a few seconds you will mark the top with the pattern of the wires.

This may not bother you but if it does follow this method:-

A   Place a folded clean and dry teacloth (dish towel) on the palm of your left hand (if you are right-handed). Use the right hand if you are left-handed.

B   Invert the first sponge on to the teacloth then carefully turn it on to the tray, so keeping the top of the sponge uppermost. When cool you can lift the sponge, which has now become much firmer in texture, to remove the greaseproof paper or baking parchment.

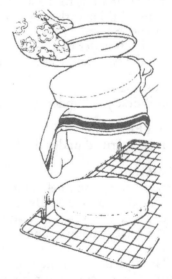

If this method worries you the other alternative is to place the teacloth on the wire cooling tray and invert the sponge on to it. This has the disadvantage that you do not get good air circulation under the sponge and it could become slightly over-moist on the side touching the teacloth.

TO BAKE THE MIXTURE AS ONE LARGE CAKE

1. Use an 18 cm/7 inch round or 15 cm/6 inch square cake tin. And line this as stage 1 in the basic recipe above.
2. Preheat the oven to 160°C/325°F, Gas Mark 3 or 140 to 150°C with a fan oven.
3. Use exactly the same ingredients as given on the left. Put into the cake tin, smooth flat on top.
4. Bake for 55 to 60 minutes or until firm to the touch. Turn out as suggested above.

TO BAKE THE MIXTURE AS ONE SHALLOW CAKE

1. Use a 20 cm/8 inch round or an 18 cm/7 inch square tin and line it as before.
2. Preheat the oven to 180°C/350°F, Gas Mark 4 or 160 to 170°C with a fan oven. If your oven is on the fierce side use 160°C/325°F, Gas Mark 3 or 150°C with a fan oven.
3. Bake for 30 minutes or until firm to the touch. Turn out as suggested above.

FLAVOURING THE VICTORIA SANDWICH

Treat the Victoria Sandwich on page 84 as THE basic recipe for a range of other flavoured light sandwich cakes or large cakes, see pages 87 to 92.

ALMOND
Use almond extract or essence instead of the vanilla flavouring. You can increase the almond flavour by adding 2 (2½) tablespoons finely chopped blanched almonds to the mixture at stage 2 or substitute 50 g/2 oz (½ cup) of flour with 50 g/2 oz (½ cup) ground almonds. In this case sift ½ teaspoon baking powder into self-raising flour or increase the amount of baking powder by this amount with plain flour.
  Fill the two sandwiches with apricot jam.

CHOCOLATE
This is described under the **Chocolate Layer Cake** right.

COFFEE
This is described under the **Coffee and Walnut Cake** on page 88.

LEMON
Cream 1 teaspoon finely grated lemon zest with the fat and sugar when making the Victoria Sandwich, page 84.
  Use 3 medium eggs instead of the large ones given in the recipe.
  Mix 1 tablespoon lemon juice with the beaten eggs and proceed as the recipe.
  This is delicious if the two cakes are sandwiched together with lemon curd or lemon curd and whipped cream.

ORANGE
Cream one or two teaspoons finely grated orange zest with the fat and sugar when making the Victoria Sandwich, page 84.

Use 3 small eggs instead of the large ones given in the recipe.

Mix 1½ tablespoons orange juice with the beaten eggs and proceed as the recipe.

Fill with orange curd or marmalade or with well-drained canned mandarin segments and whipped cream.

CHOCOLATE LAYER CAKE 1

This recipe is based on the Victoria Sandwich on page 84. The only alteration is that you use slightly less flour and add cocoa or chocolate powder instead. Use the same oven setting, baking time and sized sandwich tins (layer pans) as shown on page 84.

1. Preheat the oven and prepare the sandwich tins as stage 1 page 84.
2. Cream 175 g/6 oz (¾ cup) butter or margarine with the 175 g/6 oz (¾ cup) sugar and vanilla flavouring as stage 2 on page 84.
3. Gradually beat in the 3 large whisked eggs as stage 3 on page 84.
4. Sift 150 g/5 oz (1¼ cups) self-raising flour with ¼ teaspoon baking powder (or plain (all-purpose) flour with 1½ teaspoons baking powder) and 25 g/1 oz (¼ cup) cocoa powder, if you like a strong chocolate flavour, or 25 g/1 oz (¼ cup) chocolate powder if you prefer a milder taste.
5. Continue as stages 5 to 7 on page 84.

When cold the chocolate flavoured sponges can be sandwiched together with apricot jam, then topped with caster or sifted icing sugar or they can be filled and topped with the icing (frosting) as given on page 88.

CHOCOLATE LAYER CAKE 2

This is a richer cake than the previous one; it is flavoured with melted plain (semi-sweet) chocolate. The light cake is baked in one tin then split. While it may be quicker to bake two sandwich cakes, you will find you have a cake that is more moist in the centre if you use one tin (pan).

Oven Setting: 160°C/325°F, Gas Mark 3 or 140 to 150°C with a fan oven
Baking Time: 55 minutes
Baking Equipment: one 20 cm/8 inch cake tin
Makes: one 20 cm/8 inch iced cake which keeps well for several days. Open-freeze to save damaging the icing and pack when firm.

Metric/Imperial	Ingredients	American
150 g/5 oz	plain chocolate	5 squares
1½ tablespoons	water	1¾ tablespoons
150 g/5 oz	butter or margarine	⅝ cup
150 g/5 oz	caster sugar	⅝ cup
5 medium	eggs, whisked	5 medium
150 g/5 oz	self-raising flour or plain	1¼ cups

	(all-purpose) flour with	
	1¹/₄ teaspoons baking powder	
	Chocolate icing (frosting)	
115 g/4 oz	*plain chocolate*	*4 squares*
85 g/3 oz	*butter*	*³/₈ cup*
115 g/4 oz	***icing (confectioners) sugar, sifted***	*good 1 cup*

1. Break the chocolate into pieces, place in a basin with the water; melt over a pan of hot, but not boiling, water or on a low setting in the microwave. Allow to cool, but still remain a liquid, add to the butter or margarine.
2. Preheat the oven. Line the tin with greased greaseproof (wax) paper or baking parchment.
3. Cream the chocolate, butter or margarine and sugar until soft and light. Gradually beat in the eggs, add a little of the flour if the mixture shows signs of curdling, see information on page 72.
4. Sift the flour, or flour and baking powder, fold into the other ingredients then spoon into the tin.
5. Bake until firm to the touch and the cake has shrunk from the sides of the tin. If you insert a skewer into the centre do this very gently for the cake is fragile while hot. Cool in the tin for 5 minutes then turn out on to the wire cooling tray. Leave until quite cold.
6. **To cut a cake evenly:** place the **cold** cake in the freezer for about 30 minutes, it becomes very firm and you can then cut it into two layers.
7. **Chocolate filling and topping:** melt 85 g/3 oz (3 squares) of the chocolate, as stage 1 above. Cool then mix with the butter and icing sugar. Cream until soft and light. Spread half over one cake, add the second cake. Spread the remainder of the chocolate mixture evenly over the top of the cake.
8. Coarsely grate the remaining chocolate and sprinkle it evenly over the top of the cake. Keep for several hours before serving, so the icing can stiffen.

COFFEE AND WALNUT CAKE

Coffee and walnuts are an excellent combination and this cake has been very popular for some decades. It is made by flavouring the sponge mixture with coffee and adding chopped walnuts. The cake can be served plain or split and filled then topped with a soft coffee icing (frosting), as in the Coffee Layer Cake on pages 89–90.

Do NOT chop the walnuts for the cake too finely. It is quite easy for this to happen if you use a liquidizer (blender) or food processor. If the nuts are too fine they become like walnut flour and make the cake drier than it should be. The coffee essence referred to in the recipe is very easy to obtain. Instead of this you could use instant coffee powder dissolved in a very small amount of boiling water.

Oven Setting: 160°C/325°F, Gas Mark 3 or 140 to 150°C with a fan oven

Baking Time: 55 minutes to 1 hour

Baking Equipment: one 18 cm/7 inch cake tin (pan)
Makes: one plain cake or one iced and decorated gâteau, which keeps well for some days. The cake freezes well. Open-freeze so the icing is not damaged then pack.

Metric/Imperial	Ingredients	American
175 g/6 oz	**butter or margarine**	¾ cup
175 g/6 oz	**caster sugar**	¾ cup
1 tablespoon	**coffee essence or 1 to 1½ teaspoons instant coffee powder dissolved in 1 tablespoon boiling water**	1 tablespoon
3 medium	**eggs, whisked**	3 medium
175 g/6 oz	**self-raising flour or plain (all-purpose) flour with 1½ teaspoons baking powder**	1½ cups
85 g/3 oz	**walnuts, chopped**	¾ cup

1. Preheat the oven. Grease and flour or line the tin with greased greaseproof (wax) paper or baking parchment.
2. Cream the butter or margarine and sugar then add the coffee essence and beat again until soft and light. If using dissolved coffee powder make sure this is cold before adding it to the butter or margarine and sugar.
3. Gradually beat in the eggs, if the mixture shows signs of curdling fold in a little of the flour.
4. Sift the flour, or flour and baking powder, add to the creamed mixture with the walnuts. Fold together thoroughly, to ensure the nuts are evenly distributed.
5. Spoon into the cake tin and bake until firm to the touch and the cake has shrunk away from the sides of the tin. This is a cake that can be tested by inserting a fine skewer in the centre, see page 183.
6. Cool in the tin for 5 minutes then turn out on to a wire cooling tray.

Variations

- Bake in one 20 cm/8 inch cake tin for about 45 minutes.
- Bake in two 18 cm/7 inch sandwich tins (layer pans) for 25 to 30 minutes at the setting above.
- Use chopped pecan nuts instead of walnuts.

COFFEE WALNUT LAYER CAKE

Make the cake as the method for Coffee and Walnut Cake. When cold cut the cake horizontally into two layers, see the advice about freezing on page 88. If preferred bake the mixture in two sandwich tins (layers pans), see under Variation below.

For the Coffee Icing (Frosting)

1.   Cream 50 g/2 oz (¼ cup) butter with 225 g/8 oz (good 2 cups) sifted icing (confectioners) sugar until soft and light. Add 2 teaspoons coffee essence or 1 to 1½ teaspoons instant coffee powder dissolved in 2 teaspoons boiling water (this should be cooled before using). Beat in about 1 tablespoon milk or single (light) cream.
2.   Use half the icing to sandwich the two layers together. Spread the rest of the icing evenly over the top of the cake.
3.   Take a small flat-bladed knife and drag this over the top icing to make neat lines. Place a few walnut halves around the edge of the cake.

Variation

- Instead of decorating the cake with walnut halves chop 50 g/2 oz (½ cup); sprinkle these evenly over the icing on the top of the cake. Press the nuts against the icing with the back of a metal spoon.

American Frosting

This is the classic filling and icing for a Coffee Walnut Cake. It is not easy to make but the following steps should guide you to success.

   You have to boil the sugar and water to a given temperature, see stage 2. If you have a sugar thermometer this is easier, but you can test without a thermometer. Have a basin of cold water ready before you begin.

1.   Put 150 ml/¼ pint (⅔ cup) water with 350 g/12 oz (1½ cups) granulated or caster sugar into a saucepan. Stir over a low heat until the sugar has dissolved.
2.   Bring the mixture to the boil and let it boil, **without stirring**, until it reaches 114.5°C/238°F – always read the setting while the thermometer is in the sugar syrup. **To test without a sugar thermometer:** when the sugar mixture looks syrupy drop a little into the cold water. Wait for a few seconds then lift the mixture out of the water and see if you can roll it into a soft ball. That is the stage you **must** reach. You may have to continue boiling and testing several times. Always remove the pan from the heat while you test so there is no danger of the sugar mixture over-heating.
3.   While the sugar mixture boils, whisk the white of 2 medium eggs in a good-sized basin until stiff.
4.   When satisfied the sugar syrup has reached the right stage add a pinch of cream of tartar to this and beat the syrup in the saucepan with a wooden spoon or whisk until it changes from being transparent to looking cloudy.
5.   Pour the hot syrup on to the stiffly whisked egg whites in a steady stream, beating all the time – use a hand or electric whisk for this stage. **As you have to beat the icing and pour at the same time it would be helpful to have someone assist you by doing one of these jobs.**
6.   When the icing is cold and beginning to stiffen use about ⅓rd to sandwich the two halves of the cake together. Spoon the rest of the icing into the centre of the top of the cake.
7.   Spread it from the centre down the sides of the cake. Check the whole cake is evenly coated. Decorate with walnut halves. Allow to stand for several hours before serving.

LEMON CAKE

This light textured cake has a refreshing flavour because of the fairly high amount of lemon zest and juice. When grating the lemon rind take care to use only the top coloured part (known as the zest). If you include any of the white pith you will give the cake a bitter taste.

This cake is made by the creaming method, so it is wise to check on the various points given on page 71. It could be made by the one-stage mixing technique if you use soft butter or margarine, this is described on page 72. The inclusion of cornflour (cornstarch) helps to give a fine texture to the cake. It is not essential; see under Variations.

Oven Setting: 160°C/325°F, Gas Mark 3 or 150°C with a fan oven
Baking Time: 1 hour 10 minutes
Baking Equipment: one 20 cm/8 inch cake tin (pan) but see under Variations
Makes: one cake that keeps moist for several days, especially if soaked with lemon juice, freezes well.

Metric/Imperial	Ingredients	American
175 g/6 oz	**butter or margarine**	3/4 cup
175 g/6 oz	**caster sugar**	3/4 cup
1 1/2 level teaspoons	**lemon zest**	1 1/2 level teaspoons
4 medium	**eggs, whisked**	4 medium
200 g/7 oz	**self-raising flour with 1/4 teaspoon baking powder or plain (all-purpose) flour with 2 teaspoons baking powder**	1 3/4 cups
25 g/1 oz	**cornflour**	2 tablespoons
2 tablespoons	**lemon juice**	2 1/2 tablespoons

1. Preheat the oven. Line the cake tin with greased greaseproof (wax) paper or baking parchment.
2. Cream the butter or margarine with the sugar and lemon zest until soft and light. Hints on efficient creaming by hand or with a mixer are given on page 71.
3. Gradually beat in the eggs, if the mixture shows signs of curdling (separating) stir in some of the flour.
4. Sift the flour and baking powder with the cornflour and gently fold into the rest of the ingredients with the lemon juice.
5. Spoon into the cake tin and bake until firm to the touch. Cool in the tin for 5 minutes then turn out on to a wire cooling tray. Serve the cake plain or decorated as the details below.

Variations

- Bake in an 18 cm/7 inch cake tin. It will then take about 1 hour and 20 to 25 minutes baking time because of the greater depth. If the cake is becoming too brown after 1 hour reduce the heat to 150°C/300°F, Gas Mark 2 or 140°C with a fan oven for the last 20 to 25 minutes.

To Decorate the Lemon Cake

The Lemon Cake is delicious served plain or just topped with sifted icing (confectioners) sugar. There are however several ways to make it more elaborate.

When the cake is cold spread the top with a layer of firm lemon curd then top with sifted icing sugar.

Crisp Topped Cake: mix 2 (2½) tablespoons lemon juice with 2 (2½) tablespoons Demerara (raw) sugar. Remove the hot cake from the oven and carefully spoon this mixture evenly over the top. Leave in the cake tin until cold then remove from the tin.

A cake tin with a removable base would make this easier, for you simply push up the base, without disturbing the topping. Top the cold cake with:

Lemon Glacé Icing: sift 175 g/6 oz icing sugar (1⅓ cups confectioners sugar) into a basin. Add 2 teaspoons lemon juice then gradually, drop by drop, enough hot water to make a stiff spreading consistency. Dip a flat-bladed palette knife (spatula) into hot water, pat dry but use while warm. Spread the icing over the top of the cake to give a thin layer. Allow 2 or 3 hours for the icing to dry before cutting the cake.

Use of Cornflour (Cornstarch) in Cakes

Victorian cooks frequently added a proportion of cornflour to ordinary flour in cakes to produce a lighter texture. Of course the flour of that era was not nearly as refined or good as the flours we can obtain today.

The proportions of cornflour used varied a great deal from 100% cornflour (often a cake made like this was called a Sand Cake) to 25% cornflour and 75% ordinary flour or completely the reverse, i.e. 75% cornflour and 25% ordinary flour.

Cornflour certainly gives a very light and fine texture to a cake mixture; it must be treated as plain (all-purpose) flour and the same amount of raising agent added.

If avoiding wheat flour: use all cornflour in the Cup Cakes and Queen Cakes on pages 64 and 65 and the Victoria Sandwich on page 83 and the cakes based upon this. I found there was just one slight disadvantage, i.e. there is a faint taste of cornflour in the cooked cakes. This can be over-come by adding a little finely grated lemon or orange zest to the cake mixture or by topping the cake(s) with a fairly strong flavoured icing, such as the Lemon Glacé Icing above.

Storing Cakes

Information about the keeping qualities of the various cakes is given in the information at the top of each recipe. This provides an approximate idea of just how well the cake will keep under normal storage conditions.

You can prolong the keeping quality of cakes though if you pack them carefully, as **soon as absolutely cold**. To pack a cake while hot would mean an excessive amount of condensation, which would result in an over-moist cake on the outside and a possibility that it would become mouldy.

When the cake is quite cold put it into a tin or plastic container and seal this tightly, to exclude the maximum amount of air. If you consider the airtight way many commercially made cakes are packaged you will see this is what has been done.

One of the very best ways of storing cakes is to freeze them **when absolutely cold**. In the case of very light cakes I often think the flavour is improved. Do let the cake defrost at room temperature if possible or, if you want to hasten this process, use the microwave at a low setting. This prevents the cake becoming over-dry.

It is a good idea to slice the cake and separate the slices with pieces of greaseproof (wax) paper or baking parchment before freezing. In this way exactly the required number of slices can be removed, without the necessity of defrosting the whole cake.

CARROT CAKE

This cake is a source of healthy ingredients for it contains carrots, nuts and olive oil as well as eggs and ground almonds. Often if is called a Passion Cake, although there seems no logical explanation for the title. It is a good cake to make with wholemeal (wholewheat) flour but that is not essential, see under Variations.

It is better not to peel or grate the carrots until just before making the cake to make sure they do not lose their crisp freshness. Never put the carrots into water after peeling them, that would make them too damp.

Oven Setting: 180°C/350°F, Gas Mark 4 or 170°C with a fan oven
Baking Time: 1 hour
Baking Equipment: one 20 cm/8 inch cake tin (pan)
Makes: one cake; this keeps well for several days. It freezes well.

Metric/Imperial	Ingredients	American
175 g/6 oz	soft light brown sugar	3/4 cup
175 ml/6 fl oz	olive oil	3/4 cup
3 large	eggs, whisked	3 large
175 g/6 oz	wholemeal self-raising flour or plain wholemeal flour with 1 1/2 teaspoons baking powder	1 1/2 cups
50 g/2 oz	ground almonds	1/2 cup
175 g/6 oz	carrots, weight when peeled and grated	1 2/3 cup
85 g/3 oz	walnuts or pecan nuts, coarsely chopped	3/4 cup
1 tablespoon	milk	1 tablespoon

1. Preheat the oven; grease and flour or line the tin even if it has a non-stick finish.
2. Put the sugar into the mixing bowl, add the oil and mix thoroughly. Stir in the eggs.
3. Sift the flour, or flour and baking powder, into the egg mixture then stir in the rest of the ingredients. Mix thoroughly.
4. Spoon the mixture into the prepared tin and bake until firm to the touch. Cool for 5 minutes in the tin then turn out on to a wire cooking tray. This cake can be served plain or it can be decorated.

Variations

- Instead of using oil you can substitute 175 g/6 oz (¾ cup) butter or margarine; cream this with the sugar, add the eggs and proceed as the recipe.
- Use white flour instead of wholemeal and caster sugar instead of light brown. When using white flour omit the milk as the cake mixture is sufficiently moist without this.
- Sift 1 teaspoon mixed spice with the flour.
- Add 85 g/3 oz sultanas (good ½ cup seedless white raisins) to the other ingredients. Other dried fruit could be used instead.

To make a change

Orange Carrot Cake: follow the basic recipe but **add** 2 teaspoons finely grated orange zest to the eggs and add 85 g/3 oz chopped crystallized peel (⅓ cup candied peel). Use 1 tablespoon orange juice instead of the milk with wholemeal flour.

CARROT AND BANANA CAKE

This is an unusual cake, combining the flavour of bananas with carrots and a topping of a sweetened cream cheese. Like the Carrot Cake on page 93 the fat used is oil but butter or margarine could be substituted if you prefer. Plain (all-purpose) flour with the bicarbonate of soda (baking soda) and baking powder are best.

Oven Setting: 160°C/325°F, Gas Mark 3 or 150°C with a fan oven
Baking Time: 1 hour 5 minutes
Baking Equipment: one 23 cm/9 inch cake tin (pan)
Makes: one 23 cm/9 inch cake. This keeps well for 2 to 3 days but can be frozen.

Metric/Imperial	Ingredients	American
175 g/6 oz	carrots, weight when peeled	6 oz
50 g/2 oz	walnuts	½ cup
2 medium	bananas, ripe but not over-ripe	2 medium
175 g/6 oz	light brown sugar	¾ cup
3 large	eggs, whisked	3 large
300 g/10 oz	plain flour	2½ cups
½ teaspoon	bicarbonate of soda (baking soda)	½ teaspoon
1½ level teaspoons	baking powder	1½ level teaspoons
175 ml/6 fl oz	sunflower oil	¾ cup
	Coating	
175 g/6 oz	icing (confectioners) sugar, sifted	1½ cups
85 g/3 oz	butter	⅜ cup
85 g/3 oz	cream cheese	⅜ cup

1. Preheat the oven. Line the cake tin with greased greaseproof (wax) paper or baking parchment.
2. Finely grate the carrots, do this just before mixing the cake and do not put them in water.
3. Chop the walnuts, do not make them too fine; peel and mash the bananas and mix with the sugar.
4. Gradually blend the eggs with the bananas and the sugar. Sift the flour with the bicarbonate of soda and baking powder. Stir into the egg mixture.
5. Gradually stir in the oil and beat well, then stir in the carrots and walnuts. Mix briskly again immediately before baking.
6. Spoon into the tin and bake until firm. Cool in the tin for 10 minutes then turn out on to a wire cooling tray. Leave until cold before decorating.
7. **For the coating:** mix all the ingredients together then cream the mixture very well.
8. Spoon all the coating on the top of the cake then spread from the top down the sides. When the cake is evenly coated take a small flat knife and sweep up the coating to give a slightly rough effect.

Variation

- Instead of using oil in the cake substitute 175 g/6 oz (¾ cup) butter or margarine. Cream this with the sugar then add the bananas and the eggs and proceed as the recipe above.

DUNDEE CAKE

This is one of the most famous of all Scottish cakes. It should be quite light in texture even though it is full of flavour with its generous quantity of fruit. The small amount of ground almonds in the recipe gives a pleasantly moist texture. It is essential that plain (all-purpose) flour, with only a small amount of baking powder, is used. This ensures that the weighty mixture of dried fruit will not sink to the bottom of the cake during baking.

Oven Setting: 160°C/325°F, Gas Mark 3 or 150°C with a fan oven for the first 30 minutes then 150°C/300°F, Gas Mark 2 or 140°C for the remaining time

Baking Time: 2 hours

Baking Equipment: one 20 cm/8 inch cake tin (pan)

Makes: one cake that keeps well for several weeks in an airtight tin but can be frozen.

Metric/Imperial	Ingredients	American
175 g/6 oz	butter	¾ cup
175 g/6 oz	caster or light brown sugar	¾ cup
3 large	eggs, whisked*	3 large
225 g/8 oz	plain flour with 1 teaspoon baking powder	2 cups
25 g/1 oz	ground almonds	2 tablespoons

2 tablespoons	*dry sherry or milk*	2½ tablespoons
50 g/2 oz	*glacé (candied) cherries, quartered*	¼ cup
50 g/2 oz	*mixed candied peel, chopped*	¼ cup
450 g/1 lb	*mixed dried fruit ***	*1 lb*
	To decorate	
25 to 50 g/1 to 2 oz	*whole blanched almonds*	⅓ cup

* save a little white from one or two egg shells
** it is possible to buy mixed fruit. If buying separate fruits use equal amounts of currants, sultanas (seedless white raisins) and raisins.

1. Preheat the oven to the first temperature. Line a 20 cm/8 inch cake tin with greased greaseproof (wax) paper or baking parchment.
2. Cream the butter and sugar until soft and light, gradually beat in the eggs. Advice on creaming by hand or electric mixer is on pages 70 to 72.
3. Sift the flour, baking powder and ground almonds, stir into the creamed ingredients. Lastly add the sherry or milk then the cherries, peel and fruit and mix thoroughly but do not over-beat the mixture.
4. Spoon into the tin and smooth flat on top with a knife. Arrange the almonds over the top of the cake in a neat pattern.
5. Brush these with the egg white, saved in the egg shells, to give a shine.
6. Bake for 30 minutes at the first temperature then lower the heat and bake for a further 1½ hours or until firm to the touch.
7. Cool in the tin for 15 minutes then turn out on to a wire cooling tray.

Variations

- This cake can be made by the one-stage method, see page 72.
- To give more flavour cream 1 teaspoon finely grated orange zest with the butter and sugar at stage 2.

VANILLA CHEESECAKE

This is an excellent basic cheesecake since it can be served plain, as the recipe that follows, or topped with seasonal fruit. It is possible to add other flavourings; these are described under Variations.
   To crush biscuits: either put the biscuits into a food processor and crush or put them gradually into a liquidizer (blender). If you do not have either of these appliances put the biscuits into a plastic bag, lay this flat then press down with a rolling pin until the biscuits are evenly crushed.

Oven Setting:	150°C/300°F, Gas Mark 2 or 140°C with a fan oven
Baking Time:	1 hour to 1 hour 15 minutes
Baking Equipment:	one 20 to 23 cm/8 to 9 inch cake tin (pan) with a loose base or a springform tin (this has a lock which makes it easy to remove the cake when cooked)
Makes:	one cake that can be served for tea or as a dessert. It can be kept in the refrigerator for several days and freezes exceptionally well.

Metric/Imperial	Ingredients	American
	For the base	
50 g/2 oz	**butter, melted**	*¼ cup*
175 g/6 oz	**digestive biscuits (Graham crackers) crushed**	*1¼ cups*
50 g/2 oz	**caster sugar**	*¼ cup*
	For the topping	
85 g/3 oz	**butter**	*⅜ cup*
85 g/3 oz	**caster sugar**	*⅜ cup*
½ to 1 teaspoon	**vanilla extract* or essence**	*½ to 1 teaspoon*
3 large	**eggs**	*3 large*
450 g/1 lb	**cream cheese**	*1 lb*
3 tablespoons	**double (heavy) cream**	*3¾ tablespoons*

*this gives the best result

1. Preheat the oven. Brush the sides of the tin with a very little of the melted butter. Mix the remaining butter with the biscuit crumbs and sugar and press into the base of the tin.
2. **For the topping:** cream the butter, sugar and vanilla until soft and light. Separate the egg yolks from the whites. Drop the yolks into the creamed mixture and the whites into another basin.
3. Add the cream cheese and unwhipped cream and mix very thoroughly. Whisk the egg whites until they stand up in soft peaks. Take 1 tablespoon of the whites and beat into the creamed mixture, this gives a softer consistency and makes it easier to fold in the remaining whites. These should be folded in gently but thoroughly – use a metal spoon or spatula for this.
4. Spoon the cheese mixture into the tin and bake for 1 hour 5 to 15 minutes. It is advisable though to check the cheesecake after about 1 hour's cooking. It should be quite firm to a **gentle** touch but remain uncoloured.
5. When cooked **do not take it out of the oven**. It will wrinkle if you do so. If using a gas oven turn off the heat but with an electric oven, which tends to retain heat longer, switch off the heat and have the oven door slightly ajar. Leave the cheesecake in the oven until quite cold.
6. To remove the cheesecake from an ordinary cake tin with a loose base, put a milk bottle or small jar under the cake tin and push up gently so the cake comes out of the sides of the tin. You can then gently remove the base. With a springform tin undo the lock and take out the cheesecake. Gently remove the base of the tin.

Variations

- Use vanilla sugar and omit the extract or essence.

Chocolate Cheesecake: melt 115 g/4 oz plain (4 squares semi-sweet) chocolate. Add with the cream cheese then proceed as the recipe above. This cheesecake looks very attractive topped with lightly whipped cream.

Coffee Cheesecake: use 2 (2½) tablespoons strong coffee and 1 tablespoon double cream instead of all cream. The cheesecake can be decorated with whipped cream and halved walnuts.

Fruit Cheesecake: add about 6 (7½) tablespoons diced canned or cooked apricots, pineapple or other fruit to the cheese mixture. Decorate the cooked cheesecake with whipped cream or crème fraîche and whole fruit.

Lemon Cheesecake: omit the vanilla flavouring. Cream 1 to 1½ teaspoons finely grated lemon zest with the butter and sugar. Use 2 (2½) tablespoons lemon juice and 1 tablespoon cream instead of all cream.

Orange Cheesecake: omit the vanilla flavouring. Cream 2 teaspoons finely grated orange zest with the butter and sugar. Use 3 (3¾) tablespoons of orange juice and omit the cream.

About 6 (7½) tablespoons well-drained and chopped canned mandarin oranges can be added to the cheese mixture and the cheesecake can be decorated with whipped cream and whole mandarin oranges.

Using Vanilla Sugar

Packets of vanilla sugar are on sale but it is easy to prepare this. On page 13 you will find details. Always leave the vanilla pods (beans) in the sugar sufficiently long to flavour it. When a recipe, such as the Vanilla Cheesecake, lists both sugar and vanilla simply weigh out the required amount from the container and omit the vanilla extract or essence.

Always fill up the container again with fresh sugar.

If you want a concentrated vanilla flavouring in some recipes, you can slit a vanilla pod and scrape out the seeds and add these to the other ingredients. They would add an interesting taste and texture to the cheesecake. In this case omit the vanilla extract or essence.

To melt butter

In several recipes butter is melted. Take care when doing this so the butter does not discolour or burn. The easiest way is to put the butter into a basin and balance this over a saucepan of simmering water. Leave until melted.

Another method is to melt the butter in the microwave. Use a low setting, so there is no fear of the butter sputtering around the microwave.

TOSCA CAKE

This is an ultra-light sponge cake with an interesting topping. It is ideal if you want something special. A little butter is used in the cake so it is beautifully moist. Melt this early so it has time to cool.

The eggs and sugar are whisked until thick and creamy. If doing this by hand use a good hand or small electric whisk; stand the bowl on a folded cloth so it doesn't slip. Use the whisk of a large electric mixer not the beater. A food processor is not suitable for this type of mixture.

Having beaten a considerable amount of air into the eggs and sugar it is essential that you do not lose this. The secret is to sift the flour to aerate it. Special sponge self-raising flour is ideal but you could use ordinary self-raising flour or plain (all-purpose) flour with baking powder. The flour is then folded in. Folding is explained on page 100.

Oven Setting:	180°C/350°F, Gas Mark 4 or 170°C with a fan oven then 160°C/325°F, Gas Mark 3 or 150°C with a fan oven	
Baking Time:	25 to 30 minutes then another 10 minutes	
Baking Equipment:	one 20 cm/8 inch round or 18 cm/7 inch square cake tin (pan)	
Makes:	one cake. This should be eaten within one or two days of cooking. It freezes exceptionally well.	

Metric/Imperial	Ingredients	American
50 g/2 oz	*butter*	1/4 cup
3 large	*eggs*	3 large
115 g/4 oz	*caster sugar*	1/2 cup
85 g/3 oz	*self-raising flour or plain (all-purpose) flour with 3/4 teaspoon baking powder*	3/8 cup
	Topping	
50 g/2 oz	*blanched almonds, cut into thin strips*	1/2 cup
50 g/2 oz	*butter*	1/4 cup
50 g/2 oz	*caster sugar*	1/4 cup
3 tablespoons	*single (light) cream*	3 3/4 tablespoons
2 teaspoons	*self-raising or plain flour*	2 teaspoons

1. Preheat the oven, grease and flour the cake tin or line with greased greaseproof (wax) paper or baking parchment.
2. Melt the butter in a saucepan over a low heat or in a basin over boiling water or in the microwave (see page 98) then allow it to cool.
3. Break the eggs into a large mixing bowl or the bowl of an electric mixer, add the sugar and whisk on a fairly high speed until thick and creamy.
4. Sift the flour, or flour and baking powder, and **fold** into the whisked eggs and sugar. Page 100 explains the process very clearly.
5. Add the cooled butter and gently fold this into the rest of the ingredients.
6. Pour into the prepared tin and bake until just firm to a gentle touch. As the cake is being returned to the oven it is essential it is not over-cooked but it must be adequately cooked otherwise it would be heavy. Lower the oven temperature before adding the topping.
7. While the cake is baking prepare the topping. The slivers of almonds must be very thin. You may be able to buy these, if not use a very sharp knife on a chopping board to cut them into long thin strips. Beat the butter and sugar together then add the almonds, cream and flour.
8. Spread this mixture over the top of the cake the moment you take it out of the oven. Return to the oven and cook for a further 10 minutes.

9.   Cool in the tin for 5 minutes then carefully remove the cake and
place it on a wire cooling tray.

CORRECT METHOD OF FOLDING

In many recipes the term 'folding' is used. It is particularly important
when making the light true sponge mixture on the next pages. The word
'folding' is mentioned in other recipes to remind the cook that you do
not use too brisk an action when mixing the ingredients.

Folding basically indicates a gentle method of combining ingredients.
Experiment to find the tool you like best for this purpose. A wooden
spoon is NOT good, a metal or plastic spatula or flat-bladed knife or a
metal spoon are considered the most suitable.

The action of folding means incorporating the ingredients together by
slow and gentle movements. Each time though guide your tool to go
right through the mixture to make sure the ingredients are evenly
blended. Flour tends to sink to the bottom of the mixture and you do not
want to find unmixed flour when you are spooning the sponge into the
cake tin (pan). There was a belief that if you followed a figure of eight
action you would have a good folding movement. That is not necessarily
the case but you might like to try it and see if you find it helpful.

If you have a sneaking feeling you are being too rough and vigorous
and not folding sufficiently gently here is a tip I was given years ago.

If you are right-handed:- hold your right wrist with the forefinger and
thumb of your left hand – now try folding with your right hand.
Immediately you feel restricted – but it will show you just how slow and
gentle you should be. If you are left-handed hold the left wrist with your
right hand, finger and thumb.

If using an electric mixer you **MUST** restrict the brisk energetic
movement and use the lowest speed possible. I am still a believer in
folding the flour in by hand in the recipes on the next pages.

What happens if you overbeat the flour?
You lose so much of the light texture that has been beaten into the eggs
and the sugar and the sponge has a tight and somewhat heavy texture.

**Here are some other important points about making what is
described as a 'true' sponge.**
As you will see, I suggest sifting the flour on to a plate and leaving it in
the warmth of the kitchen before use. Why? Because the flour becomes
drier and therefore lighter in texture. You would also be wise to use the
special Sponge Flour that is now on sale, which is made especially for
light sponges.

Some people like to put the sugar on a plate and warm this slightly in
the oven, set to a very low heat. Be careful though it does not become too
hot, you are just warming it.

Is adding a little butter or oil a good idea?
Yes, it adds a certain pleasantly moist texture to the sponge.

Some recipes suggest adding a little water – is this a good idea?
Yes, if using small, rather than the large eggs, add 1 tablespoon warm
water at stage 5.

SPONGE CAKE

This is sometimes called a 'fatless' sponge, as it is generally made without the addition of any fat. As you will see under Variations, it is possible to add a small amount of melted butter or oil.

Expert cooks pride themselves on making the sponge with plain flour and no raising agent, for they feel there has been enough air beaten into the mixture by whisking the eggs and sugar together. Frankly when you begin making this not-too-easy mixture I would 'play for safety' and use self-raising flour, especially the special Sponge Flour, or add a little baking powder to ordinary plain (all-purpose) flour.

Oven Setting:	180°C/350°F, Gas Mark 4 or 160 to 170°C with a fan oven
Baking Time:	30 minutes
Baking Equipment:	one 18 to 19 cm/7 to 7½ inch cake tin (pan)
Makes:	one plain sponge that can be split and filled with jam and/or cream. Freezes exceptionally well.

Metric/Imperial	Ingredients	American
85 g/3 oz	**self-raising flour or plain (all-purpose) flour with ³/₄ teaspoon baking powder**	³/₄ cup
3 large	**eggs**	3 large
115 g/4 oz	**caster sugar**	¹/₂ cup
few drops	**vanilla extract* or essence**	few drops
	Topping	
little	**caster or sifted icing (confectioners) sugar**	little

* this gives the better flavour

1. Preheat the oven and line the tin with greased greaseproof (wax) paper or baking parchment. Good lining of the tin is especially important with this type of sponge, which is inclined to stick – even in a 'non-stick' tin.
2. Sift the flour, or flour and baking powder, on to a large flat plate so you have just a thin layer and leave it in the warmth of the kitchen while following stages 3 and 4.
3. Put the eggs and sugar into a large mixing bowl or the bowl of the electric mixer. If mixing with a hand whisk or small electric whisk, stand the bowl on a folded teacloth (dish towel) to prevent the bowl moving as you whisk energetically.
4. Whisk the eggs and sugar together until thick and creamy. To judge if sufficiently whisked you should see the trail of the whisk in the mixture when it is ready for the next stage.
5. Sift the flour, or flour and baking powder, into the eggs and sugar. Gently fold this in until the mixture is evenly blended, see advice on page 100.
6. Spoon or pour the mixture into the prepared tin, use a spatula to

scrape any mixture left in the bowl into the tin.

7. Bake in the centre of the oven until firm to a very gentle touch in the middle of the cake – an over-firm pressure leaves a mark even if the sponge is cooked.

8. Cool for 2 to 3 minutes in the tin then turn out on to a folded teacloth as described on page 85, then place on the wire cooling tray. Dust with sugar when cold.

Variations

Sponge Sandwiches: Instead of baking the sponge in one tin, bake it in two 18 to 19 cm/7 to 7½ inch sandwich tins (layer pans). Place these just above the centre of the oven except in a fan oven where they can be put on any shelf.

You can use the same oven setting as in the recipe above and bake for 10 to 12 minutes. If your oven is on the cool side then raise the oven setting to 190°C/375°F, Gas Mark 5 or 170 to 180°C with a fan oven and bake for 9 to 10 minutes.

Adding Fat
Melt 25 g/1 oz (2 tablespoons) butter or use 1 generous tablespoon olive oil. Fold this into the sponge mixture at the end of stage 5, after adding the flour.

Flavouring the Sponge
The sponge can be turned into a very light flavoured cake as follows:-

Almond: use almond extract instead of vanilla or use 25 g/1 oz (¼ cup) ground almonds and omit 25 g/1 oz (¼ cup) flour. There should be no need to alter the amount of raising agent.

Chocolate: with a delicate sponge like this do not use too much cocoa powder. It is quite sufficient to omit 15 g/½ oz flour (2 tablespoons) and substitute this amount of cocoa powder or omit 25 g/1 oz (¼ cup) flour and use 25 g/1 oz (¼ cup) chocolate powder instead. Sift the cocoa or chocolate powder with the flour and warm it as suggested in stage 2 above. There is no need to adjust the amount of baking powder.

Coffee: whisk the eggs and sugar, as stage 4 above. When thick add 1 to 2 teaspoons coffee essence and whisk again to restore the thick consistency. As this adds more liquid use 3 medium eggs instead of large ones.

Lemon or Orange: use 3 medium eggs instead of large ones.
Add ½ teaspoon very finely grated lemon zest or at least 1 teaspoon very finely grated orange zest to the eggs and sugar before whisking them. Fold ½ tablespoon lemon or 1 tablespoon orange juice into the mixture at the end of stage 5 after adding the flour.

Nut Sponges
One of the easiest ways to provide a wheat-free sponge is to substitute very finely chopped nuts instead of the flour in the recipe on page 101.

This is ideal for everyone following a no-wheat diet but it makes a delicious cake for everyone. Use 85 g/3 oz (¾ cup) of very finely chopped blanched almonds, hazelnuts, pecan nuts or walnuts. Fold them into the whisked eggs and sugar at stage 5 together with 1 level teaspoon baking powder. Bake as the sponge on page 101.

Whisking Over Hot Water

An accepted way of making a sponge mixture was to place the bowl of eggs and sugar over a saucepan of simmering water and whisk until the eggs and sugar were thick. You can try that method but in these days of excellent hand and large whisks it is really more bother and not necessary.

This method has certain problems:

a) Make sure there is adequate space between the bowl and the water in the pan, so you do not cook the eggs.

b) You must not stop whisking for a second for, unless the eggs and sugar are kept moving, they tend to set and even cook.

c) When the warm egg mixture is thick you must continue whisking until cold.

LARGE SWISS (JELLY) ROLL

While you can make a Swiss Roll with the same mixture as given for a Victoria Sandwich on page 83 this is rarely chosen, for it does give a somewhat 'solid' sponge roll. The ideal recipe to use is the one given for Sponge Cake (page 101) with 85 g/3 oz (¾ cup) flour, etc. This makes a large Swiss Roll, for a smaller one use the quantities in the recipe which follows. The baking temperature and timing for a Swiss Roll is slightly different, for the mixture is spread out more thinly so it can be baked in a shorter time at a slightly higher setting.

The golden rules for success with a Swiss Roll are:

a) Choose the correct balance of ingredients, see page 101.

b) Time the baking; do it carefully – if over-cooked the sponge cracks badly – but see advice on page 105.

c) Have everything ready for rolling the sponge, so that it is not kept waiting when it comes out of the oven.

Oven Setting:	190°C/375°F, Gas Mark 5 or 170 to 180°C with a fan oven. If your oven is on the cool side you may prefer to use 200°C, 400°F, Gas Mark 6.
Baking Time:	approximately 9 minutes
Baking Equipment:	one baking (cookie) tray measuring approximately 30 x 23 cm/12 x 9 inches
Makes:	one large Swiss Roll that keeps surprisingly well for 2 or 3 days in an airtight tin (especially if the 25 g/1 oz (2 tablespoons) melted butter or a generous tablespoon oil is added, as suggested on page 100. The sponge freezes very well but you may need to add a dusting of sugar when defrosted.

Ingredients and method of mixing as page 101. Here are extra preparations:-

1. Prepare the tin by lining it with greased greaseproof (wax) paper or baking parchment.

2. Spoon or pour the mixture into the prepared tin, tilt this carefully from side to side to make sure the mixture is spread absolutely evenly. It must not be thinner at the corners for this means an uneven sponge.
3. Bake until firm to a gentle touch.
4. While the sponge is baking:-
    a) Warm about 6 (7½) tablespoons jam (jelly), this makes it easier to spread; you can do this on a low setting in the microwave or in a saucepan. It must NOT be too hot for this makes it soak into the sponge and gives a soggy cake, rather than a light one. If the jam is a consistency that spreads easily there is no need to warm it.
    b) Place a sheet of greaseproof paper or baking parchment on the working surface and coat this with 2 (2½) tablespoons caster sugar.
    c) Have a basin of cold water with a pastry brush ready, see stage 5.
5. Remove the sponge from the oven and turn the tin upside down over the sugared paper. Have one of the shorter sides TOWARDS you. If the baking paper shows signs of sticking to the sponge (parchment will not) brush the paper with a few drops of cold water, this will solve the problem. Carefully pull away the baking paper or parchment.
6. If baked correctly the sponge edges should not be unduly crisp and they do not need cutting away. If they are crisp then cut them off.
7. Make a shallow cut across the sponge about 2.5 cm/1 inch from the edge near you. Spread the jam evenly over the sponge.
8. Lifting the sugared paper or parchment to help you, first fold the sponge over at the shallow cut then, lifting the paper or parchment to help, roll the sponge firmly away from you.
9. When completely rolled lift the sponge on to a wire cooling tray, do not unwrap at this stage, the covering helps to keep it moist. Cool away from a draught. When ready to serve, remove the paper or parchment.

SMALL SWISS ROLL

Oven Setting: as given for Large Swiss Roll
Baking Time: approximately 7 minutes
Baking Equipment: one oblong (cookie) tray measuring 25 x 18 cm/ 10 x 7 inches
Makes: one small Swiss (Jelly) Roll.

Metric/Imperial	Ingredients	American
50 g/2 oz	self-raising flour or plain (all-purpose) flour with ½ teaspoon baking powder	½ cup
2 large	eggs	2 large
85 g/3 oz	caster sugar	⅜ cup
few drops	vanilla extract or essence	few drops
scant 25 g/1 oz	melted butter	scant 2 tablespoons
or	or	or
scant 1 tablespoon	oil, optional	scant 1 tablespoon

	Filling and coating	
5 tablespoons	**jam (jelly)**	6¼ tablespoons
scant 2 tablespoons	**caster sugar**	scant 2 tablespoons

Make and bake the Swiss Roll as the directions for Large Swiss Roll but using the ingredients above.

If the sponge is slightly over baked
Moisten a clean teacloth (dish towel) in warm water, place it under the sugared paper or baking parchment before turning out the sponge. This helps to prevent the sponge cracking as it is rolled.

To fill the Swiss Roll with whipped cream and jam or fruit
a) Turn out the sponge. Remove the baking paper or parchment.
b) Place a fresh piece of greaseproof paper or baking parchment on top of the warm sponge and roll over that or allow the sugared paper or parchment to be rolled inside the sponge.
c) When cold carefully un-roll the sponge, remove all paper or parchment.
d) Spread the sponge with 5 to 6 (6¼ to 7½) tablespoons whipped cream and then top with rather less jam or sliced fruit or thick fruit purée.
e) Carefully re-roll the sponge and dust the outside with more sugar.

A NUT ROULADE
This is ideal for anyone avoiding wheat. Omit the flour in the Swiss Roll recipes but use the same weight in finely chopped walnuts or hazelnuts or other nuts instead. Add 1 level teaspoon baking powder with the nuts for the large roll or ¾ level teaspoon for the small one. Follow the mixing and baking instructions, pages 101 and 103. Fill with cream and fruit or jam, see above. You may get a few cracks when rolling the Roulade; these are acceptable.

ORANGE FRUIT CAKE

This cake is very unusual. I first learned of the method of preparing a cake mixture with sweetened condensed milk when judging a fruit cake contest. My fellow judges and I were amazed at the good texture and flavour of one of the finalists in the contest who had submitted a large cake. This is not the cake made for the competition but I have experimented with several recipes and this is the one I liked best. The recipe is for a small cake, but you will find instructions for making and baking a larger size under Variations.

There is no technique required here, just brisk mixing of the ingredients. When heating the dried fruit with the orange juice and zest be very careful that this does not scorch, for the amount of liquid is small.

Oven Setting: 150°C/300°F, Gas Mark 2 or 140°C with a fan oven
Baking Time: 1½ hours
Baking Equipment: one 15 cm/6 inch round or 12.5 cm/5 inch square cake tin (pan)
Makes: one cake that keeps well. Note the instructions

about wrapping the cake while hot in stage 5 and storing before cutting. The cake freezes well.

Metric/Imperial	Ingredients	American
350 g/12 oz	**mixed dried fruit**	scant 2 cups
2 teaspoons	**finely grated orange zest**	2 teaspoons
3 tablespoons	**orange juice**	3³/₄ tablespoons
1 x 218 g can (small size can)	**full cream sweetened condensed milk**	scant 8 oz (small size can)
1 large	**egg, whisked**	1 large
115 g/4 oz	**self-raising flour or plain (all-purpose) flour with 1 teaspoon baking powder**	1 cup

1. Preheat the oven. Line the cake tin thoroughly with greased greaseproof (wax) paper or baking parchment. This is essential even if using a non-stick type of tin.
2. Put the dried fruit with the orange zest and juice into a large saucepan (if you do this you can mix the cake in the saucepan). Heat until the juice just comes to boiling point. Remove from the heat and stir briskly, so all the fruit becomes moistened. Leave until quite cold. This stage could be done in a large bowl in the microwave.
3. Stir in all the condensed milk, make sure none is wasted in the can. Add the egg then sift in the flour, or flour and baking powder. Mix briskly, spoon into the prepared tin and bake until firm to the touch and the cake with the paper or parchment has shrunk from the sides.
4. This is the kind of cake where it is helpful to insert a fine skewer in the centre of the baked cake for it should be slightly sticky.
5. Remove the cake tin from the oven, but do NOT turn the cake out of the tin. Wrap the tin in foil to retain the heat and allow the cake to become cold then turn out of the tin. Remove the greaseproof paper or parchment.
6. If possible leave for at least 12 hours and preferably 24 hours before cutting.

Variations

Apricot and Date Cake: follow the instructions for the first recipe but instead of mixed dried fruit use 225 g/8 oz (1¹/₃ cups) of finely chopped ready-to-eat dried apricots and 115 g/4 oz (²/₃ cup) chopped dates (weight when the dates are stoned).

The cake is very delicious if the orange juice and zest are used, as in the recipe above, or you could omit these and use just 3 (3³/₄) tablespoons of water instead.

Cherry and Raisin Cake: follow the instructions in the first recipe but instead of mixed dried fruit use 5 oz/150 g (good ¹/₂ cup) chopped glacé (candied) cherries and 7 oz/200 g (1¹/₆ cup) raisins.

The orange juice and zest can be used, as in the original recipe, or omit these and moisten the fruit with 3 (3¾) tablespoons water or half water and half lemon or lime juice.

If using some lemon or lime juice you could add 1 teaspoon of the lemon or lime zest. It is not advisable to use as much of the juice and zest as when using these from an orange for the flavour would be too strong.

Ginger Fruit Cake: follow the directions for the first recipe but add 50 g/2 oz (½ cup) finely chopped crystallized (candied) ginger to the dried fruit and sift 1 level teaspoon ground ginger with the flour.

Large Cake: use exactly double the ingredients in the first recipe or in the Apricot and Date Cake and the other variations.

This means buying 2 x 218 g small cans (scant 436 g/15½ oz) of condensed milk or one large can (400 g/14 oz). I find the two smaller cans give a more moist cake as you have a slightly larger amount of condensed milk in those.

Place the mixture into a lined 18 cm/7 inch square or 20 cm/8 inch round cake tin. This generally takes about 2 hours 10 minutes at the setting given but test carefully at the end of 2 hours, for you need the cake to be slightly sticky, see stages 3 and 4 in the main recipe.

The difference in baking time between the large and the small cake may seem surprisingly small, the reason is that the mixture is spread over a much larger area in the case of the larger cake, so the depth of the cake mixture is not dissimilar.

MICROWAVE COOKING FOR CAKES

If you have a combination cooker, i.e. one in which you have both conventional cooking and microwave cooking, you can make any of the cakes on the pages from 29 to the recipe above. You will find detailed instructions on how to cook cakes in your manufacturer's instruction book, do follow those carefully to ensure success.

If you have an ordinary microwave cooker then the technique of baking cakes and puddings is very different. Most cake recipes are not suitable for microwave cooking and are better cooked in an oven but there are ways of ensuring success in the microwave. Starting on page 176 you will find several special recipes for cooking cakes and cake-like puddings in the microwave.

Output to Use
Most cakes and puddings cooked in the microwave are better if a lower output is used rather than full output.

Consult your manufacturer's manual but if in doubt use two-thirds the full output.

MAKING PASTRY

Pastry is used for a great many savoury and sweet dishes. There is a belief that if you are not a natural pastry cook there is little hope of producing first class pastry. That belief is NOT a true fact. With the right ingredients, together with the correct handling of the pastry dough and accurate baking, you will achieve good pastry, i.e. one that is light and crisp.

Shortcrust pastry (basic pie dough) is the most popular type.

Ingredients for Shortcrust Pastry
Flour: choose plain (all-purpose) flour and do not add any raising agent. White wheat flour makes the lightest pastry but modern wholemeal (wholewheat) flour produces a good result or you can use *half white flour* mixed with the same quantity of *wholemeal flour*.

A recipe for making pastry for anyone with an intolerance to wheat flour is on page 114.

Salt: while this is not essential, it helps to enhance the flavour. A 'pinch' of salt is the amount you can pick up with your forefinger and thumb.

Fat: you could use all butter or all margarine. Traditional recipes recommend *half* butter or margarine and *half* lard (shortening). It is quite interesting to vary the choice of fats from time to time.

Oil can be used to make pastry and this is described on page 111.

The usual proportions are half the amount of fat to flour. Various recipes give the correct amounts of fat and flour required for that particular dish.

Water: this is the liquid used in the majority of recipes. Make sure it is very cold before adding it to the other ingredients. In some recipes you will find a whole egg or an egg yolk is given, either instead of water, or with a very small amount of water.

An indication of the amount of water required is given in the recipe but this is only an *average amount*. Different kinds of fat and brands of flour absorb varying amounts of liquid. Wholemeal and wholewheat flours absorb more than white flour.

Always add the water gradually to the flour and fat mixture for too much makes a sticky dough that is difficult to roll out and often results in tough pastry.

Too little liquid produces a dry and crumbly dough that will break as you try to handle and roll it.

Consistency: the pastry dough is the **correct consistency** when you can gather it together into a ball, without undue pressure, so leaving the mixing bowl clean.

Stages in Making Shortcrust Pastry
1. Sift flour and salt into the mixing bowl. Sifting aerates the flour and helps to produce a light dough.
2. Cut the fat into small pieces, drop into the flour and *rub it in* until the mixture looks like fine breadcrumbs.
   Keep the mixture as cool as possible. If your hands are warm rinse them and your wrists under cold water. Shake off any surplus moisture.
   The rubbing-in movement means *lifting* small amounts of the flour and fat and applying gentle pressure between the thumbs and fingers of both hands then letting the mixture drop back into the mixing bowl. By lifting the mixture you allow air to be incorporated into it. Stop 'rubbing-in' the fat when you have the breadcrumb effect. Over-handling gives tough pastry.
3. *Add the water gradually*, pour this in from a tablespoon, rather than a jug, for you can control the amount more accurately.
4. *Place* the pastry dough on to a *lightly* floured board or working surface. *Dust* the rolling pin with a little flour and *lightly* roll the pastry into a neat shape. It can be rolled out to use but it is better to wrap it in clingfilm or aluminium foil and chill for about 30 minutes in the refrigerator. This stage is known as 'relaxing' the pastry. It is important for it allows the gluten in the flour to expand and so makes the pastry
   a) easier to roll out for the particular recipe
   b) keep a better shape.
5. Place the pastry shape back on the lightly floured board or working surface. Roll out with smooth, light movements of the rolling pin. When the pastry is the desired length *lift* the pastry dough and turn it at *right angles*, then continue rolling.
   In this way you keep the rolling pin straight ahead and you *do not roll* in all directions, which would stretch the pastry.
   The average thickness of the pastry dough will be about 6 mm/ 1/4 inch but this may vary slightly and it will be mentioned in individual recipes.
6. Use and bake the pastry as directed in individual recipes.

An Electric Mixer for Shortcrust Pastry
1. The information about the ingredients and the various steps to mixing the pastry on page 108 and above are just as important when using an electric mixer to blend the ingredients together as they are when mixing by hand.
2. To 'rub' the fat into the flour you can use the whisk, or the two whisks with a small hand mixer.
3. Always use a *low speed* to copy the deliberate action of rubbing-in by hand. Watch carefully and the moment the fat is incorporated into the flour *switch off*. Over-handling makes tough pastry.
4. While you can add the water gradually, with the machine in operation, if you are fairly inexperienced at making pastry with the mixer, I would advise adding it with the machine *switched off*, so you can judge the consistency (see page 108). After a time you may become so experienced with using an electric mixer that you can add the water steadily with the machine in operation on a low speed.

5.   Use as the information on page 109 and individual recipes.

A Food Processor for Shortcrust Pastry

1.   A food processor is more efficient than an electric mixer for mixing the ingredients for pastry. If used correctly it 'rubs' the fat into the flour very quickly and evenly. You must watch carefully for a few seconds as over-processing *forces* the fat into the flour and you produce a dough that is ultra-crumbly and difficult to handle.
     Place the cutting blade in position in the processor bowl. Put the flour, salt and fat (cut into small pieces) into the *dry* bowl of the food processor. Fix the lid and switch on. Within ½ to ¾ minute the fat will be 'rubbed in'.
2.   While you can add the liquid gradually through the feeder tube to the bowl, it can be difficult to judge the result as you cannot *feel* the texture. *It is highly dangerous to put your fingers into a processor bowl when the cutting blade is in position.* To begin with I would recommend you tip the flour and fat mixture into another container then add the water by hand as described on page 109. With experience you may feel happy to add the liquid gradually through the feeder tube with the machine operating. If your food processor has a choice of speeds use the lowest possible.
3.   When the pastry dough is mixed continue as the information on page 109 and individual recipes.

SHORTCRUST PASTRY WITH FAT (SHORTENING)

If you have not made pastry before it is advisable to read the detailed information on pages 108 to 109 before you begin. For generations the proportions of ingredients for shortcrust pastry (basic pie dough) have been half fat to flour; this produces a really good pastry that is short (hence the name) and crisp. The choice of fat has varied over the years. Once we used a great deal more lard than we do today and many people used this fat entirely. Others felt that the pastry had the best flavour if one used equal quantities of lard and butter or margarine. Vegetarians prefer all margarine. Oil is another fat you can use, see the recipe on pages 111-112. The importance of correct mixing is described on pages 108 to 109. In addition to the flour listed in the ingredients you will need a little extra to sprinkle over the working surface or pastry board and the rolling pin.

Oven Setting: as the specific recipe
Baking Time: as the recipe
Baking Equipment: as the recipe
Makes: as the recipe

Metric/Imperial	Ingredients	American
225 g/8 oz	plain (all-purpose) flour	2 cups
pinch	salt	pinch
115 g/4 oz	fat, such as half lard and half butter or margarine	½ cup
to bind	cold water, see stage 4	to bind

1. Sift the flour and salt into a mixing bowl, add the pieces of your selected fat.
2. Rub this into the flour, lifting the mixture in the air and following the advice in stage 2 of the detailed information on page 109.
3. When all the fat has been incorporated into the flour and the mixture looks like fine breadcrumbs you can start to add the water.
4. Add the water gradually from a tablespoon, stirring this in with a palette knife (spatula). Although makes of flour vary in the amount of liquid they absorb you should find you need from 2 to 2½ tablespoons to give a firm rolling consistency but one you can gather together with your fingers. After you have added nearly all the water stop using a knife and feel the consistency of the dough with your fingers.
5. Dust the board and rolling pin with a little flour and roll out the dough until a neat shape. If possible wrap and chill for 30 minutes before going any further. Stage 4 on page 109 explains the importance of this step. If you are in a hurry you will need to miss this stage.
6. You can then roll out the dough to the required thickness and shape for the particular recipe.

Variation

Sweet shortcrust pastry: in this type of pastry sugar is added and often the pastry is mixed with an egg yolk or egg as well as water (see page 114).

One Stage Pastry
Modern soft margarines and fats mean you can mix all the ingredients together by hand or with a food processor or electric mixer. Special low fat spreads are not suitable for making good pastry.

Follow the proportions of flour, salt and fat given above but use 3 (3¾) tablespoons of water, this works well with this method.

By hand: sift the flour and salt into a basin. Put the amount of soft margarine or fat into a mixing bowl, cream with a good tablespoon of the sifted flour. A fork is ideal for this purpose. Gradually work in the rest of the flour and the water, finally mix together with a knife. Proceed as stage 5 above. Stop mixing as soon as all the ingredients are incorporated.

With an electric mixer or food processor: put all the ingredients into the bowl. Use the whisk attachment with a mixer and just blend together at a low speed. Stop as soon as mixed. Put on the lid with a food processor and switch on until just blended. Do NOT over-process.

SHORTCRUST PASTRY WITH OIL

Oil makes a pastry with an excellent flavour and texture. The only drawback is that the mixture is rather difficult to handle. It is better rolled between two sheets of greaseproof (wax) paper or baking parchment. Do not use the light versions of the oil. Extra virgin oil gives the best flavour.

Oven Setting: as the specific recipe

Baking Time: as the recipe
Baking Equipment: as the recipe
Makes: as the recipe

Metric/Imperial	Ingredients	American
225 g/8 oz	plain (all-purpose) flour	2 cups
pinch	salt	pinch
120 ml/4 fl oz	olive or sunflower oil	1/2 cup
to bind	cold water, see stage 2	to bind

1. Sift the flour and salt into a mixing bowl. Make a well in the centre and pour in the oil. Mix with a flat-bladed knife.
2. Add the liquid very gradually to give a firm rolling consistency. With the amount of oil and flour given in the ingredients you will need about 1 tablespoon but brands of flour do vary in the amount of liquid they absorb. Knead gently to a neat shape. Wrap and chill for 30 minutes if possible.
3. Lay a large sheet of greaseproof paper or baking parchment on a board or working surface. Dust it very lightly with flour and also dust the top of the pastry with a very little flour.
4. Lay a second sheet of greaseproof paper or parchment over the pastry and roll out to the desired thickness and shape.
5. Use as the individual recipes. If covering fruit in a pie keep the pastry on the bottom sheet of greaseproof paper or parchment and use this to support the pastry as you invert it over the ingredients in the pie dish.

WHEN BAKING PASTRY

Place most pastry in the centre of the oven. Small tartlets can be placed just above the centre of the oven but not too high, for the base of the tartlets must be cooked and you do not want the top pastry rim to become too brown.

If you have a fan oven all shelves should give the same heat, so the pastry can be placed where convenient.

RASPBERRY TARTLETS

These tarts are an ideal way of serving small amounts of dessert fruit. While you could use shortcrust pastry (basic pie dough), made as page 110, I would suggest you use sweet shortcrust. The sugar helps to make the pastry very crisp. It is important NOT to bake sweet shortcrust pastry at too high a temperature, for the sugar content makes it likely to scorch and become over-brown.

A luxurious touch is given by filling the pastry cases with a little whipped cream before topping this with the fruit and giving the raspberries an attractive shine with a jelly glaze.

Oven Setting: 190°C/375°F, Gas Mark 5 or 180°C with a fan oven
Baking Time: 12 minutes
Baking Equipment: one tray of patty tins (shells)

Makes: 9 to 12 small tartlets. Eat when freshly baked. The cooked or uncooked pastry cases can be frozen. Freeze in the tins, remove and then pack.

Metric/Imperial	Ingredients	American
	For the pastry	
150 g/5 oz	**plain (all-purpose) flour**	1¼ cups
65 g/2½ oz	**butter**	¼ cup plus 1 tablespoon
25 g/1 oz	**caster sugar**	2 tablespoons
to bind	**water**	to bind
	For the filling	
5 tablespoons	**double (heavy) cream, whipped**	6¼ tablespoons
2 teaspoons	**caster sugar**	2 teaspoons
225 g/8 oz	**raspberries**	½ lb
	For the glaze	
1 tablespoon	**water**	1 tablespoon
2 tablespoons	**redcurrant jelly**	2½ tablespoons

1. Sift the flour into a mixing bowl, rub in the butter as described on page 109. This also explains how you could use an electric mixer or food processor for this purpose.
2. Add the sugar then gradually stir in enough water to bind (see page 109 for information on mixing pastry). Wrap and chill for about 30 minutes if possible. This will help the pastry keep a good shape.
3. Roll out the pastry until about 6 mm/¼ inch in thickness and cut into rounds to fit the size of your patty tins. Press the pastry down firmly, this helps the tarts keep a good shape. Lightly prick the base of each pastry case with the tip of a fork. If time permits cover with clingfilm and chill again for 15 minutes.
4. Meanwhile preheat the oven. Bake the pastry cases but check after 10 minutes, they should not become too brown. Cool in the tins then carefully remove on to a wire cooling tray.
5. Mix the cream with the sugar, then spoon a little into each tartlet case. Top with the raspberries.
6. Heat the water with the jelly in a small saucepan, or basin in the microwave. Cool slightly then dip a pastry brush into the glaze and carefully brush over the top of the fruit.

Variation

- Use only 2 to 3 tablespoons of whipped cream and mix this with 1 to 2 tablespoons lemon curd.

QUANTITIES FOR PASTRY

The recipes for shortcrust pastry (basic pie dough) on the previous pages make pastry based on 225 g/8 oz (2 cups) of flour, etc. Not all recipes use this amount of pastry, so sometimes you will find the following:-

Pastry made with 175 g/6 oz (1½ cups) flour etc. This means you will use the proportions of:-

A pinch of salt plus 85 g/3 oz (⅜ cup) of fat (half the amount of fat to flour) and water to bind.

Pastry made with 115 g/4 oz (1 cup) flour etc. This means you will use the proportions of:-

A pinch of salt plus 50 g/2 oz (¼ cup) of fat (half the amount of fat to flour) and water to bind.

Sweet Shortcrust Pastry

This is the pastry used for Raspberry Tartlets. As the name indicates the pastry contains a certain amount of sugar, which makes it ideal for the Raspberry Tartlets. It is very crisp and it is a pleasing contrast to the soft filling.

Do note the point made in the introduction to the recipe about baking sweet shortcrust pastry (basic sweet pie dough) a little more slowly than unsweetened pastry. Tartlets made with ordinary unsweetened pastry are given next.

Cutting Out Pastry Rounds

In order to cut the rounds for small tartlet shapes you need a metal or plastic pastry cutter. To obtain a sharp and neat edge to these rounds it helps if, from time to time, you dip the rim of the cutter into a little flour.

Replacing Wheat Flour in Pastry

In ordinary shortcrust pastry and sweet shortcrust pastry you have two alternatives.

a) Use gluten-free flour. There are many brands of these, they very slightly in flavour so, over a period of time, you may like to change the brand and decide which kind you like best. Gluten-free flours have improved enormously during the past years.

b) Use all rice flour. This gives a very short and crisp result, which is very good for tartlets. You may find it slightly more difficult to handle than gluten-free flour when making pastry for a fruit pie, or other kind of pie, where you have to handle a large piece of pastry dough.

JAM TARTS

These are a very good way to start making and using shortcrust pastry (basic pie dough). The recipe below is for making only a small amount of pastry which is easy to handle. It is important to read the instructions about pastry on pages 108 and 111 before you begin.

Oven Setting:	200°C/400°F, Gas Mark 6 or 190°C with a fan oven
Baking Time:	10 to 12 minutes
Baking Equipment:	one tray of approximately 9 small patty tins (shells)
Makes:	9 small tarts, depending on the size and depth of the tins. These are best eaten when freshly baked. When cold they can be frozen. Open-freeze before packing, so the jam does not stick to the container.

Metric/Imperial	Ingredients	American
115 g/4 oz	Shortcrust pastry made with plain (all-purpose) flour, etc, see page 110 plus a little extra flour for dusting the pastry board	1 cup
For the filling		
3 to 4 tablespoons or as required	jam	3¾ to 5 tablespoons or as required

1. Preheat the oven. There should be no need to grease the baking tins.
2. Make the pastry as page 110, if time permits wrap this and let it relax for 30 minutes.
3. Sift a little flour over the pastry board and rolling pin. Roll the pastry out until just over 6 mm/¼ inch in thickness.
4. Choose the right sized cutter for the patty tins and cut out the number of rounds required. You probably will be able to get only a few of the number required from the first rolling and will have to fold over the pieces of pastry left, so they become a neat shape. Re-roll this and cut out more rounds. Do not squeeze the pieces of pastry left, handle them carefully and gently.
5. Gently prick the base of each pastry round in the tin then add a very little jam. Do not over-fill because this would cause the jam to boil out of the pastry during the baking.
6. Bake until the pastry is firm and pleasantly pale golden in colour. Remove from the oven and add a little more jam to each tart. When slightly cooled, and less fragile, carefully remove the tarts and place them on the wire cooling tray.

Variation

Lemon Curd Tarts: make the pastry as stages 2 to 4 but prick the base of each pastry round in the tin very well, for the pastry will be baked 'blind'. That means without a filling. Lemon curd is spoiled by over-heating, so it is better to add this preserve when the pastry is cooked.

Bake as above, but you will find the pastry is ready 1 or 2 minutes earlier than above, as there is no filling. Add the lemon curd while the pastry is hot or wait until it is cold.

BAKING PASTRY 'BLIND'

The term 'baking blind' is used when describing the baking of some pastry dishes. It means that the flan or tartlet case must be baked, or partially baked, without a filling. The problem with baking blind is that you have to prevent the bottom of the pastry case from rising up and so spoiling the flat base. There are various ways to deal with this matter.

Chilling the uncooked pastry shape(s) before baking helps to keep the whole tart or flan or small tartlet cases a good shape, i.e. the pastry sides should not sink down, and so spoil the appearance, and the bottom should not rise.

a) Pricking the base of the pastry

This is more suitable for small tartlet cases than large flan or tart shapes. If you lightly prick the bottom of the pastry with the prongs of a fork then chill the pastry before baking that should be sufficient. Take care not to make holes too large or allow the prongs to go right through to the base of pastry for, if you are adding a little liquid filling such as in Quiche Lorraine, on page 135, the holes may not close up in baking and the liquid could seep through these and spoil both pastry and filling.

This method can be used when baking the uncooked pastry in larger empty cases but the methods given in b) and preferably in c) are much better.

b) Using egg white

This method is very simple; you brush the uncooked pastry with a very thin layer of unwhisked egg white. This sets during the first stages of cooking and makes a seal that helps to prevent the pastry rising and liquid filling seeping into the pastry. Chilling the uncooked pastry shape(s) is helpful here.

c) Weighing down the pastry

This is accepted as being the best method of controlling the pastry during cooking. There are several ways of doing this.

1. Insert a round or square of greased greaseproof (wax) paper, depending upon the shape of the case, into the uncooked pastry shape. Place the greased side next to the uncooked pastry. You could use baking parchment and this does not require greasing. Make sure the paper or parchment does not touch the pastry on the sides of the shape. Top the paper or parchment with something to give a light weight. This could be crusts of bread, pieces of dry short length pasta or the proper plastic baking beans, these can be used over and over again. Make certain that the beans, or other items used, are evenly distributed over the paper or parchment. You will need to remove the paper or parchment and filling before the end of the baking time to ensure that the base of the pastry case is properly cooked. By this time though the filling will have done its work. If baking small tartlet cases blind you could insert a small ball of greaseproof paper – without weights – into the pastry for half the baking time then remove these.

2. Use aluminium foil as the filling. You do not need any weights, in the form of bread, pasta or baking beans. While a round of foil is good, I find it better to make several heavier rolls of twisted foil and insert them into the shape. Here again the foil must be removed before the end of the cooking time to make certain that the bottom pastry is adequately cooked. I find that the time to remove the filling of greaseproof paper, parchment or foil is about 5 or 6 minutes before the end of the cooking time, i.e. when the sides of the pastry are just beginning to look firm and crisp. You then replace the pastry back in the oven to complete the cooking time.

FRUIT PIE

A fruit pie can be made at any time of the year; you can simply vary the fruit according to the season. The pie below is made with apples but try it with fresh apricots, greengages, plums or rhubarb. Details of preparing these fruits is given under Variations.

It is important to have sufficient fruit in the dish, otherwise the pastry will not be supported properly and will sink down. If you find you are short of fruit put a proper pie funnel in the pie dish with the fruit or use a heatproof egg cup. Either of these will help to hold the pastry in position.

The amount of pastry given is over-generous but the first time you make a pie you may find it quite difficult to cover the fruit, so it is better to have a little surplus. Any pastry left would be ideal to make a few jam tarts, as the recipe on page 114.

Oven Setting: 190 to 200°C/375 to 400°F, Gas Mark 5 to 6 or 180 to 190°C with a fan oven. In each case use the lower setting if your oven is inclined to be on the hot side. After this reduce the heat to 160°C/325°F, Gas Mark 3 or 150°C with a fan oven, see stage 14

Baking Time: 25 to 30 minutes plus an extra 10 minutes at the lower setting

Baking Equipment: 900 to 1200 ml/1½ to 2 pint (3¾ to 4½ cup) pie dish

Makes: a pie to serve 4. This can be frozen after cooking although the fruit does lose a little texture.

Metric/Imperial	Ingredients	American
225 g/8 oz	Shortcrust pastry made with plain (all-purpose) flour, etc see page 110 plus a little extra	2 cups
	For the filling	
675 to 900 g/ 1½ to 2 lb	cooking apples	1½ to 2 lb
3 tablespoons	water	3¾ tablespoons
2 to 3 tablespoons	sugar, type to personal taste	2½ to 3¾ tablespoons
	To decorate the pie	
1 tablespoon	caster sugar	1 tablespoon

1. Make the pastry as page 110 then form it into a neat shape. If time permits wrap this and let it relax for 30 minutes.
2. Meanwhile peel, core and thinly slice the apples, do not do this too far ahead for they darken with exposure to the air. Put the sliced apples into the pie dish with the water and sugar. Cover with foil while rolling out the pastry to exclude the air.
3. Sift a little flour over the pastry board or surface and the rolling pin, this is important for you have to roll out the pastry to a fairly large shape and you do not want it sticking to either the surface or the rolling pin.

4. This is the time to preheat the oven if you are NOT going to chill the pie before cooking but see NOTE at the end of the recipe.
5. Roll out the pastry until it is of a sufficient size to be about 3.5 cm/ 1½ inches larger than the top of the pie dish. It should be about 1.25 cm/½ inch in thickness.
6. Brush the rim of the pie dish with a very little water, it should feel slightly moist for it has to hold the pastry strips in position.
7. Cut several strips of pastry the width of the rim of the pie dish and press these in position. This edging of pastry is very important, for if you omit it you do not have a slightly thicker layer of pastry around the edge of the pie and this could become over-cooked and brown too much.
8. Lift up one side of the large piece of pastry, slip the rolling pin underneath so it is roughly in the centre of the pastry, the rolling pin acts as a support. Lift the pastry with the rolling pin underneath.
9. Lay the pastry over the top of the pie dish. Slip away the rolling pin.
10. Press the edges of the top pastry to the pastry rim – do not cut away any surplus until you have done this.
11. Cut away the surplus pastry from the top covering, taking care not to stretch the pastry in any way. You will now have a neat looking pie covering.
12. Press the edges of the two layers of pastry together then **flute** them. This simply means pinching the pastry at regular intervals, so you get a scalloped effect. Make a slit in the centre of the pastry covering, this allows steam from cooking the fruit to escape and keeps the pastry crisp.
13. Stand the pie dish on a baking tray, this is a precaution in case any juice bubbles out during cooking.
14. Bake until the pastry is pleasantly golden in colour, then turn down the oven to 160°C/325°F, Gas Mark 3 or 150°C with a fan oven and leave the pie for another 10 minutes to make sure the fruit is cooked. If you are worried that the pastry may become over-brown lay a piece of foil over the top of the pie.
15. Top with a good sprinkling of sugar and serve hot or cold.

NOTE: the instructions above suggest preheating the oven while preparing the pastry. If time permits it is better to make the pie, lay clingfilm (saran wrap) over the top of the uncooked pastry and chill it for about 30 minutes before baking. This helps the pastry to keep a perfect shape. In this case you do not need to preheat the oven until almost ready to bring the pie dish out of the refrigerator.

Variations

- Cooking apples should be perfectly cooked in the time given. You can make this filling more interesting by a) using orange juice instead of water for the filling; b) adding several tablespoons of raisins or chopped dates or other dried fruit; c) flavouring the apples with 2 or 3 cloves or a pinch of ground cloves or ground cinnamon.
- Large fruit, such as **apricots, extra large greengages** and **plums** could be halved and stoned before putting them into the pie dish. They fit more neatly into the pie dish but take up less room, so you need to be generous with the amount of fruit.

- Sometimes the fruit is very firm and under-ripe, this happens with early **gooseberries**. In this case pre-cook the fruit for about 10 minutes with the water and sugar then allow it to become quite cold before making the pie.
- **Rhubarb** contains a high percentage of water. The sticks should be cut into 2.5 cm/1 inch pieces and the amount of water can be reduced to half.

A little diced crystallized (candied) or preserved ginger could be added to the fruit. Orange juice is an excellent liquid to use with rhubarb.

A FRUIT TART

In this dish the fruit is sandwiched between two layers of pastry, so all the flavour is maintained. The dish is sometimes called a 'plate pie'. The problem some people experience is that the juices from the fruit can make the bottom pastry slightly soggy. To avoid this:-

a) Try and use a metal container for the pastry. The proper tins (pans) are sold as 'plate' or 'tart tins'. A large flat metal plate or shallow dish could be used or a proper flan tin (see page 125). A metal container helps the bottom layer of pastry become crisp more readily than a ceramic one. If you have no metal container always place a baking sheet or tray (pan) in the oven when preheating this and stand the fruit tart on the hot metal. This ensures that the maximum amount of heat is given to the pastry at the bottom of the tart. It also helps to safeguard the oven in case a little fruit juice should bubble out during cooking.
b) Use the filling of cornflour (cornstarch), or the alternative ingredients given under **Variations** with a little of the sugar from the **recipe before adding the fruit**. This helps to 'mop up' and thicken any natural juices that flow from the fruit during the process of cooking.
c) While you need a good heat to cook the pastry, the fact that you have two layers of the dough plus a central layer of moist fruit means that you will find it more satisfactory if you bake on a fairly high setting at first then lower the heat to ensure that all layers are adequately cooked.

NOTE: I have given a generous amount of pastry here for, as explained under the Fruit Pie on page 117, it is not easy when first handling pastry to make sure you have sufficient dough. Any uncooked pastry left could be used to make a few jam tarts, as the recipe on page 114.

Choosing the Fruit
Any of the fruits given under the Fruit Pie on page 117 can be selected for this tart. Fruits, such as apricots, plums or large greengages should be halved and stoned; rhubarb cut into even-sized lengths. Moderately under-ripe gooseberries should cook within the time given. If very hard and sour simmer for 5 to 6 minutes in a very little water to taste, then strain away the surplus liquid and allow the fruit to cool. The sugar should be added to the fruit at stage 6. Soft berry fruits, such as blackcurrants, loganberries, raspberries, etc. are ideal for this tart. The weight is for the prepared fruit, i.e. apples would be peeled, cored and sliced.

Oven Setting: 190 to 200°C/375 to 400°, Gas Mark 5 to 6 or 180 to 190°C with a fan oven. In each case use the lower setting if your oven is inclined to be on the hot side. After this reduce the heat to 160°C/325°F, Gas Mark 3 or 150°C with a fan oven, see stage 9

Baking Time: 20 to 25 minutes plus an extra 15 minutes at the lower setting

Baking Equipment: one 18 to 20 cm/7 to 8 inch pie plate, see above

Makes: A tart to serve 4. This can be frozen after cooking although the fruit filling can become somewhat softened.

Metric/Imperial	Ingredients	American
	Shortcrust pastry	
300 g/10 oz	plain (all-purpose) flour plus a little extra	2½ cups
pinch	salt	pinch
150 g/5 oz	fat, see page 110 for details	⅝ cup
to bind	cold water	to bind
	For the filling	
450 g/1 lb	fruit, for details see page 119	1 lb
50 g/2 oz	caster sugar or to taste	¼ cup
1 tablespoon	cornflour but see page 119	1 tablespoon
water	see stage 6	water
	For the topping	
1 tablespoon	caster sugar	1 tablespoon

1. Make the pastry as the details on page 109 then form into a neat shape. If time permits, wrap the pastry and let it relax for 30 minutes.
2. Meanwhile prepare the fruit, see details in the introduction.
3. Divide the pastry into two portions, have one slightly larger than the other; this is for the base of the tart.
4. Sift a little flour over the pastry board or surface and the rolling pin. Roll out the large half of the pastry until about 0.8 to 1.25 cm/⅓ to ½ inch in thickness and the size to cover the tin. Place the pastry over the tin, pressing it down gently. Do NOT cut away any surplus.
5. This is the time to preheat the oven if you are NOT going to chill the tart before baking but see NOTE in stage 9.
6. Sprinkle about half the sugar and all the cornflour evenly over the centre of the bottom pastry. Add the fruit then the rest of the sugar. Make sure the fruit and sugar are kept away from the pastry rim. Unless the fruit is very firm, such as apples, there is no need to add any liquid. In the case of apples, or equally firm fruit, sprinkle just a few drops of water on top of the fruit.
7. Brush the edges of the bottom pastry with a few drops of water then roll out the smaller round of pastry, support this over the rolling pin and lower over the fruit. This top pastry can be a little thinner than that used for the bottom layer.

8. Seal the edges of the two layers of pastry together using gentle pressure then cut away any surplus dough. Flute the edges together to make a neat edging, see stage 12 under Fruit Pie on page 117. Make a slit in the centre of the pastry lid, so steam from the fruit juices can escape. If time permits loosely cover the tart with clingfilm (saran wrap) and chill for a short time. This helps the pastry keep a good shape.
9. NOTE this would be the time to preheat the oven. Bake the pastry as the timing given. Reduce the heat when the top pastry becomes golden-coloured.
10. Sprinkle the cooked tart with sugar and serve hot or cold.

Variations

- Instead of using cornflour on the bottom of the tart you could use fine semolina or polenta or rice flour or very fine stale breadcrumbs.
- A little dried fruit, such as chopped dates, raisins or other dried fruits can be mixed with the fresh fruit.

LEMON MERINGUE PIE

This is a very special pie, consisting of a crisp pastry case, filled with a refreshing lemon mixture then topped with a soft meringue. It is a dessert that has been popular for decades. It is NOT easy to make but each stage is explained very carefully on this and the next page, so you should have great success. It certainly will be appreciated by your friends and family.

Oven Setting:	190 to 200°C/375 to 400°F, Gas Mark 5 to 6 for the initial stage to set the pastry or 170 to 180°C with a fan oven. If your oven is on the hot side use the lower setting. After this time the heat is reduced as the information given in stages 10 or 11, according to whether you are having the pie hot or cold
Baking Time:	**For the pastry:** 15 to 20 minutes see stage 3 **For the filling and meringue:** 20 minutes to 1 hour, for details see stages 10 and 11
Baking Equipment:	one 20 cm/8 inch flan tin (pan) or dish, which should be at least 3.5 cm/1½ inches in depth
Makes:	one pie to serve 4 to 6. Serve hot or cold. This does not freeze well.

Metric/Imperial	Ingredients	American
175 g/6 oz	*Shortcrust pastry made with plain (all-purpose) flour, etc. see page 114*	*1½ cups*
	For the lemon filling	
1 large or 2 small	**lemons**	*1 large or 2 small*
water	**see method, stage 5**	*water*
25 g/1 oz	**cornflour (cornstarch)**	*¼ cup*
25 g/1 oz	**butter**	*2 tablespoons*

85 to 100 g/3 to 4 oz	*caster sugar, see stage 6*	³/₈ to ¹/₂ cup
2	*egg yolks from large eggs, whisked*	2
	For the meringue	
2	*egg whites, from large eggs*	2
50 to 100 g/2 to 4 oz	*caster sugar, see stage 10*	¹/₄ to ¹/₂ cup

1. Make the pastry as the method on page 109. Form into a neat shape. If time permits wrap and chill for 30 minutes.
2. Preheat the oven then roll out the pastry as explained on page 109 and line the tin. At this stage the pastry is to be baked 'blind', so you need to insert the greaseproof paper or parchment and bread, pastry or baking beans to weigh it down as explained on page 116. If preferred use rolls of foil instead.
3. Bake the pastry 'blind' for 15 minutes only, then remove from the oven and take out the greaseproof paper or parchment and filling or the foil. At this stage the pastry should hardly have changed colour; it should be quite pale. If the bottom of the shape is very soft return the pastry case to the oven for about 5 minutes only. It will have more baking when the lemon filling and meringue are added.
4. While the pastry is in the oven prepare the lemon filling. Wash the lemon(s) in cold water then dry. Stand a grater on a large plate and rub the lemon(s) against the finest side to give very finely grated lemon zest (the top part of the lemon rind). Be careful not to take any white pith for that has a bitter taste. You need a minimum of 1 teaspoon of the zest but you can prepare a little more if you like a strong taste.
5. Halve the lemon(s) and squeeze out the juice. You need no more than 3 (3³/₄) tablespoons and only 2 (2¹/₂) tablespoons if you do not like a strong lemon taste. Tip the juice into a measuring jug then add enough water to give a total of 300 ml/¹/₂ pint (1¹/₄ cups) of lemon-flavoured liquid.
6. Put the cornflour into a basin, gradually add the lemon liquid and stir well until blended. Tip into a saucepan, add the lemon zest and the butter. Stir over a low heat until thickened and smooth. Take the pan off the heat and stir in the sugar, do this gradually so you can ascertain the flavour and adjust the amount of sugar to personal taste.
7. Whisk the beaten yolks into the mixture then return to a very low heat until the mixture thickens again, this takes about 4 minutes. Do not stop stirring throughout this time, for there must be no possibility of the mixture boiling, in which case it would curdle (separate).
8. Spoon the hot lemon mixture into the partially baked pastry.
9. Whisk the egg whites until very stiff, page 57 tells you about making meringues, gradually beat in the amount of sugar, given below in either stage 10 or stage 11.
10. **If you plan to have the dessert hot** you need to use only 50 g/2 oz (¹/₄ cup) of sugar for a soft meringue. You could add the greater amount of sugar, as stage 11 but the meringue will not become crisp in the shorter baking time. In this case reset the oven to 160°C/325°F, Gas Mark 3 or 150°C with a fan oven.

Spoon the meringue over the lemon filling, making sure it comes right to the pastry edge. Bake for 20 minutes or until the meringue is topped with golden coloured peaks and the filling is piping hot and the pastry is crisp and completely cooked. Serve as soon as baked.

11. **If you plan to have the dessert cold** or want a crisper meringue you need to use 115 g/4 oz (½ cup) sugar to give a crisp meringue. In this case reset the oven to 130°C/250°F, Gas Mark ½ or 240°C with a fan oven.

Here again you spoon the meringue over the lemon filling and take it right to the pastry edge. Bake for 1 hour or until the meringue is pale golden but has become really crisp. Allow to become quite cold then serve.

Q. **Why must the meringue come to the pastry edge?**
A. Because you need to cover the moist lemon filling completely. This could produce excess moisture to soften the meringue and make it 'weep'.

TREACLE TART

Although this is given the name of 'treacle tart' the main ingredient in the filling is golden (corn) syrup. This adds both flavour and sweetness to the pastry dish. Treacle Tart was a favourite for generations and now, like many traditional dishes, it is returning to high favour.

A difficulty that some people have experienced is that the pastry in the tart tends to rise and the filling sinks. The solution is to bake the pastry 'blind' for a short time. Detailed information about baking 'blind' is given on page 112.

Oven Setting: 190 to 200°C/375 to 400°F, Gas Mark 5 to 6 or 180 to 190°C with a fan oven, see stage 2 then 170 to 180°C/325 to 350°F, Gas Mark 3 to 4 or 150 to 160°C with a fan oven, see stage 5. Use the lower setting if your oven is on the hot side

Baking Time: To partially cook the pastry:10 minutes, see stage 3

To complete the cooking: 20 minutes, see stage 6

Baking Equipment: one 20 to 23 cm/8 to 9 inch pie plate or an 18 to 20 cm/7 to 8 inch deeper flan tin (pan)

Makes: one tart to serve 4. Can be served hot or cold and freezes well.

Metric/Imperial	Ingredients	American
175 g/6 oz	Shortcrust pastry made with plain (all-purpose) flour, etc see page 110	1½ cups
	For the filling	
1 small	lemon	1 small
6 tablespoons	golden syrup	7½ tablespoons
50 g/2 oz	soft breadcrumbs	1 cup

1. Make the pastry as page 109. Form into a neat shape. Wrap and chill for 30 minutes if time permits.
2. Roll out the pastry to a large round to cover the pie plate or insert in the flan tin. It is a good idea to cover this loosely with clingfilm (saran wrap) and chill for a short time. This helps the pastry keep a perfect shape. Preheat the oven at the first setting.
3. Top the uncooked pastry shape with greaseproof paper or parchment or foil and bake 'blind' as the instructions on page 115.
4. Meanwhile wash the lemon in cold water, dry and grate enough zest (the top part of the rind) to give ½ to 1 teaspoon depending on personal taste. Halve the fruit and squeeze out 1 tablespoon of juice. Mix with the syrup and breadcrumbs.
5. Bring the partially cooked pastry out of the oven, reduce the heat to the lower setting given above.
6. Spoon the golden syrup mixture over the pastry and complete the cooking. Serve the tart hot or cold.

Variation

*   Top the syrup mixture with 2 to 3 (2½ to 3¾) tablespoons soft breadcrumbs or rolled oats then bake the tart. This gives a crisp topping to the filling.

TAFFERTY TART

This is an old name for an apple tart. Choose really good cooking apples such as Bramleys. The tart is excellent served with cheese for it blends well with an apple pie or tart.

The small amount of semolina in the filling is to absorb the fruit juice so the bottom pastry is kept crisp. It is an advantage to use a metal pie plate or dish to ensure crisp pastry. A sandwich tin (layer pan) is a good alternative. By heating a baking (cookie) tray in the oven and placing the tart on this you also help to ensure crisp pastry on the bottom of the tart.

Oven Setting: 200°C/400°F, Gas Mark 6 or 190°C with a fan oven for 20 minutes then 180°C/350°F, Gas Mark 4 or 170°C with a fan oven
Baking Time: 40 to 45 minutes
Baking Equipment: one 20 cm/8 inch pie plate or flan dish or a shallow sandwich tin (layer pan)
Serves: 4 to 6. This tart can be frozen.

Metric/Imperial	Ingredients	American
For the pastry		
300 g/10 oz	plain (all-purpose) flour, etc., see pages 109 and 110	2½ cups
Filling		
675 g/1½ lb	cooking apples, peeled cored and sliced	1½ lb
1 teaspoon	finely grated lemon zest	1 teaspoon

pinch	**ground or grated nutmeg**	pinch
85 g/3 oz	**light brown sugar**	3/8 cup
25 g/1 oz	**butter, melted, optional**	2 tablespoons
2 teaspoons	**semolina**	2 teaspoons

1. Make the pastry as the directions on page 109 or page 110. Wrap this and allow to rest for 30 minutes.
2. Preheat the oven. Mix the apples with all the other ingredients except the semolina but leave out 1 tablespoon of the sugar.
3. Roll out the pastry, use just over half to line the tin or dish; sprinkle the semolina and the 1 tablespoon of sugar over this. Add the apple mixture.
4. Damp the edges of the bottom layer of pastry with a few drops of water. Use the remaining pastry to cover the apple mixture. Cut away the surplus pastry from the edges then seal and flute these as directions on page 118.
5. Make a slit in the pastry lid with a knife to allow steam to escape. Bake at the higher temperature to set the pastry. After 20 minutes lower the heat as the second temperature and complete the cooking. Serve the tart hot or cold.

A FRUIT FLAN

A flan (pie case) filled with fruit, is a delicious dessert. The most popular fruit fillings are cherries, strawberries, raspberries and other berries, but cooked or canned fruit can be used, see under Variations.

Before making the flan please read the information about 'baking blind' on page 115, for the flan must be baked without a filling.

There are several containers in which the pastry can be cooked:-

a) Special flan rings, these can be plain or fluted. The latter is regarded as being correct for a sweet flan. You will need to place the flan ring on a baking (cookie) tray or sheet. Always turn the tray or sheet upside down, this makes it easier to gently slide the cooked flan off the base, for there is no rim in the way.

b) A metal flan tin (pan), where you have both the sides and base.

c) There are attractive ceramic and ovenproof glassware flan dishes available. However it is far better to cook the pastry in a metal tin since it becomes more crisp. If you only possess a ceramic or glassware flan dish then always preheat a metal tray or sheet in the oven and place the dish, filled with the pastry, on this. The extra heat from below helps to crisp the base of the pastry. This step is not necessary if using a metal flan tin or flan ring.

A CHERRY FLAN

Choose ripe, but not over-ripe, dessert cherries and stone these first, the method of doing this is given in stage 1. If the cherries are small you will need 550 g/1¼ lb for the stones account for much of the weight; if large 450 g/1 lb should be enough. The cherries are prepared, poached in the sugar syrup, then allowed to become cold before placing them into the cold cooked flan. The syrup is used to make the glaze to cover the fruit, see stage 7.

Oven Setting:	190°C/375°F, Gas Mark 5 or 180°C with a fan oven
Baking Time:	approximately 20 minutes, but see stage 5 and allow about 10 minutes to make the sugar syrup and poach the cherries
Baking Equipment:	one 20 cm/8 inch flan ring plus a baking tray or a flan tin or dish, see above. Ideally the sides should be 2.5 cm/1 inch in depth
Makes:	one flan, giving 4 to 6 servings. Serve within 24 hours after cooking but allow time for the glaze to set (this takes about 1 hour). Freezes quite well. Open-freeze the flan then pack. The fruit tends to soften in freezing.

Metric/Imperial	Ingredients	American
For the filling		
225 ml/7½ fl oz	water	scant 1 cup
50 g/2 oz	caster sugar	¼ cup
450 to 550 g/ 1 to 1¼ lb	cherries, see stage 1 and page 125	1 to 1¼ lb
For the pastry		
175 g/6 oz	plain (all-purpose) flour	1½ cups
pinch	salt	pinch
85 g/3 oz	butter or margarine	⅜ cup
50 g/2 oz	caster sugar	¼ cup
1	egg yolk	1
little	cold water or use the egg white or part of this	little
For the glaze		
150 ml/¼ pint	sugar syrup, see stage 2	⅔ cup
1 level teaspoon	arrowroot	1 level teaspoon

1. Stone the cherries. Do this over a basin so no juice is wasted. There are proper cherry stoners that you push through the fruit. If one is not available a new fine hairpin can be used. Insert the bent end of the hairpin into each cherry, feel it hook around the stone and pull.
2. Pour the cherry juice into a large saucepan or frying pan (skillet) add the water and sugar, stir over a low heat until this has dissolved then put in the cherries. Ideally you need just one layer of fruit, hence the emphasis on a large saucepan. If the fruit is ripe just bring the syrup to the boil then remove from the heat. If the fruit is slightly firm simmer for 2 to 3 minutes then remove from the heat. Allow the cherries to cool in the syrup.
3. Sift the flour and salt into a mixing bowl, rub in the butter or margarine, add the sugar, then the egg yolk and enough egg white or cold water to make a firm rolling consistency. Form into a neat shape, wrap and (relax) chill for about 30 minutes.
4. Roll out to make a round to fit into the flan ring, tin or dish. Take

time to press the pastry down well. Either cut away the surplus pastry with a knife, taking care to leave a neat edge at the top or, if the ring or tin has a sharp edge, roll the rolling pin over the top. This cuts away the surplus pastry without stretching it. If time permits cover and chill for a short time before baking. Page 115 gives another hint about the pastry case.

5.   Preheat the oven. Fill the pastry, as described under 'baking blind'. Bake for 15 minutes or until the pastry is beginning to just turn colour and feel firm then carefully remove the greaseproof (wax) paper, parchment or foil. Return the empty flan to the oven and bake for a further 5 minutes or until the sides and base are firm. Cool slightly then remove from the container on to a wire cooling tray. When cold place on a serving dish.

6.   Strain the cherries through a sieve, put on kitchen paper (paper towels) for a few minutes. Measure out 150 ml/¼ pint (⅔ cup) of the syrup from the saucepan. Arrange the cherries in the flan.

7.   Blend the syrup with the arrowroot, pour into a saucepan, stir over a low heat until thickened and clear. Cool slightly then brush the syrup over the top of the cherries with a pastry brush. Allow this to stiffen then serve with cream, ice cream or yoghurt.

Variations

- For greater flavour boil the cherry stones in the syrup for 5 minutes, strain then return the syrup to the pan, add the cherries, continue as stage 1.
- If using **canned** or **cooked fruit** drain and dry the fruit as stage 6 then continue as stage 7. Use the syrup from the can or from cooking the fruit.
- If using ripe strawberries, raspberries or other dessert fruit make a sugar syrup as stage 1 with the water and sugar. Add 2 (2½) tablespoons redcurrant jelly for extra colour and flavour. Bring the syrup to the boil and stir until the jelly and sugar have dissolved. Cool slightly, add the fruit to the **warm syrup**. When cold continue as stage 6 and 7.

USING COMMERCIAL PASTRY

Two types of ready-prepared pastry are included in this book. You can of course buy commercially made shortcrust pastry (basic pie dough) but I am sure you will agree that your home-made pastry is much nicer. If you have no time to make shortcrust pastry and you buy the commercial type remember that you need to buy 350 g/12 oz (¾ lb) of the frozen shortcrust pastry to take the place of home-made pastry made with 225 g/8 oz (2 cups) of flour and 115 g/4 oz (½ cup) of fat etc. The baking times and temperature will be very similar to that given in the recipes in this book.

The first type of pastry used in recipes for Eccles Cakes and similar cakes, and for Sausage Rolls on page 136 with interesting Variations on these, is **frozen puff pastry**. On the whole this is very good and it is an elaborate pastry that is both difficult and time-consuming to make successfully at home.

When you buy frozen puff pastry keep it in your freezer until shortly before you need to use it. If this pastry is allowed to become over-thawed it will be very soft and difficult to handle, it must of course be defrosted at room temperature in order to use it in any recipe. You cannot use it when frozen, it is too hard. Defrosting does not take very long.
The pastry is at its best when cold and firm.

Although the pastry is ready prepared there are certain golden rules to make sure it keeps a good shape and you have it at its best.

You can buy either blocks of the pastry or sheets. I would suggest that the latter is better for the Sausage Rolls but the block of pastry is more versatile for the Eccles Cakes. When the pastry is defrosted and ready for use just lay it on a very lightly floured pastry board, or working surface, dust the rolling pin with a little flour and you are then ready to handle the dough.

The sheets may be the ideal size and need very little rolling out, as in the case of the Sausage Rolls, but there are occasions when you have to roll it out, as for the Eccles Cakes. In this case remember the golden rule with this richer pastry – keep the rolling pin straight ahead of you, do not turn it in all directions. If you do you will stretch the pastry and the cakes or savouries will be misshapen. Lift up the pastry and turn it at right angles, then roll out again. Continue like this all the time – turn the pastry, not the rolling pin.

Follow the directions for baking given in the individual recipes in this book or, if you are doing other recipes, those given on the packet. Remember in the case of the Eccles Cakes and the Sausage Rolls that you are not only cooking the pastry but the filling inside. This is particularly important with the sausagemeat content in the Sausage Rolls.

Puff pastry must be baked at a hotter setting than shortcrust pastry and it is essential that the oven is thoroughly preheated before baking. If the oven is too cool the fat in the pastry oozes out and, instead of being beautifully crisp and light and rising dramatically, the pastry will just be rather greasy and you will be left with excess grease on the baking (cookie) tray or sheet.

The second commercial pastry that has become very popular in this country is Filo Pastry. This is quite different from puff pastry, as it contains no fat. The way to use this pastry is explained in great detail on page 130 and there is a very interesting recipe given with the information. You could use filo pastry as an alternative to puff pastry when making Sausage Rolls. That version would be of interest to anyone who is anxious to cut down on fat intake, see page 130.

ECCLES CAKES

Up to the time of Queen Elizabeth I, 'wakes' – the Lancashire name for holidays – were celebrated in the town of Eccles. The Queen abolished these holidays but they were reinstated in the reign of her successor, King James I and they continued for some centuries.

Oven Setting: 220°C/425°F, Gas Mark 7 or 210°C with a fan oven
Baking Time: 20 minutes
Baking Equipment: one baking (cookie) tray

Makes: 10 to 12 cakes; serve freshly made; they freeze well.

Metric/Imperial	Ingredients	American
350 g/12 oz	frozen puff pastry (paste)*	3/4 lb
	For the filling	
50 g/2 oz	butter	1/4 cup
50 g/2 oz	caster or light brown sugar	1/4 cup
50 g/2 oz	sultanas (seedless white raisins)	1/3 cup
50 g/2 oz	currants	1/3 cup
2 tablespoons	finely chopped mixed crystallized peel	2 1/2 tablespoons
1 teaspoon	finely grated lemon zest	1 teaspoon
1/2 teaspoon	mixed spice	1/2 teaspoon
1/2 to 1 tablespoon	lemon juice	1/2 to 1 tablespoon
	To glaze	
	1 egg white and caster sugar	

* This can be obtained in sheets which defrost quicker than a block of pastry

1.   Allow the pastry to defrost to a firm rolling consistency (see left) and roll out thinly on a lightly floured pastry board.
2.   Soften the butter slightly by leaving it at room temperature then mix with the other ingredients for the filling. The amount of lemon juice used is a matter of personal taste.
3.   Roll out the pastry until 3 mm/1/8 inch in thickness. Cut into rounds about the diameter of a small saucer. Place a little filling in the centre of each pastry round, moisten the edges of the pastry with water and gather together to form neat balls, completely enclosing the filling. Turn the balls over, so the joins are underneath.
4.   Roll out *gently* to form flattish rounds 6 to 7.5 cm/2 1/2 to 3 inches in diameter. Make several slits on top of the cakes, then place the cakes on an ungreased baking tray. Brush the top of the cakes with unwhisked egg white and sprinkle with the caster sugar. It helps to keep the cakes a good shape if they are chilled for a short time in the refrigerator before baking.
5.   Preheat the oven. Bake the cakes until crisp and golden brown. Check the baking after 12 minutes and reduce the heat by 10°C or 25°F or 1 Mark with gas if the pastry is becoming too brown.

NOTE: you can use milk to glaze the pastry instead of egg white.

To make a change

Banbury Cakes: if you follow tradition these cakes are oval in shape, so you need to buy oval, rather than round, cutters. You can, of course, make them as the recipe above.

The main difference is the filling, which is more substantial than the one given. Use all the same ingredients, as for Eccles Cakes, but add 50 g/ 2 oz (1 cup) fine soft cake or macaroon crumbs and mix well at stage 2.

FILO PASTRY

Over the past years this pastry has become very popular. It differs from other kinds of pastry dough in that it is already prepared and rolled out, so the pack you buy contains sheets. The packs are sold as chilled or frozen, so choose the most convenient type for your purpose.

If you buy frozen filo pastry you will need to let it defrost at **room temperature** before use.

One problem about filo pastry is that it dries out in the air, since it is made of flour and water only. So you should keep the sheets not being handled well covered with a damp (not wet) teacloth (dish towel). If the pastry dries out it crumbles so badly that it cannot be used.

The sizes of the sheets of filo pastry do vary slightly, according to the particular make, so you may have to adjust the size of the slices in the recipe below. In several pastry recipes in this book you will find hints on how the pastry given can be replaced with filo pastry.

Using Filo Pastry

Take off one sheet and brush this with a little melted butter or oil; add a second sheet and do the same thing.

The number of sheets required will vary with the dish you are making.

In the case of the Palma Slices below, you have a fairly heavy amount of fruit, so it is advisable to use 5 sheets of pastry for the base of the slices but only 3 for the topping **for this is to cover the fruits, and not to bear the weight**.

You will find that, because of its low fat content, filo pastry browns quickly. It is therefore advisable to check on the baking as it cooks. If it is becoming over-brown before the end of the cooking time then reduce the oven heat by at least 10°C or 25°F or 1 Mark with a gas cooker, to complete the baking time.

PARMA SLICES

These are made from layers of filo pastry, filled with an interesting mixture of dried fruits, bound together with honey and a very little cream.

Oven Setting: 190°C/375°F, or 180°C with a fan oven
Baking Time: 15 minutes
Baking Equipment: one baking (cookie) tray
Makes: 8 to 10 slices, according to the size of the sheets of filo pastry. Better when freshly baked. The cooked pastry tends to crumble in freezing.

Metric/Imperial	Ingredients	American
	Filling	
50 g/2 oz	*dried figs, chopped*	*⅓ cup*
100 g/3½ oz	*dates, chopped*	*⅔ cup*
	(weight when stoned)	
50 g/2 oz	*raisins*	*⅓ cup*
50 g/2 oz	*sultanas (white seedless raisins)*	*⅓ cup*

50 g/2 oz	*walnuts, chopped*	½ cup
1 tablespoon	*clear honey*	1 tablespoon
2 tablespoons	*water*	2½ tablespoons
2 tablespoons	*double (heavy) cream*	2½ tablespoons
	For the slices	
8 sheets	*filo pastry, see comments above*	8 sheets
50 g/2 oz	*butter*	¼ cup
	Topping	
2 tablespoons	*icing (confectioners) sugar*	2½ tablespoons

1. Preheat the oven; lightly grease the baking tray.
2. Put the fruits and nuts into a saucepan with the honey and water, stir over a very low heat until the water has evaporated then add the cream and continue heating until a thick purée, with no liquid left. Leave until cold.
3. Count out the number of sheets of filo pastry needed, place on the table and cover, as instructions on page 130.
4. Melt the butter in a saucepan, or in a basin in the microwave, do not allow it to become too hot and discolour.
5. Take the first sheet of filo pastry; keep the rest covered; lay on the baking tray and brush with a little butter. Repeat until you have 5 sheets coated with butter, piled on top of one another on the baking tray.
6. Spread with the cold fruit mixture.
7. Take a sheet of filo pastry, brush with the butter and lay on top of the fruit filling; repeat this process until you have 3 sheets covering the fruit mixture. Brush the top pastry with butter.
8. Bake the pastry until golden brown and firm, check on the baking as suggested on the left.
9. Remove the pastry from the oven, leave until nearly cold or you may prefer to serve them warm. When ready to serve cut into slices with a sharp knife and dust with the sifted icing sugar.

Variations

Using Oil: instead of using melted butter to brush the sheets of filo pastry use sunflower, olive or groundnut oil.

Palma Purses
Instead of making slices you can make the mixture into attractive purse shapes, a little like old-fashioned 'dolly bags'.

Use 4 oblong sheets of filo pastry and brush each with butter and put them on top of one another. Cut through the pile of sheets down the centre in half. You have then made 2 squares of pastry to make 2 purses.

Put a spoonful of the fruit mixture into the centre of each of the squares of buttered filo pastry.

Gather the corners of the pastry together and press them firmly with your fingers, so they seal well. This is very easy.

Brush the outside of the pastry purses with melted butter, carefully lift on to the baking tray.

Cook as the temperature for Parma Slices, but allow just 10 to 12 minutes cooking time. Dust with sifted icing sugar when ready to serve.

Continue with more sheets of filo pastry until all the filling is used or bake just 2 purses and freeze the rest of the fruit filling, ready to use on another occasion.

CORNISH PASTIES

These pastry cases, filled with an interesting mixture, were created years ago as a packed meal for the tin-miners in Cornwall. In those days it was quite usual to pack a meat filling at one end of the pastry and a thick fruit purée or jam at the other end, so providing a complete meal in one pasty. It is important to use good quality beef (or other meat) in the filling, as stewing meat would not be adequately cooked within the time.

Oven Setting: 220°C/425°F, Gas Mark 7 or 200°C with a fan oven
                  for 15 minutes then 160°C/ 325°F, Gas Mark 3 or
                  150°C with a fan oven for a further 30 minutes
Baking Time: 45 minutes
Baking Equipment: one baking (cookie) tray
Makes: four pasties, which can be served hot or cold. The
                  cooked pasties can be frozen.

Metric/Imperial	Ingredients	American
	For the pastry	
350 g/12 oz	**plain (all-purpose) flour etc.**	*3 cups*
	For the filling	
350 g/12 oz	**rump or lean sirloin steak**	*¾ lb*
2 medium	**potatoes, peeled**	*2 medium*
2 medium	**onions, peeled**	*2 medium*
to taste	**salt and freshly ground black pepper**	*to taste*
to taste	**few chopped mixed herbs, optional**	*to taste*
2 to 3 teaspoons	**beef stock**	*2 to 3 teaspoons*
	To glaze	
1	**egg whisked**	*1*

1. Make the pastry as the directions on page 109. Wrap and allow it to relax in the refrigerator for 30 minutes. Lightly grease the baking tray.
2. Cut the meat into 1.5 cm/½ inch dice; chop the potatoes and onions into slightly smaller pieces. Mix the meat, vegetables, seasoning, herbs and stock.
3. Roll out the pastry on a lightly floured board until just about 8 mm/⅓ inch in thickness. Cut into four equal sized large rounds. In order to do this invert a small plate or large saucer on the pastry and cut around this with a sharp knife.
4. Take one round of pastry and put ¼ of the filling in the centre.

Brush the edges of the pastry with a few drops of water on the pastry brush. Bring these edges together to form an oval pasty shape.
Lift on to the baking tray.
5. Repeat stage 4 with the rest of the pastry and filling.
6. When the pasties are all on the tray seal and flute the edges. This means firstly pressing the edges together then depressing them at regular intervals with your forefinger and thumb to give a scalloped effect.
7. Brush the pastry with the egg to give a shine. Bake at the higher temperature for 15 minutes to set the pastry; lower the heat for the remaining time to make sure the filling is adequately cooked.

Variations

• Use diced raw lean lamb, cut from the fillet (top of the leg) or lean shoulder meat or used diced raw young chicken or rabbit.
• Add a diced raw swede (rutabaga) to the vegetables.

Vegetarian Cornish Pasties: substitute the same weight of cooked or well-drained canned red kidney beans or broad (fava) beans or chickpeas (garbanzo beans) for the meat; use vegetable stock and plenty of chopped herbs.

MEAT PLATE PIE

The ingredients used for Cornish Pasties can be turned into a plate pie.
The amount of pastry and ingredients for the filling are the same.
The filling ingredients are prepared as stage 2 above.

Oven Setting: 220°C/425°F, Gas Mark 7 or 200°C with a fan oven for 15 minutes then 160°C/ 325°F, Gas Mark 3 or 150°C with a fan oven for a further 30 minutes
Baking Time: 45 minutes
Baking Equipment: one metal 20 cm/8 inch pie plate or shallow flan tin (pan)
Makes: one pie to serve 4 people. This freezes well after cooking. Do not freeze the uncooked pie; the potatoes lose texture.

1. Make the pastry as directed on page 109, wrap and relax (chill) as suggested under all pastry recipes. Obviously if short of time this stage must be omitted.
2. Divide the pastry into two portions; make one portion slightly larger for the base of the pie.
3. Insert this into the pie plate, pressing it down firmly so it will form a good shape. Cut away the surplus pastry or use the rolling pin, as described on page 127 or wait and cut it away with the top pastry.
4. Top the pastry with the filling ingredients, spreading these out evenly.
5. Damp the edges of the pastry with a few drops of cold water.
6. Roll out the remaining pastry to make a round to cover the filling. Place this over the filling. You may find it easier to do this if you slide the rolling pin under the centre of the round of pastry and use

this to support the pastry, then slip it away as the pastry covers the filling.

7. Seal the top pastry round to the bottom pastry. Cut away the surplus with a knife; flute the edges, as under Cornish Pasties stage 6 .

8. Make a slit in the top of the pastry, to allow the steam to escape. Brush the pie with the beaten egg. You can chill it at this time if wished. Preheat the oven.

9. Bake as for the Cornish Pasties, lowering the heat after 15 minutes. Serve hot or cold.

Variation

Steak and Kidney Plate Pie: use cooked stewing steak and kidney as the filling, drain the cooked meat well and make sure it is cold before adding it to the pastry. In this case the cooking time at the lower setting could be reduced slightly to 20 minutes. Any gravy from cooking the meat can be served with the pie.

BACON AND EGG PIE

This is an old traditional farmhouse pie; it makes an excellent hot dish or it is ideal to take on a picnic. Break the eggs one by one on to a saucer or plate, so it is easy to slide them on top of the bacon.

Oven Setting: 190°C/375°F, Gas Mark 5 or 180°C with a fan oven
Baking Time: 35 minutes plus a few minutes for cooking the bacon
Baking Equipment: one metal 20 cm/8 inch pie plate or flan tin (pan)
Serves: 4 to 6. Do not freeze this dish, the eggs become rubbery.

Metric/Imperial	Ingredients	American
	For the pastry	
350 g/12 oz	*plain (all-purpose) flour, etc.*	3 cups
	For the filling	
350 g/12 oz	*bacon rashers*	¾ lb
4 to 6	*eggs*	4 to 6
	To glaze	
1	*egg, whisked*	1

1. Make the pastry as the directions on page 109 and the information below. Wrap and allow to relax in the refrigerator for 30 minutes.

2. Grill (broil) the rashers or cook them in the microwave. Do not over-cook. If they have rinds remove these; cut the rashers into 2.5 cm/ 1 inch pieces then cool. Hot bacon would make the pastry sticky.

3. Preheat the oven and roll out the pastry until about 8 mm/1/3 inch in thickness. Use just over half to fit the pie plate or tin. Cut away the surplus pastry. Make a level layer of bacon.

4. Break the first egg and slide it over the bacon. Repeat this step with the rest of the eggs; try and get them evenly spaced.

5. Damp the edges of the bottom pastry with a few drops of water on a

pastry brush. Place the rest of the pastry over the top of the filling do not press down too firmly, for you do not want to break the eggs. Cut away the surplus pastry then seal and flute the edges, see stage 6 on page 133.

6. Cut a slit in the centre of the pie to allow the steam to escape so giving crisp pastry. Brush with the egg. Bake until the pastry is golden brown.

NOTE: you may find it easier to cut away the surplus pastry from the bottom and top layers together, not one by one, as in stages 3 and 5.

Variation

Bacon, Egg and Mushroom Pie: discard the stalks form 225 g/8 oz (½ lb) mushrooms, wipe the caps then slice thinly. Heat 25 g/1 oz (2 tablespoons) butter in a frying pan (skillet) and cook the mushrooms for 3 or 4 minutes. Season to taste then cool. Put over the bottom pastry before adding the bacon.

QUICHE LORRAINE

This is one of the most famous of all the savoury custard flans. In order to keep the pastry as crisp as possible, under the moist topping, follow the advice about 'baking blind' on page 115 and stage 5.

Oven Setting:	200°C/400°F, Gas Mark 6 or 190°C with a fan oven then 160°C/325°F, Gas Mark 3 or 150°C with a fan oven
Baking Time:	the pastry case about 15 minutes or until set but still pale in colour, plus a few minutes to cook the bacon. When the filling is added allow about 30 to 35 minutes
Baking Equipment:	one 20 cm/8 inch flan tin (pan) or dish
Makes:	one quiche to serve 4 to 5 people. This freezes very well especially if a little cream is used.

Metric/Imperial	Ingredients	American
	For the pastry	
175 g/6 oz	plain (all-purpose) flour, etc, see page 110	1½ cups
	For the filling	
1	egg white, see stage 5	1
3 or 4	lean bacon rashers (slices), see stage 3	3 or 4
100g/3½ oz	Gruyère or Cheddar cheese, grated	scant 1 cup
2	eggs	2
1	egg yolk	1
150 ml/¼ pint	milk	⅔ cup

5 tablespoons	*single (light) cream*	6¼ tablespoons
to taste	*salt and freshly ground black pepper*	to taste

1. Make the pastry as the directions on page 109. Form into a neat shape, wrap and chill for about 30 minutes if time permits.
2. Line the flan ring or dish and prepare this to 'bake blind', see page 115. Chill for about 20 minutes then bake.
    Meanwhile cook the bacon rashers under the grill (broiler) or in the microwave; drain on kitchen paper (towels), then chop into small pieces and cool.
3. Take the partially baked flan case out of the oven, remove the filling then lower the heat as directed above.
4. Brush the bottom pastry with a very little of the egg white, this forms a good seal.
5. Sprinkle the bacon and cheese over the bottom pastry.
6. Whisk the eggs and egg yolk, add the milk, cream and seasoning. Pour carefully through a strainer (to make sure there are no undissolved pieces of egg) over the bacon and cheese. Sometimes it may appear that you have a little too much custard mixture, save this. Return the flan to the oven for about 5 minutes and you will find the filling sinks slightly and you can pour on the extra custard.
7. Bake until the filling is firm. Remove from the oven and allow to cool or serve hot.

Variation

- Use mixed cooked vegetables, cooked fish or chicken instead of the bacon.

SAUSAGE ROLLS

Sausage Rolls are generally made with light pastry and frozen puff pastry is ideal for this purpose. Details about using this pastry are on page 128. The sheets of frozen puff pastry are an excellent choice as you need strips of pastry to coat the rolls of sausagemeat.

As puff pastry rises quite dramatically when it is baked make sure it is rolled out quite thinly, although the thickness of the coating for the sausagemeat is a matter of personal taste. The recipe uses equal quantities of sausagemeat and commercially made puff pastry. This is enough for a thin pastry coating.

As stressed on page 128 it is essential that you allow sufficient baking time to ensure that the sausagemeat is thoroughly cooked. The initial setting in the oven is high to make certain the pastry rises well. After it has risen, and become lightly browned, it is sensible to reduce the oven heat slightly, as given in the recipe right, this cooks the sausagemeat without over-cooking the pastry.

Other kinds of pastry can be used and details of these are given under Variations.

Oven Setting: 220°C/425°F, Gas Mark 7 or 200°C with a fan oven; after this reduce the heat to 190°C/375°F, Gas Mark 5 or 180°C with a fan oven

Baking Time:	approximately 20 minutes at the higher setting then 5 to 10 minutes at the lower heat	
Baking Equipment:	one or two baking (cookie) trays	
Makes:	this varies with the size of the rolls. If making medium sized rolls you should produce about 12. If making cocktails sized ones about 24 to 30 from the quantities below. The cooked or uncooked rolls can be frozen but make sure they are frozen soon after making or baking, as sausagemeat is highly perishable. The cooked rolls must be cold before being put into the freezer. Defrost in the microwave or in the oven, do NOT leave out at room temperature.	

Metric/Imperial	Ingredients	American
225 g/8 oz	*frozen puff pastry, preferably in sheets*	½ lb
little	**plain (all-purpose) flour**	little
225 g/8 oz	**sausagemeat, flavour to suit personal choice**	½ lb
	To glaze the pastry	
1	*egg, whisked*	1

1. Allow the pastry to defrost, then dust the pastry board and rolling pin with a small amount of flour, do not use too much, for this would spoil the texture of the pastry.
2. The thickness of the puff pastry varies slightly, according to make, but the sheets should be rolled out until about 6 mm/¼ inch in thickness.
3. Form the sausagemeat into several long thin rolls. If using sausages, simply remove the skins before doing this.
4. Cut the pastry into long strips, they should be sufficiently wide to cover the sausagemeat rolls with a little pastry over to give a good seal along the edges.
5. Place the sausagemeat in the centre of each pastry strip, damp the edges of the pastry with a small amount of water.
6. Fold the pastry over the sausagemeat; then press the side edges together. You can 'flake' these to encourage the pastry to rise. To do this hold a small sharp knife horizontally and make light cuts into the pastry edges.
7. Cut each strip into the required number of sausage rolls, then place on the baking tray.
8. Make 2 slits on the top of each sausage roll then brush them with a little egg. Place in the refrigerator to chill for 25 to 30 minutes. This stage is important in setting the shape and encouraging the pastry to rise.
9. Bake as the instructions at the beginning of the recipe. When cooked place on the wire cooling tray. Serve hot or cold. Store cold sausage rolls for a very short time only in the refrigerator.

Variations

- Use Shortcrust Pastry (basic pie dough) made with 225 g/8 oz (2 cups) flour etc., see page 110. This seems a thicker crust when rolling out the pastry but it does not rise in the same way. Bake at 200°C/400°F, Gas Mark 6 or 190°C with a fan oven then reduce to 190°C/375°F, Gas Mark 5 or 180°C with a fan oven.

Use Filo Pastry: read the directions for using this pastry on page 130. Stack 5 sheets of filo pastry, brushing each one with melted butter or oil. Divide the layers into strips, as the basic recipe, then add the sausagemeat. Continue as stage 6 onwards. Use more filo pastry and sausagemeat as required. When the rolls are ready brush these with melted fat or oil and not with egg. Bake as for shortcrust pastry above.

Sardine Rolls: use cooked, boned and mashed fresh sardines or well-drained canned sardines in oil or tomato sauce instead of sausagemeat.

Salmon Rolls: use flaked cooked or canned salmon instead of sausagemeat.

Anchovy Batons: cut strips of puff pastry, about 1.25 cm/½ inch wide and 7.5 cm/3 inches in length. Brush with beaten egg and bake for about 12 minutes or until crisp and brown at the oven setting given. When cooked and cold take very well-drained canned anchovy fillets and twist these around the pastry batons.

Mille Feuilles

Cut the sheets of puff pastry into equal sized squares or fingers. Place on baking sheets and brush with beaten egg. Chill as stage 8 then bake as the instructions at the top of the recipe for about 15 to 20 minutes.

When cooked you can make thick Mille Feuilles by sandwiching two together or thinner ones by carefully cutting the pastry through the centre.

Savoury Mille Feuilles: fill with cream cheese, flavoured with chopped mixed herbs.

Sweet Mille Feuilles: fill with whipped cream and jam. Top with sifted icing (confectioners) sugar.

MAKING BREAD

If you have never made bread before I am going to suggest you buy a small packet of bread mix first. There are many interesting and different kinds, including some favourite Italian types. By buying the complete mix, which only needs the addition of liquid, you will feel very sure that you have the **right flour**, the **right type and quantity** of dried yeast, which is mixed with the flour in the packet. You can then practise and become proficient in the **right handling** of a yeast mixture, see below.

Read and follow the directions very carefully. After this you are then better equipped to make the bread with the flour and yeast you buy.

Using Fresh Yeast

Nowadays it is not easy to buy fresh baker's yeast. Some health food stores sell it and so do some supermarkets. I am therefore going to give you the method using fresh yeast, which I have called Bread No. 1, see page 141 and a second recipe, with the modern easy-to-use and speedy-action dried yeast called Bread No. 2. It is on page 143.

Fresh yeast has advantages. The bread tends to have a better taste and texture and sometimes rises better too. On the other hand if you use fresh yeast it has the disadvantage that you need to 'prove' the dough in bulk and then as a loaf. The word 'prove' is used in yeast cookery to denote the rising of the dough. When making up the ready-packaged bread mixtures, or using sachets of the modern dried yeast, this double action proving is not necessary, so you save a considerable amount of time.

I stress you save *time*, rather than you save *effort* for while the dough is rising you can be doing other things.

Freezing bread: it is sensible to slice the bread before freezing then you can extract just the number of slices required, without defrosting the whole loaf.

Some Terms Used When Handling Yeast Dough

Cooking with yeast as the raising agent means you use a considerable number of special expressions. Here are the most important.

The sponge breaks through: this term is used when you mix fresh yeast with the liquid and a sprinkling of flour. After a short time the surface of the yeast liquid is covered with bubbles, this denotes the 'sponge breaks through'.

Kneading: this is the action when handling the dough to make it smooth and in doing this to distribute the yeast evenly. The right way to knead – and this applies when using bread mixes too – is to pull and push the dough, so stretching it. You use the 'heel' of the hand, i.e. the base of the palm for this.

How can you tell when the dough is sufficiently kneaded?
Press it with a lightly floured finger. This will leave an impression. If the impression **does not** come out the dough is insufficiently kneaded and you should continue. When ready, the impression slowly comes out.

Do not continue kneading after this stage.

Proving: as already explained, this is the term used when you are allowing the dough to rise.

Where should it rise?
You can hasten the proving stage if you place the lightly covered dough or loaf or buns in a warm – but not too hot – a place, such as the airing cupboard or leave it at room temperature.

Some people like to put the dough, or the loaf, into the refrigerator and allow it to prove slowly. Often they do this over-night to give them freshly baked rolls for breakfast. This slow proving is particularly successful when using fresh yeast. It may not be so foolproof with the quicker action dried yeast, as you would not be there to see when the dough has risen correctly.

Can one prove for too long?
Yes, the dough should never rise more than twice its original bulk.

Knocking back: this term applies when the dough rises in bulk and you then turn it out on to a floured surface and knead it until it returns to its original size, ready to be made into loaves or other shapes.

Testing: this is covered in the individual recipes.

Using Yeast
Whether you choose fresh or dried yeast you are using a very special form of raising agent, quite unlike baking powder.

Basically yeast is a living organism, which needs warmth and liquid to make it active. When subjected to heat, as in the oven, it will continue to make the dough rise for a short time, then its purpose is over and dough will no longer rise but will cook through.

Quantities of fresh and dried yeast
Generally speaking you need twice as much fresh yeast as dried yeast, i.e. for each 15 g/½ oz (½ cake compressed) fresh yeast you need 7 g/¼ oz dried (¼ cake compressed) yeast.

Choosing the right flour
In many yeast recipes you should use strong flour, either white or wholemeal (wholewheat). To make brown bread, use equal quantities of white and wholemeal flours. Strong flour ensures the best result for the bread or the particular mixture. It has a high gluten content, which helps to give the dough the capacity to expand and rise well, so producing a light texture, a good shape and a pleasantly crisp crust to the baked bread.

In a few recipes plain flour is given, for that is better for that specific recipe.

Enriched Yeast Dough
Although buns and similar recipes can be made from the same basic plain
yeast dough used for bread, they are much more appetising if they
contain a certain amount of fat, and egg or eggs, and sugar.

This is the reason why the proportion of yeast is often higher in these
recipes than the quantity for the plain dough. The yeast has to raise the
weight of the fat and sugar, and sometimes dried fruit, as well as the flour.

The recipes from page 153 onwards are based upon the enriched
dough. You could make up the relatively small amount given in each
recipe or make up a larger quantity then divide this into portions and add
the extra ingredients for each set of buns.

WHITE BREAD 1

*Do read pages 139 and 140 first, so you are familiar with the special
terms used and you feel confident about embarking on one of the most
pleasurable forms of baking.*

*You can make bread with fresh yeast or with dried yeast. The method
when using modern dried yeast is under Bread 2 on page 143. The classic
recipe below is for bread made with fresh yeast. The instructions cover
the preparation of the bread dough by hand.*

*Information on preparing the bread dough in an electric mixer or food
processor is on page 145. If you become very fond of home-made bread it
would be worthwhile examining the advantages of buying a bread-
maker. This prepares and cooks the bread so the job is virtually done for
you.*

Flour: in either case strong flour (known as hard wheat flour in America)
is the best to use, for reasons to choose this see page 140.

The recipe is based upon 675 g/1½ lb (6 cups) flour to match Bread 2.

If intolerant to wheat you will have to substitute gluten-free flour.

Yeast: if fresh yeast is really fresh it should be evenly creamy-putty
coloured, have a strong smell and crumble easily.

If you buy a considerable amount of fresh yeast it is wise to weigh it
out in 15 g/½ oz amounts, wrap these and store the quantity not being
required in the freezer, for it lasts only about 4 days in a container in the
refrigerator. When you take out the frozen yeast grate this to hasten
creaming.

Sugar: add just a little caster sugar to the yeast liquid.

Salt: do not omit this, it brings out the flavour in the bread.

Fat: not essential but it helps to keep the bread moist.

Oven Setting:	230°C/450°C, Gas Mark 8 or 210 to 220°C with a fan oven
Baking Time:	25 to 30 or 35 to 40 minutes, see stage 12
Baking Equipment:	depends upon the shape required, but for round loaves, one or two flat heavy baking (cookie) sheets or trays
Makes:	one or two loaves. The bread freezes perfectly. Page 139 suggests slicing before freezing.

Metric/Imperial	Ingredients	American
450 ml/¾ pint	water, see stage 1	scant 2 cups
1 teaspoon	caster sugar	1 teaspoon
15 g/½ oz	fresh yeast	½ oz (½ cake)
675 g/1½ lb	strong flour plus a little extra on the board	1½ lb (6 cups)
2 teaspoons	salt	2 teaspoons
15 g/½ oz	butter or lard (shortening) or margarine or olive oil, optional	1 tablespoon

1. To obtain the right temperature water, bring about half the quantity to the boil, add to the remaining cold water. It is now pleasantly warm.
2. Add the sugar to the warm water. Crumble the yeast in a basin then pour about half the warm water on to the yeast, add a dusting of the flour and leave in a warm place until the 'sponge breaks through', i.e. it is topped with bubbles. This takes about 10 minutes.
3. Meanwhile mix or sift the salt with the flour into a large mixing bowl, if using fat rub this into the flour at this stage. If using oil leave until the liquid has been added.
4. Add the yeast liquid to the flour mixture, then gradually add the rest of the liquid. This is the time to add the oil, if using this. Mix well with a knife then with your fingers. The dough should be soft but sufficiently firm to gather together and roll into a ball. Makes of flour vary in the amount of liquid they absorb but you should find the quantity in the recipe is exactly correct.
5. Turn the dough on to a lightly floured board and knead until smooth, see definition of this on pages 139 to 140 and way to tell if sufficiently kneaded. This stage takes about 10 minutes by hand.
6. Put the dough back into the mixing bowl and cover the bowl with lightly greased clingfilm (saran wrap) or a cloth. If preferred put into a large lightly oiled polythene bag, allowing plenty of space for the dough to 'prove' (rise).
7. Put in a warm place or leave in the kitchen until risen almost double the original size. In the kitchen this would take about 1½ to 2 hours, depending on the temperature in the room. In an airing cupboard it would take about 50 to 60 minutes. In a refrigerator about 12 hours.
8. When the dough has risen return it to the board and 'knock back' (knead again); form into a loaf or loaves.
9. The easiest shape is to make one large or two smaller neat rounds of dough and place them on to one or two greased and slightly warmed baking sheets or trays. Allow plenty of space between two loaves for them to rise upwards and outwards.
10. Cover the loaf or loaves very lightly with clingfilm and leave to 'prove' until nearly double in size. This would take about 40 minutes for two smaller loaves at room temperature or 1 hour for a large loaf. In a warm place it would probably take 30 to 40 minutes. In the refrigerator several hours.
11. While the bread is 'proving' preheat the oven. Make sure it has

reached the right temperature before baking.

12. Bake the bread as near the centre of the oven as possible, except in a fan oven where any position should give the same heat. One large loaf will take about 35 to 40 minutes, 2 smaller loaves 25 to 30 minutes.

13. **To test if cooked:** lift the bread off the sheet or tray, give the bottom of the loaf a sharp tap. The bread should sound hollow if cooked. If it does not, replace in the oven for a further few minutes and test again.

14. When cooked place the loaf or loaves on to a wire cooling tray. When cold store in a bread bin or freeze for longer storage.

For information on making other shapes of bread see page 146. For various kinds of bread see page 148.

Adding Ascorbic Acid

Ascorbic acid, or vitamin C, will hasten the process of the dough rising. Dissolve 1 x 50 mg tablet into the warm water at stage 2 in the recipe above.

The nutritional value of vitamin C is lost in the cooking of the bread dough but you will find the 'proving' time at stages 7 and 9 in the recipe above and below will be shortened by some minutes.

WHITE BREAD 2

If you are going to make bread with the quick acting dried yeast you will still find it helpful to read pages 139 and 140 about making bread, as these define the various terms used throughout the preparation.

When using this method of bread making you omit the process where the dough proves in bulk (see stages 6 and 7 under White Bread 1 on page 142). The dough is formed into loaves when kneaded.

Flour: use strong flour (known as hard wheat flour in America). For reasons for choosing this see page 140.

The recipe is based on 675 g/1½ lb (6 cups) flour to match White Bread 1. You may however find packs of dried yeast give slightly varying amounts of flour for their sachets, i.e. from 650 g/1 lb 5 oz (5¼ cups) to 750 g /1 lb 11 oz (6¾ cups). Do not let that bother you just use the yeast with the amount of flour and other ingredients given below.

If intolerant to wheat flour you will have to substitute gluten-free flour.

Yeast: use the modern speedy (easy blend) dried yeast as the method below.

Sugar: add the teaspoon of sugar as method below.

Salt: add salt as below, do not omit for it gives flavour to the bread.

Fat: not essential but it helps to keep the bread moist.

Oven Setting:	230°C/450°F, Gas Mark 8 or 210 to 220°C with a fan oven. Some packets of dried yeast do suggest starting at 240°C/475°F, Gas Mark 9. I find that is too hot, but if your oven tends to be on the cool

side it is a good idea to preheat at this setting then
turn down to 230°C, etc.

Baking Time: 25 to 30 minutes or 35 to 40 minutes, see stage 9
Baking Equipment: depends upon the shape desired but for round
loaves one or two flat heaving baking (cookie)
trays or sheets
Makes: one or two loaves. The bread freezes perfectly.
Page 139 suggests slicing before freezing.

Metric/Imperial	Ingredients	American
675 g/1½ lb	**strong flour plus a little extra on the board**	1½ lb (6 cups)
2 teaspoons	**salt**	2 teaspoons
1 teaspoon	**caster sugar**	1 teaspoon
15 g/½ oz	**butter or lard (shortening) or margarine or olive oil, optional**	1 tablespoon
1 x 7g sachet	**speedy (easy blend) dried yeast**	1 x 7g sachet
450 ml/¾ pint	**warm water, see stage 3**	scant 2 cups

1. Sift or mix the flour, salt and sugar in a mixing bowl. Rub in the fat if using this. Do not add the oil at this stage.
2. Add the dried yeast and mix well.
3. Bring half the water to boiling point then mix with the remaining cold water, this will give the right temperature for warm water.
4. Mix in the water with a knife then with your fingers. This is the time to add the oil, if using this.
5. The dough should form into a soft elastic-textured dough. Turn on to the lightly floured board and knead until smooth. Pages 139 to 140 define kneading and a way to tell if sufficiently kneaded. This stage takes about 10 minutes by hand.
6. Form the dough into one large round loaf or 2 smaller rounds. Ways to make other shaped loaves are on page 146.
7. Place the loaf or loaves on to one or two lightly greased and slightly warmed baking sheets or trays. Cover lightly with oiled clingfilm (saran wrap) and leave to 'prove' (rise). This will take approximately 30 to 35 minutes in a warm place or about 40 to 45 minutes at room temperature. The loaves should rise to nearly twice their original size(s).
8. While the loaves are rising preheat the oven.
9. Bake the bread as near the centre of the oven as possible, except for a fan oven where any position should give the same heat. One large loaf will take 35 to 40 minutes, the smaller loaves 25 to 30 minutes.
10. **To test if cooked:** lift the bread off the sheet or tray, give the bottom of the loaf a sharp tap. The bread should sound hollow if cooked. If it does not replace in the oven for a further few minutes then test again.
11. When cooked place the bread on a wire cooling tray. When cold store in the bread bin or freeze for longer storage.

USING EQUIPMENT FOR KNEADING YEAST DOUGHS

The following information gives the method of handling the yeast dough with a large electric mixer or a food processor. Different makes of machines vary in the kind of attachments they provide but the following gives general advice.

Using an Electric Mixer
Use the dough hook.
   a) In Bread 1 recipe the initial stage of creaming yeast and rubbing in fat should be done by hand.
   b) In all yeast recipes when the liquid has been added to the flour and other ingredients, use the dough hook to knead the mixture. Set the machine to a low speed.
   c) Check the progress of kneading carefully, for the electric mixer gives a more vigorous action than hand kneading. Stop the machine.
   d) **Test the dough.** To do this press with a floured finger. If the impression comes out then the dough is ready for the next stage.
   e) The dough hook can be used for 'knocking back' the dough in Bread 1 recipe, see page 140 for the definition of this term.

Using a Food Processor
Use the kneading attachment.
   Always check with the manufacturer's instructions as to the maximum amount of dough that can be kneaded in the machine.
   a) In Bread 1 recipe the initial stage of creaming the yeast should be done by hand. After that the fat and flour, etc. can be put into the food processor with the usual cutting attachment in place, for the machine incorporates the fat into flour, as though rubbing in by hand.
   b) In all yeast recipes before the liquid has been added to the flour and other ingredients, the cutting attachment should be replaced with the kneading one. The action of a food processor is so vigorous that it is advisable to check whether the dough has been sufficiently kneaded after just a minute. The method of testing is given above in stage d).
   c) The kneading attachment can be used for **'knocking back'** the dough in the Bread 1 recipe, see page 140 for the definition of this term.

SHAPING BREAD DOUGH

Having prepared bread dough as Bread 1 or Bread 2 on pages 141 and 143 you may want to make this into a different shape from that described under the recipes. Here are some alternatives.
   In each case I would suggest you use half the amount of dough to form your chosen loaf. This means you could make two loaves of different shapes or you could make one loaf and a batch of rolls, as given on the following pages.
   Follow the baking time and temperature as given in the recipes.

Bloomer Loaf

Make the dough into a long and fat sausage shape. Place it on the baking tray. Make cuts at regular intervals along the loaf, the knife should be inserted about 1.25 cm/½ inch into the dough, no deeper.

Prove and bake as the recipe.

Cob Loaf

This is similar to the rounds of bread in the recipes. A true cob loaf should have an X shape marked on the dough with a floured knife.

Prove and bake as the recipe.

Cottage Loaf

Divide the dough into two portions; the first should be twice as large as the second. This will be the base of the loaf.

Form this into a round and place on the baking tray.

Form the smaller amount of dough into a round and place this in the centre of the larger portion, press it down gently.

Take the handle of a wooden spoon and insert the tip of this through the top ball of dough. This will give an indentation and make the two amounts of dough adhere together.

Prove and bake as the recipe.

Tin Loaf

If you divide the 675 g/1½ lb (6 cups) of flour etc. given in Bread 1 and Bread 2 into halves to make two loaves you will need two 675 g/1½ lb (6 cup) size loaf tins or you may decide to make one tin loaf and one other shape or one tin loaf and rolls as the instructions on page 147.

Put the dough on to a pastry board and firmly press it out until you have a neat oblong shape. This should measure the length of the bread tin you will use and three times its width. Fold the dough over so it now becomes the size of the tin.

Lightly grease the loaf tin then insert the dough, making sure the joins are placed at the bottom of the loaf, so you have an attractive rounded top to the loaf.

The dough should come about ⅔ up the tin, so giving plenty of space for the dough to rise.

Prove and bake as the recipe.

Flowerpot Loaf

One of the most successful containers for cooking bread made with yeast is to put the dough into a new well cleaned then greased clay flowerpot. The material is ideal for baking.

Place the dough in the flowerpot, allow room for it to 'prove' (rise) then bake in the usual way.

Because of the greater depth of the flowerpot loaf you may find you need to bake it for 5 or 6 minutes longer time than other loaves but test in the usual way.

MAKING ROLLS

Small rolls are one of the best ways to start handling yeast dough; you can enjoy creating a selection of various shapes from a basic yeast mixture.

1. Make up the dough as Bread 1 or Bread 2 recipes on pages 141 and 143. The full quantity from either of these recipes, using 675 g/ 1½ lb (6 cups) flour, etc., would make 20 to 24 medium sized rolls. It may therefore be wiser to use half the dough to make one loaf and then use the remaining half to produce rolls.
2. Divide the dough into equal sized portions, form these into the desired shapes. You can make **batons**, these are finger shapes, and they look more interesting if the dough has one or two light cuts on top before proving. You can make miniature **cobs** or **cottage loaves** as in the sketches.
3. Place the rolls on a lightly greased baking (cookie) tray, allowing space between them, for they do spread out slightly as well as rise.
4. Allow rolls to prove (rise) until nearly double the original size. The proving time will be under half the time needed for a loaf, i.e. they should be ready to bake within about 20 minutes but this will vary with the temperature of the room.
5. Preheat the oven as given for the loaves, see pages 141 and 143, i.e. 230°C/450°F, Gas Mark 8 or 210°C with a fan oven.
6. Place the tray of rolls just above the centre of the oven, except with a fan oven, where all shelves should give the same heat.
7. Allow 10 to 12 minutes baking time, or until the rolls are firm and golden in colour. Lift from the baking tray on to a wire cooling tray.

Variation

- To make soft rolls, like a **Scottish Bap**, use half milk and half water to make the yeast dough as Bread 1 or Bread 2 on pages 141 and 143. Make half the dough into a loaf. Form the remaining dough into 8 to 10 oval shapes, place on the lightly greased baking tray. Brush the tops with milk and add a light dusting of flour. Prove and bake as stage 4 to 7 above.

Make use of Seeds

Edible seeds add food value as well as interest to bread and rolls. There are many kinds from which to choose but the most popular are **poppy seeds, sesame seeds, sunflower seeds** and **caraway seeds**. These are obtainable from health food stores or supermarkets.

The seeds should be lightly sprinkled over the top of the loaf or rolls before these are allowed to prove.

You can add 1 to 1½ level teaspoons of seeds to the 675 g/1½ lb (6 cups) flour in Bread 1 or Bread 2 on pages 141 and 143. Caraway seeds, usually associated with cakes, are particularly good in the bread.

Make use of Herbs

Try adding chopped parsley, coriander (cilantro), basil, rosemary or other herbs to bread. To each 675 g/1½ lb (6 cups) of flour in Bread 1 and Bread 2 on pages 141 and 143 add 2 (2½) level tablespoons of the herbs.

VARYING THE BREAD

It is easy to adapt a basic bread recipe and produce other flavours. Here are some ideas.

Follow the method under Bread 1 on page 142 or Bread 2 on page 143.

Brown Bread: use the quantity of strong flour in either bread recipe but use half wholemeal (wholewheat) and half white flour. You will need to add approximately ½ tablespoon of extra milk as the wholemeal flour absorbs more liquid. The loaves may need a few minutes longer baking time.

Cheese Bread: sift a good shake of black pepper and 1 teaspoon dry mustard powder with the flour and salt. Add 150 g/5 oz (1¼ cups) grated Cheddar cheese to the flour, also see page 164 for another recipe.

Fruit Bread: increase the amount of sugar in either bread recipe to 1 tablespoon and add 115 to 175 g/4 to 6 oz (⅔ to 1 cup) of currants or other dried fruit to the flour.

Malt Bread: add 4 (5) tablespoons malt extract to the flour, etc. As this has a liquid content you need approximately 4 (5) less tablespoons of water. A tablespoon of black treacle (molasses) can be added with the malt.

Milk Bread: mix the dough with warm milk instead of warm water. For a richer milk loaf increase the amount of fat in either recipe to 25 g/1 oz (2 tablespoons). Butter is best. You can omit 2 (2½) tablespoons of liquid and add 1 beaten egg to the flour mixture. A **Sweet Milk Loaf** is made as above but with the addition of 2 (2½) tablespoons caster sugar.

Nut Bread: add 150 g/5 oz (1¼ cups) chopped walnuts or other nuts or mixed nuts to the flour.

Wholemeal Bread: use wholemeal (wheatmeal) flour instead of white flour. You will need 1 to 1½ tablespoons extra liquid to mix the dough and the baking time for the loaves may be slightly longer.

For information on shaping bread see page 146.

BRIDGE ROLLS

These are a very good and attractive form of bread to make and they are ideal for sandwiches. Often small bridge rolls, the type needed for a teatime or buffet party, are not readily available. The dough used is slightly richer than the usual bread dough. If you prefer to make larger rolls the quantity and baking time is given under Variations.

I have given the recipe based on making a large quantity of small rolls, for these freeze very well.

Oven Setting: 220°C/425°F, Gas Mark 7 or 190 to 200°C with a fan oven
Baking Time: 10 minutes
Baking Equipment: one or two large baking (cookie) trays
Makes: approximately 30 small rolls.

Metric/Imperial	Ingredients	American
450 g/1 lb	**strong white flour**	4 cups
1/2 teaspoon	*salt*	1/2 teaspoon
1 x 7g sachet	*speedy (easy blend) dried yeast*	1 x 7g sachet
2 teaspoons	*caster sugar*	2 teaspoons
50 g/2 oz	*butter or margarine*	1/4 cup
150 ml/1/4 pint	*boiling water*	2/3 cup
150 ml/1/4 pint	*cold milk*	2/3 cup
	To glaze	
1 or 2	*eggs, whisked*	1 or 2

1. Lightly grease the baking trays.
2. Sift the flour and salt into a mixing bowl; add the yeast and sugar. Rub in the butter or margarine.
3. Mix the boiling water with the cold milk then pour into the bowl. Stir thoroughly then gather the mixture together with your fingers and turn on to a floured surface. You should have a soft but easy to handle dough; see the detailed comments under Bread on page 139.
4. Knead the dough with the 'heel' of the hand, see page 139. It can be done on a slow speed in an electric mixer or food processor. To test if sufficiently kneaded, press the dough with a floured finger, see page 140.
5. Divide the dough into about 30 portions, form into finger shapes. Put on to trays, allowing room for the rolls to spread out slightly as well as rise. During this stage preheat the oven.
6. Brush the tops with the beaten egg(s). Place clingfilm (saran wrap) loosely over the trays and leave to prove at room temperature for about 35 minutes or until the rolls have risen almost twice their original height.
7. Place in the oven and bake. When firm remove on to a wire cooling tray.

Variations

- If using strong brown flour use 1 tablespoon extra liquid. With wholemeal flour use 1½ extra tablespoons liquid.
- If you prefer to use the whole of a 500 g/1 lb 2 oz (4½ cup) bag of flour, increase the water and milk quantity by 1 tablespoonful. Check the consistency at stage 3. There is no need to alter the amounts of yeast, sugar and butter or margarine.

Larger Bridge Rolls: make approximately 15 larger rolls and increase the baking time by 2 to 3 minutes. You may need to allow an extra 5 to 10 minutes longer proving time at stage 6.

IRISH SODA BREAD

To many people this traditional bread is one of the nicest of all varieties. It is soft and light and it does not require any yeast. It is advisable to make this bread with ordinary plain (all-purpose) flour, either white or wholemeal (wholewheat). Do not use strong flour – the kind used for many yeast breads. When ovens were not common in Irish homes the bread would be baked on a flat griddle on top of the stove but today most cooks in Ireland prefer to use an oven.

The recipe below is based upon buttermilk, which is obtainable from supermarkets. If you would rather use fresh milk see under Variations.

It is better to cook the bread on a heavy baking sheet rather than a lighter baking (cookie) tray.

Oven Setting: 220°C/425°F, Gas Mark 7 or 210°C with a fan oven
Baking Time: 30 minutes
Baking Equipment: one baking sheet
Makes: one large round loaf. Eat when fresh. Freezes well.

Metric/Imperial	Ingredients	American
450 g/1 lb	plain white or wholemeal flour	1 lb
1 level teaspoon or to taste	salt	1 level teaspoon or to taste
½ level teaspoon	bicarbonate of soda (baking soda)	½ level teaspoon
½ level teaspoon	cream of tartar	½ level teaspoon
300 ml/½ pint or amount required	buttermilk	1⅓ cups or amount required

1. Preheat the oven. There is no need to grease the baking sheet or tray.
2. Sift the flour with the salt, bicarbonate of soda and cream of tartar into a good-sized mixing bowl. Gradually add the buttermilk. Various makes of flour absorb different quantities of liquid; the dough must be soft, but not sticky.
3. Turn out on to a lightly floured surface and shape into a round with your hands. This should be from 2.5 to 3 cm/1 to 1¼ inches in thickness.

4. Place on the baking sheet then gently mark the loaf into 4 good-sized sections, known as farls, with a knife. Do not cut right through the loaf.
5. Bake for 30 minutes or until firm, in the centre of the oven. Remove on to a wire cooling tray. If you like the bread to be soft, wrap it in a teacloth (dish towel) to cool.

Variations

- Use ordinary milk to mix the bread and increase the amount of cream of tartar to 1 level teaspoon.
- Some stores sell special Irish bread flour, which already has raising agents included. Follow the directions of the packet for mixing.
- Use ordinary self-raising flour, add the salt. Mix with buttermilk. You could use ordinary milk but the bread will not be quite as light.

Freezing Bread and Cakes
It is a good idea to slice bread and cakes before freezing. This enables you to remove just the number of slices required – without defrosting the whole loaf or cake. If you have made a rather elaborate cake you could separate the slices with squares of baking parchment, so making them very easy to remove.

AMERICAN CORNBREADS

American cornbreads are quick breads without yeast that substitute cornmeal (polenta) for some or all of the flour. They can include many different flavourings such as cheese, bacon, onion, snipped fresh herbs or even chilli. Cornbreads can also be cooked to be thin and crisp or thick and light by simply varying the size and depth of the pan you use. They are traditionally served warm with butter to accompany main meals and are delicious with soups.

GOLDEN CORNBREAD

This is an excellent recipe; it was given to me by Orlando Murrin, who is the editor of the BBC, Good Food Magazine. *He extolled the recipe and he is quite right it is outstandingly good. The amount of baking powder seems excessive but is necessary for the heavy moist ingredients. Cornmeal is becoming more readily available but fine polenta is a good alternative.*

Oven Setting: 180°C/350°F, Gas Mark 4 or 170°C with a fan oven
Baking Time: 45 to 55 minutes
Baking Equipment: one 20 cm/8 inch square cake tin (pan)
Makes: one loaf giving 8 to 10 slices; keeps reasonably well for 2 days. Freezes well.

Metric/Imperial	Ingredients	American
250 g/9 oz	**cornmeal or polenta**	2¼ cups
325 g/11 oz	**plain (all-purpose) flour**	2¾ cups
100 g/3½ oz	**golden* caster sugar**	scant ½ cup

7 level teaspoons	baking powder	7 level teaspoons
3/4 level teaspoon	salt	3/4 level teaspoon
2 large	eggs	2 large
450 ml/16 fl oz	milk	2 cups
25 g/1 oz	butter, melted	2 tablespoons

* this refers to natural (unbleached) sugar

1. Preheat the oven, lightly butter the tin and if you wish line the base with baking paper, as I do find cornbread has an inclination to stick.
2. In a large bowl, mix the cornmeal or polenta, flour, sugar, baking powder and salt. Set aside.
3. Lightly beat the eggs, then add the milk and butter. Slowly stir this mixture into the cornmeal or polenta and stop immediately it is incorporated. Scrape the batter into the tin.
4. Bake until light brown and a skewer inserted into the centre comes out clean. Transfer to a wire cooling tray to cool, then cut in wedges. Serve warm or as fresh as possible after baking, with butter.

NOTE: you need a generous amount of baking powder and sugar. The baking powder raises the damp mixture.

LUXURY CORNBREAD

This cornbread, the recipe for which was given to me by my publisher, Anne Dolamore, is both rich and sweet, so it could be served with tea or coffee without butter. The baking time is short because the mixture is spread thinly over a large area. Check this early for the bread dries if over-cooked.

Oven Setting: 180°C/350°F, Gas Mark 4 or 160 to 170°C with a fan oven

Baking Time: 25 to 30 minutes

Baking Equipment: one Swiss roll tin (jelly pan) measuring 33 x 23 cm/ 13 x 9 inches, see stage 1

Makes: one large Cornbread, which should be eaten warm or freshly baked. It can be frozen.

Metric/Imperial	Ingredients	American
225 g/8 oz	self-raising flour or plain (all-purpose) flour with 2 teaspoons baking powder	2 cups
1/2 teaspoon	baking powder	1/2 teaspoon
1/2 teaspoon	salt	1/2 teaspoon
150 g/5 oz	cornmeal or fine polenta	1 1/4 cups
175 g/6 oz	caster or granulated sugar	3/4 cup
300 ml/1/2 pint	single (light) cream	1 1/4 cups
225 g/8 oz	butter	1 cup
2 large	eggs, lightly whisked	2 large

1. Preheat the oven. Grease and flour the tin; it should have a depth of at least 2 cm/³⁄₄ inches. If more shallow line the tin with greased greaseproof (wax) paper or baking parchment and allow this to stand well above the edges of the tin.
2. Sift the flour, or flour and baking powder, with the extra baking powder and salt. Add the cornmeal or polenta and sugar.
3. Pour the cream into a saucepan, cut the butter into small pieces, add to the cream and heat until the butter has melted. This could be done in a bowl in the microwave. Cool slightly then pour on to the dry ingredients and mix together.
4. Lastly add the eggs and mix well. Spoon the thick batter into the prepared tin, spreading it evenly. Bake until the bread is lightly browned and firm to the touch. Cool in the tin for a few minutes before placing on a cooling tray then cutting into fingers or squares.

Variation

- Use full-cream milk instead of cream.

ENRICHED DOUGH TO MAKE BUNS AND TEACAKES

This is the basic dough from which the recipes that follow are made, do read the extra information on page 139 too. Each recipe will have slightly different ingredients added but the technique of mixing is the same. White flour is used for all buns but if choosing wholemeal (wholewheat) strong flour, add 1 to 1½ extra tablespoons of liquid.

Metric/Imperial	Ingredients	American
350 g/12 oz	**strong white flour plus extra that may be needed for handling the dough**	3 cups
pinch	*salt*	pinch
1 x 7g sachet	*speedy (easy blend) dried yeast*	1 x 7g sachet
25 g/1 oz	*caster sugar*	2 tablespoons
50 g/2 oz	*butter or margarine*	¼ cup
150 ml/¼ pint	*warm milk, see stage 3*	⅔ cup
1	*egg, whisked*	1 egg

1. Put the flour, salt and yeast into a mixing bowl; blend well.
2. Add the sugar, then rub in the butter or margarine until the mixture is like fine breadcrumbs. Advice on 'rubbing-in' is under pastry on page 109.
3. Bring half the milk to boiling point; add to the rest of the cold milk. This gives just the right temperature.
4. Pour on to the flour mixture, add the egg and mix well with a knife then with your fingers. You should have a reasonably soft dough.
5. Turn the dough on to a lightly floured board and knead thoroughly. Follow the directions for kneading given on pages 139 or 140. The dough is now ready to make the recipes that follow.

SALLY LUNS

These are rich teacakes; you can follow the Enriched Yeast Dough exactly as above but they can be made with just 1 teaspoon of sugar.

Each teacake serves two people.

1. Follow the recipe above to stage 5 and then divide the dough into two portions.
2. Grease and slightly warm two sandwich tins (layer pans), the type used for making a Victoria Sandwich, measuring about 15 cm/6 inch in diameter. Press each portion of dough into the tin. You could use slightly larger tins if more convenient but you do not get such deep teacakes.
3. Lightly cover the top of the tins with clingfilm (saran wrap) and leave to 'prove' (rise) until nearly double in size. This should take about 25 to 30 minutes but will depend on the room temperature.
4. Preheat the oven to 220°C/425°F, Gas Mark 7 or 200°C with a fan oven.
5. Place the tins in the oven and bake for approximately 15 minutes or until well risen and firm.
6. These teacakes are generally glazed to give a sticky sweet topping. **To make the glaze:** blend 1 tablespoon caster sugar with 1 tablespoon boiling water, brush over the hot tea cakes. Leave for 5 minutes then remove these from the tins on to a wire cooling tray.
7. Serve when freshly baked with butter. They freeze well.

CHELSEA BUNS

These have a long tradition and were particularly popular in the London area. The Enriched Dough recipe should give you exactly the right texture to roll and then cover with the fruit mixture. It should be softer than a pastry dough.

Oven Setting:　220°C/425°F, Gas Mark 7 or 190 to 200°C with a fan oven
Baking Time:　15 to 20 minutes
Baking Equipment:　one 23 to 25 cm/9 to 10 inch square cake tin, see stage 3
Makes:　about 9 to 12 buns. These should be eaten when freshly cooked but they freeze well.

Metric/Imperial	Ingredients	American
	Ingredients as Enriched Dough page 153 plus:	
50 g/2 oz	butter or margarine, softened	1/4 cup
good pinch	ground cinnamon	good pinch
good pinch	grated or ground nutmeg	good pinch
50 g/2 oz	caster or soft light brown sugar	1/4 cup
100 g/3 1/2 oz	mixed dried fruit	2/3 cup

For the glaze

2 tablespoons	**caster sugar**	*2½ tablespoons*
2 tablespoons	**boiling water**	*2½ tablespoons*

1. Make the Enriched Yeast Dough and proceed as far as stage 5. Knead the dough well, see pages 139 and 140.
2. Place the dough on a lightly floured board and roll out to a large oblong shape about 1.25 cm/½ inch in thickness. You should have two long sides about 30 cm/12 inches in length and two shorter sides about 20 cm/8 inches in length.
3. Stand the butter in the kitchen to soften; do NOT melt it. Mix the spices and the butter, spread over the dough. Sprinkle the sugar and dried fruit on top of the butter.
4. Make a slight fold along one of the long sides then continue rolling up the dough; do this lightly and without pressure, for the yeast dough must have room to rise well. Grease the cake tin.
5. Cut the roll into 9 larger or 12 smaller portions and place these into the greased tin, they should be fairly tightly packed so the buns keep a good shape. Cover the top of the tin with clingfilm (saran wrap) and allow them to 'prove' until nearly double in size. This will take about 35 to 40 minutes at a warm room temperature.
6. Meanwhile preheat the oven. Place the tin of buns in the oven and bake until these are firm. Check after about 12 minutes and, if the buns are becoming rather too brown, lower the heat slightly.
7. Mix the sugar and water; bring the buns out of the oven and brush with the glaze. Leave for about 5 minutes then remove from the tin on to a wire cooling tray.

FRUIT BUNS

While these can be made by adding several tablespoons of mixed dried fruit to a small quantity of an ordinary bread dough, such as the recipes on pages 141 and 143, then shaping the mixture into balls, as stage 6, you will have much richer and more interesting buns if you use a richer dough as below.

Oven Setting: 220°C/425°F, Gas Mark 7 or 190 to 200°C with a fan oven

Baking Time: 12 to 15 minutes, depending upon the size

Baking Equipment: one or two flat baking (cookie) trays (pans)

Makes: 10 to 12 buns. Eat when freshly baked although they can be split and toasted if they become stale. They freeze very well. Defrost at room temperature or on a low setting with the microwave or at 150 to 160°C/300 to 325°F, Gas Mark 2 or 3 or 140°C with a fan oven.

Metric/Imperial	Ingredients	American
350 g/12 oz	**strong white flour**	*3 cups*
pinch	**salt**	*pinch*

1 x 7g sachet	*speedy (easy blend) dried yeast*	*1 x 7g sachet*
25 g/1 oz	*caster sugar*	*2 tablespoons*
50 g/2 oz	*butter or margarine*	*¼ cup*
85 g/3 oz	*mixed dried fruit*	*½ cup*
2 tablespoons	*chopped mixed crystallized (candied) peel*	*2½ tablespoons*
150 ml/¼ pint	*warm milk or milk and water, see stage 3*	*⅔ cup*
1	*egg, whisked*	*1*
	For the glaze	
2 tablespoons	*caster sugar*	*2½ tablespoons*
2 tablespoons	*boiling water*	*2½ tablespoons*

1. Put the flour, salt and yeast into a mixing bowl, blend well.
2. Add the sugar, then rub in the butter or margarine until the mixture is like fine breadcrumbs. Advice on 'rubbing-in' is under pastry, page 109.
3. Add the dried fruit and peel. Bring half the milk, or milk and water, to boiling point, add to the remainder of the cold liquid. This gives just the right temperature.
4. Stir the warm liquid and then the egg into the other ingredients. Mix with a knife and then with your fingers. You should have a reasonably soft dough.
5. Turn out and knead until smooth, there are full directions for kneading on pages 139 and 140. If the dough seems a little sticky you can sprinkle a little flour on to the working surface and your fingers but do not make the dough too dry, this will spoil the buns.
6. Divide the dough into 10 or 12 equal-sized portions, roll each into a neat ball and place on the lightly greased baking tray(s). Leave plenty of space between the balls for the buns rise and spread out too.
7. Leave to 'prove' until almost double in size, this will take an average of 30 to 35 minutes at a warm room temperature.
8. Meanwhile preheat the oven. Place the tray(s) of buns into the oven and bake for 12 to 15 minutes or until firm and golden brown.
9. Mix the sugar with the boiling water. Take the buns out of the oven but leave on the tray(s). Brush the top of each bun with the glaze. Leave for a few minutes then remove from the tray(s) on to a wire cooling tray. Serve when freshly made.

RICH FRUIT LOAF

1. Make the mixture in exactly the same way as the Fruit Buns above but instead of forming the mixture into buns, as stage 6, shape the dough into one round loaf.
2. Place on a greased baking sheet or tray and allow to prove until almost double the original size. As it is a fairly large amount of a richer dough this may take up to 45 minutes or more in the temperature of an average kitchen.
3. Preheat the oven to the temperature given in the recipe above.

4. Place the loaf in the oven then bake for 20 minutes. At the end of this time check on the baking progress; if the loaf is becoming rather brown lower the heat to 190°C/375°F, Gas Mark 5 or 180°C with a fan oven and continue baking for a further 10 to 15 minutes, or until the loaf is completely cooked.
5. Remove on to a wire cooling tray. Cut into thin slices and spread with butter. This loaf will keep for 2 or 3 days in an airtight container.

HOT CROSS BUNS

These are made like the Fruit Buns on page 155 but traditionally Hot Cross Buns are well-flavoured with spice.

1. Sift 1 teaspoon ground cinnamon or mixed spice and ½ teaspoon grated or ground nutmeg with the flour at stage 1 opposite. Proceed as stages 1 to the end of stage 5 in the Fruit Buns.
2. Divide the buns into equal-sized portions, roll into balls and place on the baking tray(s).
3. **To make the cross on each bun:**
   Method 1: mark a X in the centre of each bun; allow the knife to penetrate through the dough to a depth of at least 2 cm/¾ inch; this is important for as the dough rises in proving then in baking, the marks could be obliterated unless sufficiently deep.
   Method 2: make a flour and water paste by mixing 4 (5) tablespoons of plain white flour with enough water to give a firm rolling consistency. Roll out until quite thin, then cut short lengths. Form two of these into a cross shape on top of each bun, press them down firmly on to the dough.
4. Let the buns prove as stage 7 of Fruit Buns; preheat the oven, as stage 8.
5. Bake the buns as stage 8. If you are going to eat them immediately after baking they can be glazed as stage 9.
6. If you have made the buns before Good Friday it is quite sensible to glaze the buns after they have been reheated in the oven or microwave.
   To reheat the buns on Good Friday: use a very low setting in the microwave, this prevents the mixture becoming over-firm and dry. Two buns take about ½ a minute only. Allow 8 to 10 minutes in a preheated oven 150 to 160°C/300 to 325°F, Gas Mark 2 to 3 or 140°C in a fan oven. Glaze the buns after heating.

BATH BUNS

These are one of the most interesting traditional yeast buns. They have become very scarce in recent years so it would be a treat for people to enjoy home-made ones. The dough is quite rich but, like all yeast buns, they should be eaten when fresh, or frozen for eating later.

Oven Setting: 220°C/425°F, Gas Mark 7 to 190 to 200°C with a fan oven
Baking Time: 15 to 20 minutes
Baking Equipment: two baking (cookie) trays

| **Makes:** | 10 to 12 buns. These should be eaten when freshly made but they freeze well. | |

Metric/Imperial	*Ingredients*	*American*
350 g/12 oz	**strong flour**	*3 cups*
pinch	*salt*	*pinch*
1 x 7g sachet	**speedy (easy blend) dried yeast**	*1 x 7g sachet*
25 g/1 oz	**caster sugar**	*2 tablespoons*
115 g/4 oz	**butter or margarine**	*¹/₂ cup*
50 g/2 oz	**chopped mixed crystallized (candied) peel**	*¹/₃ cup*
115 g/4 oz	**mixed dried fruit**	*²/₃ cup*
150 ml/¹/₄ pint	**warm milk, see stage 3**	*²/₃ cup*
2	*eggs, whisked*	*2*
	For the topping	
5 lumps	*loaf sugar*	*5 lumps*

1. Put the flour, salt and yeast into a mixing bowl; blend well.
2. Add the sugar then rub in the butter or margarine, until the mixture looks like fine breadcrumbs. Advice on 'rubbing-in' is given under pastry on page 109. Add the peel and fruit.
3. Bring half the milk to boiling point then add it to the cold milk, this gives exactly the right temperature to the liquid.
4. Pour nearly all the milk into the flour mixture then add the eggs, stir together with a knife then with your fingers. The dough should be soft, but sufficiently firm to handle. Bath Buns need a softer dough than other buns.
5. Gradually add the last of the liquid or enough to give this soft dough.
6. Turn on to a lightly floured board and knead. You will find the more it is kneaded the better the texture becomes. See advice on kneading on pages 139 and 140.
7. Divide into 10 to 12 portions and form these into soft rounds, they are too soft to make balls, as Fruit Buns. Place on the lightly greased baking trays. Allow plenty of space for the mixture to spread out in proving and baking.
8. Lightly crush the lumps of sugar. The easiest way to do this is to put them into a plastic bag and press down with a rolling pin. You should have small pieces. Spoon these evenly over the top of the buns.
9. Allow the buns to prove until twice their original size. In view of the amount of fat and fruit they may take at least 45 minutes in the average kitchen heat.
10. Meanwhile preheat the oven. Bake until firm. Check the baking after about 12 minutes and, if the buns are getting too brown, lower the heat to 190°C/375°F, Gas Mark 5 or 180°C with a fan oven. Lift off the trays on to a wire cooling tray.

TEABREADS

Teabreads of various kinds make a pleasant change from ordinary bread and often can take the place of a cake. Slices of teabread, such as the one below and the Banana Bread, are excellent with cheese salads or vegetable soups. They can make an unusual basis for cheese sandwiches too.

WALNUT AND DATE TEABREAD

This recipe produces a pleasantly moist loaf. Do not chop the walnuts too finely, it will make the loaf too dry as very finely chopped walnuts become like a flour.

Oven Setting: 160°C/325°F, Gas Mark 3 or 150°C with a fan oven
Baking Time: 1¼ hours
Baking Equipment: one 900 g/2 lb loaf tin (pan)
Makes: one loaf. Keeps for several days, freezes well.

Metric/Imperial	Ingredients	American
225 g/8 oz	cooking dates, chopped	1⅓ cup
50 g/2 oz	butter or margarine	¼ cup
100 g/3½ oz	caster sugar	scant ½ cup
150 ml/¼ pint	water	⅔ cup
1	egg, whisked	1
225 g/8 oz	self-raising flour or plain (all-purpose) flour with 2 level teaspoons baking powder	2 cups
½ level teaspoon	bicarbonate of soda (baking soda)	½ level teaspoon
115 g/4 oz	walnuts, chopped	1 cup

1. Preheat the oven. Grease and flour or line the loaf tin.
2. Put the dates, butter or margarine, sugar and water into a good-sized saucepan and bring the liquid to the boil. Remove from the heat and leave until cold.
3. Add the egg to the mixture. Sift the flour, or flour and baking powder, with the bicarbonate of soda, stir into the other ingredients together with the walnuts.
4. Spoon into the tin and bake until firm to the touch. Allow to cool in the tin for 5 minutes then turn out.
5. Serve thinly sliced and spread with butter.

Variations

- Use 3 (3¾) tablespoons olive or sunflower oil instead of the butter or margarine, do not heat this at stage 2. Add before the egg at stage 3.

Walnut and Cranberry Loaf: substitute 175 g/6 oz (1½ cups) fresh whole cranberries for the dates. Increase the sugar to 150 g/5 oz (⅝ cup). Heat the cranberries at stage 2 with the butter, sugar and water until the berries are softened then allow to cool. Proceed as the recipe from stage 3 onwards.

BANANA BREAD

This is a very pleasant teabread that keeps remarkably moist for several days. Use ripe, but not over-ripe, bananas. As these vary so much in size I have given the weight of the bananas in their skins, as this provides the most accurate measurement.

Oven Setting:	180°C/350°F, Gas Mark 4 or 160 to 170°C with a fan oven	
Baking Time:	45 to 50 minutes	
Baking Equipment:	one 900 g/2 lb loaf tin (pan)	
Makes:	one loaf that keeps well for several days and freezes moderately well for up to three weeks, after that it seems to lose a lot of flavour.	

Metric/Imperial	*Ingredients*	*American*
115 g/4 oz	**butter or margarine**	*½ cup*
115 g/4 oz	**caster sugar**	*½ cup*
½ teaspoon	**vanilla extract* or essence**	*½ teaspoon*
1 large	**egg, whisked**	*1 large*
225 g/8 oz	**self-raising flour or plain (all-purpose) flour with 2 teaspoons baking powder**	*2 cups*
pinch	**salt**	*pinch*
450 g/1 lb	**bananas, weight in their skins**	*1 lb*
85 g/3 oz	**walnuts, chopped, optional**	*¾ cup*
50 g/2 oz	**raisins**	*⅓ cup*

* this gives the better flavour

1. Preheat the oven. Grease and flour or line the base, or base and sides, of the tin with greased greaseproof (wax) paper or baking parchment.
2. Cream the butter or margarine and sugar with the vanilla extract or essence until soft and light. Beat in the egg.
3. Sift the flour, or flour and baking powder, and salt into the creamed mixture, but do not try to mix it together at this stage.
4. Peel, then mash the bananas until a very smooth soft pulp, add to the flour mixture and stir briskly.
5. Add the walnuts and the raisins and mix with the rest of the ingredients.
6. Spoon into the prepared tin and bake in the centre of the oven, except with a fan oven where all shelves should be the same temperature.
7. Check at the end of 40 minutes for although the timing above is right for most ovens if your oven is on the fierce side the loaf may be cooked. The loaf should rise well and be firm to the touch. A fine

skewer inserted should come out clean. Do not over-bake this loaf, for it has a fairly dry consistency and over-cooking could make it crumble badly.

<hr>

Variations

<hr>

- Use 120 ml/4 fl oz (½ cup) extra virgin olive oil instead of butter or margarine. This means simply mixing all the ingredients together.

Date and Banana Loaf: omit the raisins and walnuts in the recipe and add 175 g/6 oz (1¼ cups) chopped dates (weight when stoned). If the dates are dry put into a basin, add 1 tablespoon of boiling water; stir well to moisten all the dates. Allow to stand for 15 minutes then add to the mixture at stage 5.

ORANGE AND APRICOT BREAD

This is one of the many teabreads that are made without yeast. The modern ready-to-eat apricots mean that overnight soaking is no longer necessary.

Oven Setting:	180°C/350°F, Gas Mark 4 or 170°C with a fan oven for the first 30 minutes then 160°C/325°F, Gas Mark 3 or 150°C with a fan oven for the remaining 1 hour
Baking Time:	1½ hours
Baking Equipment:	one 900 g/2 lb loaf tin (pan)
Makes:	one large loaf, which keeps well for several days and can be frozen. Leave for 24 hours to mature before cutting.

Metric/Imperial	Ingredients	American
175 g/6 oz	read-to-eat apricots, finely chopped	good 1 cup
225 ml/7½ fl oz	orange juice	scant 1 cup
2 level teaspoons	finely grated orange zest or to personal taste	2 level teaspoons
85 g/3 oz	butter or margarine, melted	⅜ cup
50 g/2 oz	chopped crystallized (candied) orange peel	⅓ cup
350 g/12 oz	self-raising flour or plain (all-purpose) flour with 3 level teaspoons baking powder	3 cups
115 g/4 oz	caster sugar	½ cup
2	eggs, whisked	2

1. Put the chopped apricots with the orange juice and zest into a good-sized mixing bowl. Leave to soak for 30 minutes.
2. Grease and flour the loaf tin or line the base, or base and sides, with greased greaseproof (wax) paper or baking parchment.

3. Preheat the oven. Stir the melted butter or margarine then the chopped peel into the apricots and orange juice.
4. Sift the flour, or flour and baking powder, into the apricot mixture then add the sugar and eggs. Mix thoroughly and spoon into the prepared tin.
5. Bake in the centre of the oven, except with a fan oven when all shelves should be at the same temperature. After 30 minutes reduce the heat. Although this loaf generally needs the full 1½ hours baking, it is wise to check the oven after 1 hour and 20 minutes for, in a fairly fierce oven, it may be cooked. The loaf is ready when it is firm to the touch, is well-risen and has shrunk away from the sides of the loaf tin. It is not an easy loaf to check with a fine skewer as it has the moist apricots and peel among the ingredients.
6. Cool in the tin for 10 minutes then turn out on to a wire cooling tray.

Variations

- Add about 50 g/2 oz (½ cup) chopped nuts – walnuts, pecans or hazelnuts are particularly suitable – with the flour at stage 4.

Orange and Prune Loaf: use ready-to-eat stoned prunes instead of apricots. Use wholemeal (wheatmeal) flour and add 1 extra tablespoon orange juice or lemon juice to give a slight 'bite' to the mixture.

BARM BRACK

The famous 'speckled bread' was originally made using balm, the froth that forms on the top of fermenting liquor, hence its name. Today yeast is used as the raising agent instead of balm and the quick acting yeast is excellent for this loaf. While you can use strong flour I prefer the result with plain (all-purpose) flour.

Oven Setting:	190 to 200°C/375 to 400°F, Gas Mark 5 to 6 or 180 to 190°C with a fan oven. Use this setting for the first 30 minutes and select the lower setting if your oven is on the fierce side. After this time reduce the heat to 160°C/325°F, Gas Mark 3 or 150°C with a fan oven to complete the baking.
Baking Time:	1 hour and 15 minutes
Baking Equipment:	one 23 cm/9 inch round cake tin (pan)
Makes:	one rich loaf that keeps for several days. It freezes very well.

Metric/Imperial	Ingredients	American
450 g/1 lb	**plain flour**	*4 cups*
1 teaspoon	**grated or ground nutmeg**	*1 teaspoon*
1 to 2 teaspoons	**caraway seeds, depending on personal taste**	*1 to 2 teaspoons*
1 x 7 g sachet	**speedy (easy blend) dried yeast see under Variation**	*1 x 7 g sachet*
175 g/6 oz	**butter or margarine**	*¾ cup*

115 g/4 oz	caster sugar	½ cup
115 g/4 oz	**mixed candied peel, chopped**	½ cup
225 g/8 oz	currants	1¼ cups
225 g/8 oz	raisins	1¼ cups
250 ml/ 8 fl oz	**milk, see stage 3**	1 cup
3	**eggs, whisked**	3

1. Grease and flour the cake tin. Preheat the oven at stage 5.
2. Sift the flour with the nutmeg into a large mixing bowl, add the seeds and dried yeast. Mix together then rub in the butter or margarine, add the sugar, peel, currants and raisins.
3. Heat the milk to blood heat, the easiest way to do this is to bring half the milk to the boil then add this to the remaining cold milk. Pour on to the ingredients in the mixing bowl, mix well with a knife then add the whisked eggs and continue to mix with a knife then with your fingers.
4. Gather the dough together and turn on to a floured pastry board. Knead until quite smooth and any impression left with a floured finger comes out, (see page 140).
5. Press into the prepared cake tin. Cover the top of the tin with a cloth and leave the dough to 'prove' in a warm place until risen to almost twice the original depth. This will take about 1 hour. During this time preheat the oven at the higher setting shown.
6. Bake the bread for 30 minutes then lower the heat, as instructed above and continue baking for 45 minutes or until firm and golden brown. Cool for a few minutes in the tin then turn out on to a cooling tray.

Variations

- This is the minimum of dried yeast you can use; for a slightly lighter loaf use 1 x 7 g sachet plus another scant teaspoon of the dried yeast.
- If you would prefer to use fresh yeast you need 20 g/¾ oz (¾ cake). Cream this with a teaspoon of the sugar then add the warm milk and a sprinkling of the flour. Stand until the surface is covered with bubbles then add to the flour and continue as above.
- If using fresh yeast you need to knead then prove the dough in bulk before placing into the cake tin when it should be allowed to prove for a second time. For more information on fresh yeast read page 139.

OATCAKES

Although these are called 'cakes' I have included them in the section with bread, for oatcakes are often served at breakfast time in Scotland as an alternative to rolls (baps) or toast. They are excellent with cheese.

*When first making these choose **fine** oatmeal for the dough is easier to bind. **Medium** oatmeal gives a more nutty taste to the oatcakes.*

Oven Setting: 180 to 190°C/350 to 375°F, Gas Mark 4 to 5 or 160 to 170°C with a fan oven but see the alternative cooking instructions under Variations

Baking Time: 15 minutes but see stage 7
Baking Equipment: one or two baking (cookie) trays
Makes: about 12 to 14. Store in an airtight tin away from
                       biscuits and bread.

Metric/Imperial	Ingredients	American
225 g/8 oz	**fine or medium oatmeal** **plus a little extra**	1⅓ cups
½ teaspoon	**salt**	½ teaspoon
1 tablespoon	**melted lard (shortening)**	1 tablespoon
150 ml/¼ pint	**water**	⅔ cup

1. Preheat the oven. Lightly grease the baking trays.
2. Put the oatmeal and salt into a mixing bowl, add the melted lard and mix this in with the oatmeal.
3. Bring the water to boiling point, this is important for the heat makes the oatmeal easier to handle.
4. Gradually add the boiling water; stop just before you add the full quantity and mix the ingredients together. You should have a dough that binds together and forms a firm rolling consistency. Continue adding the water until you reach this stage.
   Dust your fingers with oatmeal and form the oatmeal dough into a ball in the mixing bowl then transfer it to the pastry board, which should be lightly dusted with oatmeal.
5. Shake a little oatmeal on to the rolling pin then roll the dough out until it is approximately 6 mm/¼ inch in thickness.
6. Cut into rounds or triangles and lift on to the baking trays.
7. Bake until firm. Cool on the baking trays then carefully lift off, use a fish slice or palette knife (metal spatula) for the oatcakes are very fragile. Do not pack until cold.

Variations

Griddle Cooking: lightly grease then preheat the griddle, see page 168. Cook the oatcakes for about 3 minutes on either side or until firm, do not let them become brown in colour.
   Substitute butter or margarine for the lard. You can use up to 2 (2½) tablespoons of these fats or the lard for slightly richer oatcakes.

Sweeter Oatcakes: add up to 2 (2½) tablespoons caster sugar to the oatmeal.
   In this variation and the recipe above some people like to add ½ teaspoon baking powder. I have not found this makes better oatcakes.

GLUTEN-FREE CHEESE BREAD

The original recipe was given to me by a friend. She made a bread that was low in wheat, using only 115 g/4 oz (1 cup) plain (all-purpose) flour with the cornmeal or polenta. This would not be suitable for anyone who was allergic to wheat flour so I experimented with various other flours and found that rice flour, plus the cornmeal or polenta, gave the most pleasant flavour. You will see that under Variations you can use other types of flour if you prefer these. My friend recommended that the loaf was cut into squares, rather than being sliced, and this is the way I have enjoyed it.

Oven Setting: 200°C/400°F, Gas Mark 6 or 190°C with a fan oven
Baking Time: 30 minutes.
Baking Equipment: one 20 cm/8 inch square cake or deep sandwich tin (layer pan)
Makes: one loaf which keeps well for 24 hours but can be reheated on a low heat. Freezes well too.

Metric/Imperial	Ingredients	American
115 g/4 oz	rice flour	1 cup
1 level tablespoon	baking powder	l level tablespoon
115 g/4 oz	polenta, fine type if possible	1 cup
2	eggs	2
85 g/ 3 oz	Cheddar cheese, finely grated	1 cup
284* ml/½ pint	milk	1⅓ cups
to taste	salt and freshly ground black pepper	to taste

* use this metrication

1. Preheat the oven; grease and flour or line the tin with greased greaseproof paper or baking parchment.
2. Sift the flour with the baking powder, add the rest of the ingredients and mix thoroughly. Spoon into the tin and bake until firm to the touch.
    Cool in the tin for 5 minutes then turn out. Serve warm or cold.

Variations

• Add 2 teaspoons chopped coriander (cilantro) to the mixture.

Tomato Cheese Bread: mix the ingredients with half tomato juice and half milk instead of all milk or use the recipe above and add 3 to 4 (3¾ to 5) tablespoons very finely chopped sun-dried tomatoes at stage 2.
  Use gluten-free flour instead of rice flour.
  Use buckwheat flour instead of rice flour.
  Return to the original recipe and use ordinary plain flour instead of rice flour.

PIZZA

When you have made bread you will be well equipped to produce a home-made pizza. Although these can be cooked in a domestic oven the result is not exactly the same as when they are produced in proper pizza ovens, since the heat in these is very intense.
  Pizzas consist of basic bread dough, with a topping. The most usual and popular toppings consist of a savoury tomato mixture with cheese,

anchovies and olives but there are many others; brief suggestions are under Variations.

There are many commercial sauces that could be chosen to take the place of the tomato mixture below, but this has an excellent flavour. If you are very fond of pizzas you could make a larger amount of the topping and freeze batches for future use. You can buy ready-made pizza bases that need just a topping. Bake them as the instructions on the packet.

Pizzas have become so popular that special heavy duty pizza plates and 'stones' are now sold. The reason for specifying a metal baking **sheet**, rather than a baking tray (pan) is that the heavier sheet holds the heat better.

It is wise to make the topping first to allow it time to cook before it is added to the bread dough.

Oven Setting:	220°C/425°F, Gas Mark 7 or 190 to 200°C with a fan oven
Baking Time:	15 to 20 minutes
Cooking Time for Topping:	20 to 25 minutes
Baking Equipment:	a proper pizza stone or a baking sheet, see stage 6 plus an extra baking sheet, see stage 7
Makes:	one 25 to 28 cm/10 to 11 inch pizza, serving 2 to 4. Serve when freshly baked. Open-freeze, when frozen wrap carefully. Defrost and reheat in a low setting in the microwave or at 150 to 160°C/300 to 325°F, Gas Mark 2 to 3 in the oven. A fan oven should be set to 140°C.

Metric/Imperial	Ingredients	American
	For the tomato mixture	
1 tablespoon	olive or sunflower oil	1 tablespoon
2 medium	onions, finely chopped	2 medium
1 to 2	garlic cloves, crushed, see page 168	1 to 2
1 x 425 g can	chopped plum tomatoes	2 cups
1 to 2 teaspoons	chopped fresh oregano or 1/2 to 1 teaspoon dried oregano	1 to 2 teaspoons
to taste	salt and freshly ground black pepper	to taste
1 tablespoon	tomato purée, optional	1 tablespoon
	For the dough	
225 g/8 oz	strong flour	2 cups
good pinch	salt	good pinch
1 teaspoon	speedy (easy blend) dried yeast	1 teaspoon
150 ml/1/4 pint	warm water, see stage 4	2/3 cup
1 1/2 tablespoons	olive oil	scant 2 tablespoons

For the topping

few drops	*olive oil*	*few drops*
85 g/3 oz	*Mozzarella cheese, grated* *see Variations*	*¾ cup*
few	*canned anchovy fillets, optional*	*few*
few	*black olives, optional*	*few*

1. Heat the oil in a saucepan, add the onions and cook gently for 5 minutes then put in the garlic, tomatoes, with all the liquid from the can, the oregano and a little salt and pepper.
2. Simmer gently in an uncovered pan, stirring from time to time, until the mixture becomes a thick pulp. The tomato purée from a tube or a small can could be added if you want a stronger taste; allow sauce to become quite cold. If making some time ahead cover and store in the refrigerator.
3. Put the flour and salt into a mixing bowl; add the yeast.
4. Bring half the water to boiling point, add to the remaining cold water then pour this warm liquid on to the flour, add 1 tablespoon of the oil. Mix well with your fingers then turn on to a lightly floured board and knead as fully explained on page 139.
5. When sufficiently kneaded put the dough back into the mixing bowl, brush the top with the remaining oil, cover the bowl and leave for 45 minutes or until well risen.
6. Turn the dough out of the bowl and knead again. Dust a rolling pin with a very little flour if the dough is slightly sticky, roll out the dough into a large 25 to 28 cm/10 to 11 inch round.
7. Preheat the oven and place the second baking sheet in the oven to heat.
8. Rub the pizza stone or metal sheet with a few drops of oil; add the round of dough. Spread the cold tomato mixture over the top leaving the edges of the dough free of topping. Top with the cheese.
9. If using the anchovy fillets and olives, use only **half** the cheese over the tomato mixture; save the rest to cover the anchovy fillets and olives.
10. Place the pizza on its base over the heated baking sheet, this gives extra heat underneath the dough and helps it to become firm.
11. Bake until the bottom dough is firm. If the filling seems to be getting over-cooked top this with a piece of foil; do not wrap the foil around the pizza or it will hinder the cooking of the bread base.
12. Serve the pizza when cooked, cutting it into wide segments.

Variations

- Use cooked vegetables over the tomato mixture and under the cheese.
- Use cooked sliced ham or salami over the tomato mixture and under the cheese.
- Substitute grated Cheddar or Cheshire cheese or a mixture of Parmesan and other cheese.

Crushing Garlic
Take 1 or 2 cloves (segments) from the garlic head. Remove the skin(s). Sprinkle a little salt on a chopping board, place the cloves on this and crush with a weight or heavy pressure on the blade of a strong knife.

If preferred chop finely.

You can buy special garlic crushers.

USING A GRIDDLE

A griddle, often known as a bakestone, is a solid plate that is placed over a gas burner or electric hotplate and heated ready for cooking various teacakes and even special cakes, as those given on this page.

The use of the griddle goes back through the ages, when ovens were not part of many coal-fired ranges.

Older models of electric cookers had solid hotplates or grill-boilers and these took the place of the griddle. If you are anxious to make the cakes on this page or other recipes on pages 169, 170 and 171 and have no special equipment, you could use a very heavy frying pan instead. Treat that like a griddle, brush it with a very little oil or melted lard (shortening) and preheat it as the instructions given for heating a griddle in the various recipes.

SINGING HINNIES

These have been a favourite teacake in Northumberland for decades. The rather strange name is because the teacakes give a singing sound as they cool and the word 'hinnie' is a term of endearment in the north of England so it denotes that the teacakes were very popular. The recipe below gives the traditional ingredients. Years ago lard (shortening) was the prefered fat for baking and in those days it was of a very high quality, generally coming from a family butcher. However as you will see, butter or margarine can be substituted.

Oven Setting: the oven is not used. The griddle must be preheated well, see stage 4
Cooking Time: 8 to 10 minutes
Cooking Equipment: griddle (often called a bakestone)
Makes: 10 to 12 large teacakes or 15 smaller ones. It is worthwhile making a good number for they freeze remarkably well.

Metric/Imperial	Ingredients	American
450 g/1 lb	plain (all-purpose) flour plus a little extra	4 cups
pinch	salt	pinch
scant ¾ level teaspoon	bicarbonate of soda (baking soda)	scant ¾ level teaspoon
scant 1½ level teaspoons	cream of tartar	scant 1½ level teaspoons
115 g/4 oz	lard (shortening) or butter or margarine	½ cup

175 g/6 oz	*currants*	*1 cup*
300 ml/½ pint	*milk*	*1¼ cups*

To grease the griddle

few drops	*sunflower or groundnut or olive oil*	*few drops*

1. Sift the flour with the salt, bicarbonate of soda and cream of tartar.
2. Rub in the lard or alternative fat (hints of rubbing fat into flour are given under pastry on page 109).
3. Add the currants then gradually add the milk. The quantity given should be right but makes of flour vary slightly in the amount they absorb. The dough should be of a firm rolling consistency.
4. Brush the griddle with a little oil then preheat. It is ready when a little flour, shaken over the surface, turns golden (not brown) in 1 minute.
5. Sift a small amount of flour over the working surface and the rolling pin. Roll out the dough until 1.25 cm/½ inch in thickness then cut in rounds. Traditionally these should be quite large.
6. Place these on the hot griddle and cook for 4 to 5 minutes, or until golden on the under side. Insert a fish slice or palette knife (metal spatula) under the teacakes; turn over and cook for the same time on the second side. Smaller rounds take almost the same cooking time as larger ones.
7. Place a teacloth (dish towel) on a wire cooling tray, add the teacakes and cover. Split through the centre and serve warm or cold with butter.

Variations

- Use wholemeal (wholewheat) flour or half wholemeal and half white flour. In either case you will need a little extra milk to give the right texture.
- Use self-raising flour and omit the bicarbonate of soda and cream of tartar.

WELSH CAKES

These are cakes, not teacakes, but because the cooking instructions are so similar to the Singing Hinnies, I have placed them together.

Oven Setting: the oven is not used. The griddle must be preheated well, see stage 3
Cooking Time: 8 to 10 minutes
Cooking Equipment: griddle (often called a bakestone)
Makes: 10 to 12 small cakes. These should be eaten when freshly made. They do freeze well.

Metric/Imperial	*Ingredients*	*American*
225 g/8 oz	*self-raising flour or plain*	*2 cups*
	(all-purpose) flour with 2 teaspoons	
	baking powder plus a little extra	

pinch	*salt*	*pinch*
115 g/4 oz	**butter or margarine**	*½ cup*
115 g/4 oz	**caster sugar**	*½ cup*
115 g/4 oz	**currants**	*¾ cup*
1 large	**egg, whisked**	*1 large*
2 tablespoons or as required	**milk**	*2½ tablespoons or as required*
	To decorate	
1 tablespoon	**caster sugar**	*1 tablespoon*

1. Sift the flour or flour and baking powder and salt into a mixing bowl. Rub in the butter or margarine as for Singing Hinnies.
2. Add the sugar, then the currants and the egg. Mix well then gradually add sufficient milk to make a firm rolling consistency.
3. Grease, preheat and test the griddle, as stage 4 of Singing Hinnies.
4. Sift a little flour over the working surface and the rolling pin and roll out the dough until 1.25 cm/½ inch in thickness. Cut into small rounds or triangles.
5. Place these on the griddle and cook as stage 6 of Singing Hinnies.
6. When cooked lift on to a wire cooling tray; do not cover these as they should be slightly crisp on both sides. Cool then top with a light sprinkling of caster sugar.

CRUMPETS

These are one of the most interesting of all yeast recipes and, of course, a very popular teacake for wintertime. You can also use crumpets for the base of a speedy Pizza. Crumpets are made from a yeast batter, so you **must** *buy metal rings to contain the soft mixture and keep the crumpets a good shape. Do not use plastic rings on the heated griddle.*

These are better made with plain (all-purpose) flour, rather than strong flour.

Oven Setting: the oven is not used. The griddle must be pre-heated well, see stage 1.
Cooking Time: approximately 6 minutes
Cooking Equipment: crumpet, or similar metal rings, see above, plus a griddle (often called a bakestone)
Makes: about 8 crumpets, depending upon the size. The cooked, but untoasted, crumpets freeze well. Defrost at room temperature then toast them as stage 9.

Metric/Imperial	*Ingredients*	*American*
few drops	**sunflower or groundnut oil**	*few drops*
115 g/4 oz	**plain flour**	*1 cup*
pinch	*salt*	*pinch*
½ sachet	**speedy (easy blend) dried yeast**	*½ sachet*

150 ml/¼ pint	*milk*	⅔ cup
15 g/½ oz	*butter*	1 tablespoon

1. Rub the griddle with a few drops of oil; it should just look greasy. When the yeast dough is almost ready to use, preheat this just before cooking the crumpets. To test the heat, shake a very little flour over the surface, this should take 1 minute to turn pale golden. If it does this more quickly lower the heat. If it takes much longer then increase the heat. Brush the inside of the crumpet rings with a little oil too.
2. Sift the flour and salt into a mixing bowl, add the yeast, mix with the flour.
3. Warm the milk with the butter until the butter melts, this can be done in a saucepan or a basin in the microwave. Allow the milk and butter to stand until the mixture feels pleasantly warm to your finger, then add to the flour.
4. Beat very well with a wooden spoon, cover the bowl and leave at room temperature until the surface is covered with bubbles, then beat again.
5. Place the rings on the heated griddle, leave for about a minute, so they also become hot, this means the yeast batter will not stick.
6. Spoon some of the yeast batter into each ring and allow the mixture to cook for 3 minutes, or until the top surface begins to bubble. After this stage it is advisable to lower the heat under the griddle, so the bottom surface does not become too darkened.
7. Cook for a further 2 to 3 minutes. To test if completely cooked, remove one crumpet from the heat, take off the ring – be careful this will be very hot – press the crumpet quite firmly on top. If it feels springy, and no batter oozes from the side, it is ready and you can lift them all from the griddle.
8. Place a dry teacloth (dish towel) on the wire cooling tray, add the crumpets and cover with the cloth, this keeps them soft.
9. **To toast the crumpets:** place in an electric toaster or under a preheated grill (broiler), toast until brown and slightly crisp on both sides. You will need to turn them if using the grill. Butter and serve hot.

Speedy Pizza: top the toasted crumpets with sliced tomatoes then grated cheese and place under the grill until the cheese melts.

LARDY CAKE

This traditional British cake depends upon a good bread dough. I suggest you delay making it until you have become accustomed to making bread with yeast.

Initial Preparations
Follow Bread 1 recipe on page 141 to stage 8 or
Follow Bread 2 recipe on page 143 to stage 5.
   In either case cut off **half** the dough. Make and bake this as a loaf. While making the bread cover the **remaining half** with clingfilm (saran wrap); keep it in the refrigerator until ready to make the cake.

Oven Setting: 230°C/450°F, Gas Mark 8 or 210 to 220°C with a
                           fan oven
Baking Time: 25 to 30 minutes
Baking Equipment: one 20 cm/8 inch square cake tin (pan)
Makes: one cake that should be eaten when freshly baked.
                           It can be frozen.

Metric/Imperial	Ingredients	American
	bread dough, see page 171	
little	*flour, for rolling the dough*	*little*
6 teaspoons	*clear honey*	6 teaspoons
150 g/5 oz	*best quality lard (shortening)*	5/8 cup
150 g/5 oz	*caster or light brown sugar*	5/8 cup
100 g/3½ oz	*mixed dried fruit*	½ cup
½ teaspoon	*ground cinnamon*	½ teaspoon
½ teaspoon	*ground or grated nutmeg*	½ teaspoon

1. Grease the base and sides of the cake tin; do not line it.
2. Lightly dust the pastry board and rolling pin with a little flour, place
    the proven dough on the board and roll out to an oblong about
    6 mm/¼ inch in thickness, have the shorter end towards you.
3. Spread 2 teaspoons of the honey over two thirds of the dough, keep
    the bottom third of the dough near you, uncovered.
4. Spread a third of the lard over the honey covered dough; add a third
    of the sugar and a third of the fruit. Sprinkle on a third of the spices.
5. Fold the uncovered part of the dough over half the covered dough (it
    should look like an opened envelope at this stage).
6. Bring down the top covered part of the dough, making it like a
    closed envelope.
7. Roll out the dough as stage 2 and repeat stages 3 to 6, so using up all
    the ingredients. Roll out the dough once more and then fold it into a
    shape to fit the cake tin.
8. Lightly cut the top of the dough to make a criss-cross pattern.
9. Cover the top of the tin with clingfilm (saran wrap) and allow the
    cake to prove (rise) until almost double the original depth. This will
    take about 30 minutes but it will vary with the temperature of the
    room.
10. Meanwhile preheat the oven. Remove the clingfilm and bake the
    proven cake until firm and golden brown. Remove from the tin onto
    a dish and pour any syrup that has run into the cake tin over the top
    of the cake.

A FEW FINAL BAKING IDEAS

BAKING FRUIT

Many fruits can be baked in the oven; here are some examples.

Apples: select a good cooking apple, Bramley Seedlings are famous for their good cooking qualities; James Grieve are another good choice. *To prepare the apples:* remove the centre core with an apple corer, or a small sharp knife. Carefully slit the skin around the centre of the fruit. Stand the apple(s) on a baking (cookie) tray or ovenproof dish.

You can fill the centre (where the core was removed) with sugar – Demerara (raw) sugar is particularly good for this purpose – and a small knob of butter or with golden (corn) syrup or clear honey or crushed blackberries and sugar. Apples weighing about 225 g/½ lb each take approximately 55 minutes in a preheated oven set to 180°C/350°F, Gas Mark 4 or 170°C with a fan oven. The baking time for one or several apples is exactly the same.

Apples can be prepared as above then cooked in a microwave on full output (HIGH). One apple takes about 3½ minutes but for several you must increase the time, so check with your manufacturer's handbook. The flavour of the pulp is excellent but the skins are tougher than when oven baked.

Bananas in their skins can be baked for about 15 minutes at the setting given under apples. After baking, peel away the skin carefully for the fruit is very hot; you have lovely soft pulp inside to serve with cream or ice cream. The fruit can also be baked in syrup.

Bananas in rum syrup: peel 4 bananas, put into a baking dish. Dilute 4 (5) tablespoons rum with the same amount of water, add 2 (2½) tablespoons caster sugar. Pour over the bananas, cover the dish and bake for 20 minutes at the setting above. If you do not like rum use 150 ml/ ¼ pint (⅔ cup) orange juice and omit the water.

Pears in red wine: peel, halve and core 4 large firm dessert pears. Put into an ovenproof dish. Mix 240 ml/8 fl oz (1 cup) red wine with 2 (2½) tablespoons sugar or clear honey, plus a pinch of ground cinnamon. Pour over the fruit, turn the pears around, so all sides are moistened. Cover the dish and bake for 30 minutes at the temperature given under apples.

Soft fruits: black, white and red currants with cherries can be baked for approximately 15 minutes at the temperature given under apples. If ripe add just 1 tablespoon water. If firm add 3 (3¾) tablespoons to each 450 g/ 1 lb with sugar to taste.

FRUIT CRUMBLES

A crumble topping on fruit is an excellent alternative to pastry; it is quickly made and tastes appetising. Make sure that the fruit base is not too liquid, for excess juice could bubble up during cooking and spoil the crispness of the crumble.

Oven Setting:	180°C/350°F, Gas Mark 4 or 170°C with a fan oven
Baking Time:	time to soften the fruit if necessary, see stage 3, plus 30 to 35 minutes for the crumble
Baking Equipment:	1.2 litre/2 pint (5 cup) pie dish
Serves:	4 to 6. Serve hot and freshly made. Not ideal for freezing; some crispness lost.

Metric/Imperial	Ingredients	American
	For the base	
550 to 675 g/1¼ to 1½ lb	**fruit, see stage 1**	1¼ to 1½ lb
as required	**water, see stage 2**	as required
to taste	**sugar, see stage 2**	to taste
	For the crumble	
175 g/6 oz	**plain (all-purpose) flour**	1½ cups
85 g/3 oz	**butter or margarine**	⅜ cup
115 g/4 oz	**granulated sugar**	½ cup

1. Prepare the fruit, **apples** should be peeled, cored and thinly sliced. **Apricots** and **plums** are better halved and stoned, for you need a flat layer of fruit, so you have a good foundation for the crumble. Soft fruit, such as **blackcurrants**, should just be washed in cold water. **Rhubarb** should be cut into 2.5 cm/1 inch lengths.
2. Place the fruit in the pie dish. If very firm add about 4 (5) tablespoons water, if moderately soft and juicy add 2 (2½) tablespoons. Soft fruit needs just 1 tablespoon. Mix in 2 to 3 tablespoons sugar, or as desired.
3. Preheat the oven. If the fruit is very firm (like apples), cover the pie dish with foil and cook for 15 to 20 minutes; if moderately firm for about 10 minutes. Soft fruit should not need pre-cooking.
4. Meanwhile prepare the crumble. Put the flour into a mixing bowl. Cut the butter or margarine into smaller pieces, drop into the flour and rub in until like fine breadcrumbs. There is more about the rubbing-in technique under Pastry on page 109. Add the sugar.
5. Spoon the mixture evenly over the fruit; gently press it down with the back of a metal spoon to give a flat layer.
6. Bake until crisp and golden brown. Serve with cream or custard.

Variations

Rich Crumble: increase the butter or margarine to 115 g/4 oz (½ cup). Increase the sugar slightly and use Demerara (raw) sugar.

Varying the flour: use wholemeal (wholewheat) flour or gluten-free flour or cornmeal or polenta if you are intolerant to wheat.

Nutty Crumble: add 4 (5) tablespoons finely chopped almonds or other nuts to the crumble.

Oatmeal Crumble: omit a quarter of the flour, replace it with rolled oats.

Spiced Crumble: sift 1 teaspoon ground cinnamon or ginger with the flour.

PWDIN EFA

This is a famous baked Welsh Pudding. It consists of a light topping over a fruit purée – this is usually apples.

Oven Setting:	160°C/325°F, Gas Mark 3 or 150°C with a fan oven
Baking Time:	35 to 40 minutes also time to prepare apples and topping
Baking Equipment:	1.2 litre/2 pint (5 cup) pie dish
Serves:	4 to 6. Serve hot and freshly made, do not freeze.

Metric/Imperial	Ingredients	American
	Fruit layer	
675 g/1½ lb	cooking apples, peeled, cored and sliced	1½ lb
150 ml/¼ pint	water	⅔ cup
50 g/2 oz	caster sugar	¼ cup
½ to 1 tablespoon	lemon juice	½ to 1 tablespoon
	Topping	
50 g/2 oz	butter	¼ cup
50 g/2 oz	plain (all-purpose) flour	½ cup
300 ml/½ pint	milk	1¼ cups
few drops	vanilla extract* or essence	few drops
50 g/2 oz	caster sugar	¼ cup
2 large	eggs	2 large
	Decoration	
1 to 2 tablespoons	icing (confectioners) sugar, sifted	1 to 2½ tablespoons

* this has a better flavour

1. Put the apples, water, sugar and lemon juice into a saucepan, stir over a moderate heat until the sugar melts then simmer gently for about 10 minutes or until a thick purée; spoon into the pie dish.
2. Preheat the oven. Heat the butter in another saucepan, stir in the flour then add the milk and vanilla extract. Bring to the boil and stir or whisk continually until a thick sauce. Stir in the sugar then remove from the heat, cool slightly.

3.   Separate the eggs, whisk the egg yolks into the warm sauce. Whisk the egg whites until stiff then fold into the egg-flavoured sauce.
4.   Spoon over the apple mixture and bake for 35 to 40 minutes or until the topping is well-risen. Top with the icing sugar and serve at once.

Variations

Other fruits to use are fresh apricots, blackberries mixed with apples, blueberries, stoned cherries, gooseberries, plums of all kinds, damsons and greengages.

For the topping: omit the vanilla extract or essence and flavour the topping with 1 teaspoon finely grated lemon zest. Use 2 (2½) tablespoons lemon juice and deduct this amount from the milk.

Gluten-free topping: use the same quantity of rice flour or cornflour (cornstarch) instead of the plain flour in the recipe.

MICROWAVE BAKING

With a combination microwave you can make all the dishes in this book for you have the capabilities of a conventional cooker plus the speed of the microwave.

    The dishes that follow are ideal for an ordinary microwave, for they have the appearance to make them look as good as they taste. They were cooked in an 18 cm/7 inch ovenproof glass soufflé dish, an ideal replacement for a cake tin.

    Mixtures baked in a microwave rise more drastically than when baked in the oven, so choose a container that is sufficiently deep. The soufflé dish used was 7.5 cm/3 inches in depth. See page 107.

PINEAPPLE UPSIDE DOWN CAKE

The steps for making the sponge are similar to the Victoria Sandwich on page 83. The difference in the sponge ingredients is there is a little less fat and sugar to give a firmer topping which supports the fruit base.

Microwave Setting: two-thirds to three-quarters of full output (HIGH)
Cooking Time: 30 seconds for the glaze then 7 minutes, see stage 4
Cooking Utensil: as above
Makes: one cake, which also can be served as a hot or cold pudding for 6 people. It can be frozen but the fruit base becomes slightly over-softened.

Metric/Imperial	Ingredients	American
	For the glaze and base	
50 g/2 oz	butter	¼ cup
50 g/2 oz	soft brown sugar	¼ cup
4 to 6	pineapple rings, canned in syrup	4 to 6
8 to 12	glacé (candied) cherries, optional	8 to 12

For the sponge

150 g/5 oz	*butter or margarine*	*⁵/₈ cup*
150 g/5 oz	*caster sugar*	*⁵/₈ cup*
3	*eggs, whisked*	*3*
175 g/6 oz	*self-raising flour or plain (all-purpose) flour with 1¹/₂ teaspoons baking powder*	*1¹/₂ cups*

1. Grease the sides of the soufflé dish with a little of the butter. Put the rest of the butter and sugar into the base of the dish and heat on full output for 30 seconds. Add 1 tablespoon of the pineapple syrup and then arrange the pineapple rings and cherries in a neat design over this.
2. Cream the butter or margarine and sugar until soft and light. Gradually beat in the eggs, then fold in the sifted flour or flour and baking powder.
3. Spoon into the dish, being careful not to disturb the fruit base.
4. Set the microwave control to two-thirds or three-quarters output; microwaves vary in their settings. Place the cake on the turntable; switch on. The timing is correct for the microwave used but you should consult your manufacturer's handbook and test as page 184.
5. Allow the cake to stand for 4 minutes then invert on to the serving dish.

Variation

- Use any canned or cooked or fresh fruit instead of the pineapple.

EVE'S PUDDING

1. Peel, core and thinly slice 550 g/1¹/₄ lb cooking apples, put into the dish, with sugar to taste and 2 (2¹/₂) tablespoons water. You can add a pinch of mixed spice or ground cloves and several tablespoons of raisins or other dried fruit.
2. Cover the dish and heat in the microwave for 3 minutes or until the apples are slightly softened.
3. Make the sponge topping as above. Spoon over the apples and cook as above. The pudding is served in the dish, so top the hot sponge with caster or sifted icing (confectioners) sugar. Serve with cream or custard.

SPICED CHOCOLATE ORANGE CAKE

1. Ingredients as sponge topping above but add 150 g/5 oz (5 squares) plain chocolate, 1 tablespoon orange juice, 1 teaspoon grated orange zest and 2 teaspoons mixed spice.
2. Break the chocolate into pieces, put into a bowl with the orange juice. Melt on a low setting in the microwave. Allow to cool, but not set again.
3. Add the orange zest with the butter or margarine and sugar. Continue as stage 2. Sift the mixed spice with the flour.

4.   Place a round of baking parchment in the bottom of the soufflé dish, grease the sides then spoon in the cake mixture.
5.   I find it a help with some microwaves to stand the dish on an upturned saucer to make sure the heat penetrates to the base. With certain microwaves there is a tendency for the base of a cake to be slightly under-cooked.
6.   This cake took 7 minutes at three-quarters of the full output. Test as page 184. Allow to stand for 4 minutes then turn out onto a wire cooling tray. When cold top with whipped cream and grated chocolate.

OVEN BAKING

For all recipes: preheat the oven at 180°C/350°F, Gas Mark 4 or 160 to 170°C with a fan oven; if necessary lower the heat slightly after 40 minutes. Bake in the centre of the oven, except for a fan oven.

Pineapple Upside Down Cake
Use an 18 cm/7 inch cake tin (pan) without a loose base. Grease the sides. Melt the butter and sugar in the tin for a few minutes in the oven. Add the syrup, the pineapple and cherries then the sponge. Bake for 1 hour or until firm. Turn out onto a serving dish.

Eve's Pudding
Put the prepared apples into a 1.2 litre/2 pint (5 cup) pie dish. Cover with foil and cook for 7 minutes in the oven. Top with the sponge and bake for 50 minutes or until firm. Sprinkle with sugar and serve hot.

Spiced Chocolate Orange Cake
Line an 18 cm/7 inch cake tin with greased greaseproof (wax) paper or baking parchment. Melt the chocolate over hot water or in the microwave then continue as the recipe. Spoon into the tin and bake for 1 hour or until firm. Turn out and when cold decorate as above.

BAKED PUDDINGS

PINEAPPLE SURPRISE PUDDING

This is a very delicious light pudding and an unexpected one. The ingredients separate during cooking, giving a light, almost soufflé type, topping with a thick sauce below. It is a good idea to stand the dish in a tin of water to prevent the sides of the pudding becoming too dry.

On page 22 I recommend you buy a 600 ml/1 pint (2½ cup) and a 1.2 litre/2 pint (5 cup) pie dish and if you have followed this advice you will need to use the larger one. If you have a 900 ml/1½ pint (3¾ cup) dish it is better, for the mixture fills it more readily. This pudding is delicious served with rings of cold fresh pineapple.

Oven Setting: 160°C/325°F, Gas Mark 3 or 150°C with a fan oven
Baking Time: 50 minutes

Baking Equipment: 900 ml/1½ pint (3¾ cup) pie dish or see above
Serves: four with small portions; serve hot, do not freeze.

Metric/Imperial	Ingredients	American
50 g/2 oz	**butter or margarine**	¼ cup
50 g/2 oz	**caster sugar**	¼ cup
1 teaspoon	**finely grated lemon zest**	1 teaspoon
2 large	**eggs**	2 large
50 g/2 oz	**self-raising flour or plain (all-purpose) flour with ½ teaspoon baking powder**	½ cup
2 tablespoons	**lemon juice, or to taste**	2½ tablespoons
225 ml/7½ fl oz	**canned pineapple juice**	scant 1 cup

1. Preheat the oven; grease the sides of the pie dish with a few drops of oil. Add a small amount of cold water to a baking tin (pan); you need to be certain this will not be too much when the filled pie dish is added.
2. Cream the butter or margarine, sugar and lemon zest until soft and light.
3. Separate the eggs, let the whites fall into a basin and add the yolks one by one to the creamed mixture and beat in thoroughly.
   Sift the flour, or flour and baking powder, into the creamed mixture, then gradually beat in the lemon and pineapple juices. You may find the mixture tends to separate 'curdle' but that does not matter.
4. Whisk the egg whites until stiff, fold into the rest of the ingredients then pour into the pie dish. Stand this in the tin of water and bake until just firm. Serve hot.

To make a change

Chocolate Soufflé Pudding: omit the lemon zest and fruit juice. Sift 2 (2½) level tablespoons cocoa powder with the flour and mix the pudding with 300 ml/½ pint (1¼ cups) cold milk.

Coffee Soufflé Pudding: omit the lemon zest and fruit juices but use 300 ml/½ pint (1¼ cups) moderately strong liquid coffee. This must be cold before adding to the other ingredients.

Lemon Soufflé Pudding: omit the pineapple juice and use a total of 3 (3¾) tablespoons of lemon juice made up to 240 ml/8 fl oz (1 cup) with water.

Orange Soufflé Pudding: follow the basic recipe but use just 1 (1¼) tablespoons lemon juice and 240 ml/8 fl oz (1 cup) orange juice.

SOME QUESTIONS WITH ANSWERS

On the following few pages you will find some typical cookery questions, the kind I have been asked, and have answered, for many years. Do not get annoyed with yourself if the first efforts at baking are not as perfect as you would wish, good cooking comes from experience and baking is the most complex of cooking processes. If you are boiling, simmering or frying in pans on top of the cooker you can see what is happening and you can adjust the heat to give the desired result. When you put food into the oven you are less in charge of the procedure. The first thing therefore is to get to know your oven and respect its particular qualities.

USING THE COOKER

In the book you mention that ovens do vary and some may be slower or more gentle in heat than others, while some may be more fierce. Is there any way one can assess the type of oven you have, so you can deal with differences between its heat and the recommended temperatures in the recipes?
An oven thermometer will help you achieve the right temperature in your own oven and help you determine variations between top and bottom within the oven (see page 7).

Trays of small cakes and even larger cakes tend to brown more on one side than on the other, why is this?
It could be a fault with the cooker, in which case have it checked. It could be that the cooker is not standing 100% level and this must be put right.
You can check this with the help of a spirit level. If you cannot rectify this yourself, then ask the store from which the cooker was purchased to help.

In this book you state that you reduce the oven setting by 10°C for a fan oven, although in some cases manufacturers do state they should be reduced by 20°C. In a few recipes you give two settings for fan ovens, why is that?
I have found from experience that those dishes are particularly affected by too much heat and I wanted to emphasise that you should check on the oven setting with extra vigilance. Even if you normally reduce the heat for most recipes with your fan oven, in those where I have given extra temperature you may need to make an extra reduction.

Following are some of the sad things that can happen to even the most experienced cook. Perhaps the telephone rang at the wrong time and you forgot to look at the oven. It is always wise to have a timer, and set this, to remind you to check on the oven.

Is there anything one can do if pastry or cakes or bread become slightly over-cooked and over-brown, or even slightly burned on the outside?
Yes, you can remove the offending surface from a cake or pastry tart or top edge of a flan with the fine side of a grater.

Stand the food on the wire cooling tray, with a plate or dish underneath to collect the over-brown or burnt particles. Very slowly and carefully rub the fine side of a grater over the offending surface.

When you have removed the dark particles you can dust the entire cake or pastry with sifted icing (confectioners) sugar.

In the case of bread it is possibly better to remove the over-cooked crust and use the crumb part to make sandwiches.

If a cake sinks in the centre, why is this and is there anything one can do?
The sinking could be for a number of reasons.

a) The mixture was too damp; never exceed the amount of heavy ingredients such as syrup, treacle (molasses) and honey given in the recipe. Remember tablespoon measures mean **level** tablespoons. You may have added too much milk or other liquid, do check on the consistency as you mix the cake.

b) You used damp dried fruit. Today the fruit in packets is pre-cleaned but if you do decide to wash it in **cold water** then you must spread it out on flat dishes and leave it at room temperature to dry out for 48 hours.

c) You used too much baking powder, this has the effect of making the cake rise and then sometimes it drops back. It is particularly important not to exceed the raising agent when making a fruit cake, like the Dundee Cake on page 95. This is why a small amount only is included in a cake with a generous amount of fruit, as in this recipe. You must not have too light a cake mixture for it cannot carry the weight of fruit. If you do the cake part rises and the fruit sinks down which could result in a cake that is heavy in the middle or a two-layer cake, i.e. fruity layer below and plainer layer above.

d) The oven was set too low for that particular cake and the mixture did not rise as it should or the oven was too hot and the outside set too quickly before the heat could penetrate to the centre of the cake. Do check on oven settings in the recipes and the advice on page 7.

What can one do?
If the cake has sunk in the centre but still is NOT heavy, you could fill the centre with a little icing and top it with chopped nuts or fruit or use whipped cream and fruit. Never worry if a gingerbread sinks slightly in the centre as that is acceptable.

If the middle of the cake is heavy take a large pastry cutter and carefully press this through the centre. Remove the heavy part, and serve the remainder as a ring cake.

If you have a two-layer cake then capitalise on this. Slice the cake carefully through the centre. Top the fruit layer with a thin coating of sieved apricot jam and chopped nuts and the plain layer with sifted icing sugar.

What can one do if biscuits are not crisp?
Replace the biscuits on a baking (cookie) tray and bake them again for about 5 minutes at the original temperature. Allow to cool, and they should be fine.

Do be careful how you store biscuits, it may be they have softened because they were stored incorrectly. Biscuits containing oatmeal in any form should be stored away from other biscuits, so should chocolate biscuits.

Is there anything one can do to rescue a cake that is drier than it should be?

One could moisten it, as one does a Christmas Cake, by pricking the top and bottom of the cake with a fork or skewer then carefully pouring or brushing sherry or other alcohol over both sides. Leave it a while for the liquid to penetrate.

You could moisten a light sponge by standing it on the serving dish and moistening it a little with sweetened apricot, raspberry, or other flavoured, syrup from canned or defrosted frozen fruit to make a really moist cake. Decorate it with whipped cream or fromage frais and fruit and you have produced an elaborate gâteau.

What is the best way to make stale bread more moist and edible again?

You can heat it on the lowest setting in the microwave if you need it urgently but it must be eaten up while hot for it becomes stale again. The best way is to reheat it in the oven.

If the crust is already firm and crisp, then dip the loaf for a few seconds only in a little cold water, place it on a flat baking (cookie) tray and heat for about 10 minutes in a preheated oven set to 180°C/350°F, Gas Mark 4 or 160 to 170°C with a fan oven.

If the crust is still fairly soft just wrap the loaf in foil and proceed as above.

Can one freshen cooked pastry that has become softer?

Yes, you can do this on a low setting in the microwave. The pastry becomes fresher but loses its crispness, unless of course you have a combination microwave when it will be fine.

The best way to freshen and re-crisp it is in the oven at the setting given for bread above.

If you have not the size tin (pan) given in the recipe and you use a slightly smaller or bigger tin, do you have to change either the time of cooking or the temperature?

Often you do need to make simple adjustments. The cake on page 86 illustrates how the baking time might vary with a slight difference in tin sizes. If a tin varies by 1.25 cm/$^1/_2$ inch in diameter that should make relatively little difference to the cooking time, maybe 5 minutes. It is when the difference is 2.5 cm/1 inch that adjustments must be made to accommodate the different depth of mixture.

Sandwich Cakes: if the recipe for light sponges states: use two 18 cm/7 inch sandwich tins (layer pans) but you only have two 20 cm/8 inch tins, shorten the cooking time by 5 to 6 minutes. Use the same temperature.

Take care not to over-bake the sponges, for they will be thinner than those cooked in the tins with a small diameter.

If the recipe states use two 20 cm/8 inch sandwich tins but you only have two 18 cm/7 inch sandwich tins you must:

a) Check that there is room in the tins for the mixture and that it will not over-flow in cooking. Having satisfied yourself on this point you will need to cook the sponges for a **longer** period because of the greater depth.

b) Start with the temperature given in the recipe but, as you will need to increase the baking time by at least 5 to 6 minutes, lower this slightly for the last 10 minutes of the total cooking time to prevent over-browning.

Large Cakes: the same rules apply as above but the difference in time will be slightly longer.

If putting into a cake tin that is 2.5 cm/1 inch larger in diameter than given in the recipe:

Shorten the cooking time by 10 minutes for fairly plain cakes, but 20 minutes for richer cakes that are baked at a fairly low temperature.
Use the same temperature as given in the recipe.

If putting into a cake tin that is 2.5 cm/1 inch smaller in diameter than given in the recipe:

a) Check there is room in the tin for the mixture, as outlined above.

b) Lengthen the cooking time by 10 to 15 minutes for fairly plain cakes but 20 to 30 minutes for richer cakes that are baked at a fairly low temperature.

In each case start with the temperature given in the recipe but as you will need to increase the baking time you need to lower the oven temperature slightly for the last 20 minutes for plainer cakes and 35 minutes for richer cakes to prevent the top of the cakes becoming over-brown.

Square and Round Cake Tins: always use a 2.5 cm/1 inch smaller square tin than a round one, e.g.

If the recipe states use a **20 cm/8 inch round** cake tin you can use an **18 cm/7 inch square** tin and allow exactly the same baking time and temperature.

How can one be certain that a cake that appears to be cooked is really ready?
There are various ways of testing:

a) Carefully draw the cake tin out of the oven and press the centre of the top with a finger. In the case of a very light sponge use a gentle pressure.
If the cake is cooked your finger should NOT leave an impression.
If it does then the cake is not quite cooked. In the case of a cake with a very firm texture, pressing like this is not entirely satisfactory and the tests below are better.

b) Check that the cake has shrunk slightly away from the sides of the tin (pan) or lining paper or parchment.

c) Insert a very fine skewer (preferably wooden) into the centre of the cake. If this comes out clean the cake is cooked. This test is virtually foolproof with plain cakes but can be slightly confusing with a cake containing dried fruits, glacé (candied) cherries or similar ingredients. If the skewer happens to pierce any of these it might well come out looking very sticky – a sign that the cake is not yet ready. It could cause one to replace the cake that *was* cooked back into the oven and continue cooking it – without cause.

If the skewer does look sticky check stages a) and b) as a precaution or do a second test with the skewer. Of course a skewer does make a mark in the top of the cake.

184 SOME QUESTIONS WITH ANSWERS

A very rich fruit cake is not included in this book but the infallible test for that is to *listen*. An uncooked rich fruit cake makes a distinct humming noise whereas a cooked rich fruit cake is silent.

If the cake is not 100% cooked, will it be spoiled by returning it to the oven?
The result varies, in some cases the cake may be slightly heavier in the middle but in many cases, providing you do not keep the cake out of the oven for too long, it will not be adversely affected. See advice on page 181.

How does one test a cake cooked in the microwave oven?
If using a combination microwave cooker, i.e. one where you have the advantages of a conventional cooker allied to microwave heating, then you can test as given above. The cake will look the same as when baked in a conventional cooker.

In the case of an ordinary microwave oven the cake **looks** different at the end of the recommended cooking time. It appears slightly over-soft on top. Do not imagine this means it is badly under-cooked. Test it by inserting a fine wooden skewer or even a cocktail stick (toothpick). Allow this to go right down to the centre of the cake, then check as stage c) above. If the skewer or cocktail stick comes out clean, with no trace of stickiness then irrespective of the top softness, the cake is cooked. Remove from the microwave and allow it to stand in a draught-free place. As the cake cools the softness from the top will disappear.

If, on the other hand, the skewer or cocktail stick comes out after testing with a sticky surface, then the cake is NOT cooked and must be replaced into the microwave oven for a little longer. In the case of a microwave this 'little longer' may only be 30 seconds, so do test frequently.

A cake that is over-cooked in the microwave becomes excessively dry, so careful testing is essential.

Why is cooked pastry sometimes rather tough and not crisp and short?
This is because too much water was used in mixing the pastry and/or because the oven heat was not sufficiently high. If you know the pastry dough is too moist then be fairly generous with the flour on the rolling pin and pastry board. This will make a less rich pastry but you may avoid it being tough.

If you leave the block of pastry to chill for some hours in the refrigerator it may well 'dry out' without the use of extra flour in rolling.

Why is uncooked pastry sometimes inclined to break as it is rolled out and also be ultra crumbly when cooked?
For the opposite reason from that given above; too little liquid was used in making the pastry. If this happens drop a very little water on to the pastry shape then fold this over so the liquid is absorbed. Chill for a while and then roll out. If you do not fold the dough over the liquid will make the pastry stick to the rolling pin.

Why does pastry lose its shape in baking, particularly in a flan or tart shape?
Because the pastry was not allowed to relax (chill) before rolling out and after forming the desired shape; these steps are very important. You will find pastry is much easier to roll out after this first relaxing.

Also because the uncooked pastry was not pressed down into the flan case or flan ring sufficiently well. Spend a little time on doing this.

If you are using self-raising flour, rather than plain (all-purpose) flour for making pastry, you will find this could happen.

Because preparations for baking 'blind' were not followed, see page 115.

A different way of lining a tin (pan) for a flan or tart

There is a rather unusual step you can take when lining the tin with pastry that is used by some cooks. Instead of cutting away the surplus uncooked pastry from the top of the flan or tart before baking they let the surplus dough hang over the top of the tin. The tart or flan is baked and then the crisp surplus pastry is cut away. It means wasting those scraps of pastry and a top edge to the tart or flan which may not look as neat as it would be if the surplus pastry was cut away before baking. On the other hand you never have the sides of the flan or tart sinking down as far, for you have the extra pastry to compensate for this.

Today many people try to avoid salt in cooking. Is the pinch of salt in pastry essential?

No, it is not, but I find it does improve the flavour of the pastry.

Does the use of an egg yolk improve the flavour of the pastry?

Yes it does, and it also helps to make the pastry easier to handle. If you have no use for the egg white on that occasion you could use this instead of adding water with the egg yolk. It is however the yolk of the egg that adds richness and a better texture to the pastry.

Does pastry made with oil instead of fat (shortening) taste as good?

It has a very good flavour but, as explained on page 111, it is difficult to handle.

Can one flavour pastry to make a change?

Yes, the choice of flour, whether white or wholemeal (wholewheat) or a mixture of these, and the fat or oil you use to make shortcrust pastry (basic pie dough) will affect the flavour. If you add sugar you give it a sweeter taste. *Avoiding wheat flour:* if you substitute gluten-free flour or rice flour for wheat flour you will make a great deal of difference in the flavour and texture of the pastry.

Try:

a) adding mixed spice, ground cinnamon or ground ginger to the flour, i.e. ½ to 1 level teaspoon to 225 g/8 oz (2 cups) of flour.

b) adding finely grated lemon or orange zest (the top part of the rind, free from bitter white pith). Use 1 teaspoon to each 225 g/8 oz (2 cups) of flour. Add a little juice to mix the pastry instead of using all water.

c) replace about a quarter of the flour in a recipe with ground almonds. This gives a lovely delicate texture to shortcrust pastry.

What is the best way to measure out very small quantities of vanilla and other extracts or essences and colourings?

It is possible to buy proper measuring spoons that give ¼, ½ and 1 teaspoon. If using an ordinary 5 ml/1 teaspoon then pour in the liquid carefully to assess the right amount. Do not do this over the bowl containing any ingredients in case you spill some of the liquid and so add too much.

Where you need just a few drops of liquid, as in the case of culinary colourings, insert a fine skewer into the bottle of colouring then hold the skewer over the ingredients to be tinted and let a few drops fall in.

Colourings are fairly strong, so add a very few drops, mix well to ascertain the tint before adding any more drops.

What gives yeast bread or buns a strong smell and taste of yeast?
Using too much fresh or dried yeast. Follow the recipes carefully and you will have just the right proportion of yeast to flour and other ingredients.

Why does bread sometimes have an uneven texture with extra large holes in the crumb?
Firstly, it is because the dough was not sufficiently kneaded before being set to prove (rise). The recipes on pages 139 and 140 indicate very clearly how you can tell when the dough has had sufficient kneading. This stage is very important whether making the bread by hand or with an electric mixer or food processor.

Another fault that can cause this texture is by letting the dough prove for too long and allowing it to rise too much. It should never rise more than twice the original volume, whether you use fresh or dried yeast. I tend to let it rise just below twice the original amount.

Would it matter if I replace strong bread flour with plain (all-purpose) flour for bread and other dishes made with yeast?
You could use plain flour but you will not get such a good texture or shape to the bread or the teacakes and buns where it is specified that you use strong flour.

Obviously if you are anxious to avoid wheat you will have to use gluten-free flour.

In some recipes in the book there are suggestions for replacing wheat flour with other ingredients, such as gluten-free flour or rice flour or polenta, will that improve the flavour of the dish?
In some cases you may prefer the newer flavour and texture of the dish. It will have a change in the taste from using wheat flour.

The object of offering different ingredients is to allow people, who are intolerant or allergic to gluten or wheat, to make up the recipe using replacement ingredients.

Do bread and cakes made with gluten-free flour keep as fresh as long as when they are made with ordinary wheat flour?
No, bread in particular does not keep as fresh. That is why it is a good idea to make small loaves with gluten-free flour so they are eaten soon after baking or place the cooked and cold bread in the freezer for storage.

The replacement flour for cakes does not seem to make the result much drier for the recipes contain appreciable amounts of fat.

INDEX